THE PERCEPTION OF PICTURES

VOLUME I

**Alberti's Window:
The Projective Model of
Pictorial Information**

ACADEMIC PRESS
SERIES IN COGNITION AND PERCEPTION

SERIES EDITORS:
Edward C. Carterette
Morton P. Friedman
Department of Psychology
University of California, Los Angeles
Los Angeles, California

Stephen K. Reed: *Psychological Processes in Pattern Recognition*

Earl B. Hunt: *Artificial Intelligence*

James P. Egan: *Signal Detection Theory and ROC Analysis*

Martin F. Kaplan and Steven Schwartz (Eds.): *Human Judgment and Decision Processes*

Myron L. Braunstein: *Depth Perception Through Motion*

R. Plomp: *Aspects of Tone Sensation*

Martin F. Kaplan and Steven Schwartz (Eds.): *Human Judgment and Decision Processes in Applied Settings*

Bikkar S. Randhawa and William E. Coffman: *Visual Learning, Thinking, and Communication*

Robert B. Welch: *Perceptual Modification: Adapting to Altered Sensory Environments*

Lawrence E. Marks: *The Unity of the Senses: Interrelations among the Modalities*

Michele A. Wittig and Anne C. Petersen (Eds.): *Sex-Related Differences in Cognitive Functioning: Developmental Issues*

Douglas Vickers: *Decision Processes in Visual Perception*

Margaret A. Hagen (Ed.): *The Perception of Pictures, Vol. 1: Alberti's Window: The Projective Model of Pictorial Information*

in preparation

Margaret A. Hagen (Ed.): *The Perception of Pictures, Vol. 2 Dürer's Devices: Beyond the Projective Model of Pictures*

THE PERCEPTION OF PICTURES

VOLUME I

Alberti's Window:
The Projective Model of
Pictorial Information

EDITED BY

Margaret A. Hagen

Department of Psychology
Boston University
Boston, Massachusetts

With a Foreword by

JAMES J. GIBSON

1980

ACADEMIC PRESS

A Subsidiary of Harcourt Brace Jovanovich, Publishers

New York   London   Toronto   Sydney   San Francisco

ACADEMIC PRESS, INC.
111 Fifth Avenue, New York, New York 10003

United Kingdom Edition published by
ACADEMIC PRESS, INC. (LONDON) LTD.
24/28 Oval Road, London NW1   7DX

Library of Congress Cataloging in Publication Data
Main entry under title:

The Perception of pictures.

(Academic Press series in cognition and perception)
Includes index.
CONTENTS: v. 1.   Alberti's window, the projective
model of pictorial information.
1.   Visual perception––Addresses, essays, lectures.
2.   Optical illusions––Addresses, essays, lectures.
3.   Art––Psychology––Addresses, essays, lectures.
I.   Hagen, Margaret A.
N7430.5.P48   760'.01'9   79–8862
ISBN 0–12–313601–6 (v. 1)

PRINTED IN THE UNITED STATES OF AMERICA

80 81 82 83   9 8 7 6 5 4 3 2 1

Contents

List of Contributors   ix
Foreword   xi
Preface   xix
Introduction   xxiii
Contents of Volume II   xxix

PART **I**

GENERAL THEORY AND FORMAL ANALYSIS OF THE PROJECTIVE MODEL OF PICTORIAL INFORMATION

CHAPTER **1**

Perceiving Space from Pictures: A Theoretical Analysis   3

RALPH NORMAN HABER

Introduction   3
The Geometrical Optics of Scenes—A Stimulus Analysis   4
Information about Depth in Light Reflected from Pictures   10
Developmental Aspects of the Dual Reality of Pictures   15
Are the Renaissance Rules Capable of Producing Errors in Perception?   21
Do We Have to Learn to Perceive Pictures?   21

Perception of Incomplete Representational Pictures   23
When Will Pictures Create an Illusion?   25
Summary   28
References   29

CHAPTER **2**

The Geometry of Spatial Layout in Pictorial Representation   **33**

H. A. SEDGWICK

Fundamental Concepts   33
Orthographic Projection   41
Perspective Constructions   48
Geometrical Information for Spatial Relations   62
References   88

CHAPTER **3**

Problems of Magnification and Minification:
An Explanation of the Distortions of Distance,
Slant, Shape, and Velocity   **91**

ERNEST A. LUMSDEN

Introduction   91
Magnification   92
Minification   126
Summary   132
References   134

CHAPTER **4**

Compensation for Viewing Point in the Perception
of Pictured Space   **137**

RICHARD R. ROSINSKI AND JAMES FARBER

Introduction   137
Decoding Spatial Layout through Linear Perspective   140
Effects of Viewing-Point Dislocation   143
Pictorial Space Perception   148
Perceptual Compensation for Geometric Distortion   156
References   175

PART **II**

APPLICATIONS AND LIMITATIONS OF THE PROJECTIVE MODEL OF PICTORIAL INFORMATION

CHAPTER **5**
The Renaissance Artist as Quantifier   179

SAMUEL Y. EDGERTON, JR.

Introduction   179
Renaissance Art Influences Scientific Development   180
The Unique Characteristics of Renaissance Art   181
Renaissance Art versus Eastern Art   185
Renaissance Art and the Advent of the Printing Press   189
Conclusion   211

CHAPTER **6**
Exceptional Cases of Pictorial Perspective   213

WILLIAM R. MACKAVEY

Introduction   213
Close Viewing   215
Far Viewing   218
Trompe L'Oeil   220
References   223

CHAPTER **7**
Perception of Movement in Pictures   225

SARAH L. FRIEDMAN AND MARGUERITE B. STEVENSON

Introduction   225
Representational Information   226
The Effectiveness of Pictorial Movement Information—
Experimental Evidence   236
A Continuum of Information Correspondence between
Pictorial Indicators and the Environment   246
Summary   251
Appendix 1   252
Appendix 2   252
References   254

CHAPTER **8**

Convention, Context, and Caricature 257

D. N. PERKINS AND MARGARET A. HAGEN

Introduction   257
A for Instance   261
Measuring Consistency in Caricaturing   268
A Test of Transfer   271
Negation and Recognition   275
Three More Theories of Caricature   278
Caricature and Convention   282
References   285

Subject Index   **287**

List of Contributors

Numbers in parentheses indicate the pages on which the authors' contributions begin.

SAMUEL Y. EDGERTON, JR. (179), Department of Art History, Boston University, Boston, Massachusetts 02215

JAMES FARBER (137), Department of Psychology, Cornell University, Ithaca, New York 14850

SARAH L. FRIEDMAN (225), Laboratory of Developmental Psychology, National Institute of Mental Health, Bethesda, Maryland 20014

RALPH NORMAN HABER (3), Department of Psychology, University of Illinois at Chicago Circle, Chicago, Illinois 60680

MARGARET A. HAGEN (257), Department of Psychology, Boston University, Boston, Massachusetts 02215

ERNEST A. LUMSDEN (91), Department of Psychology, The University of North Carolina at Greensboro, Greensboro, North Carolina 27412

WILLIAM R. MACKAVEY (213), Department of Psychology, Boston University, Boston, Massachusetts 02215

DAVID N. PERKINS (257), Project Zero, Harvard Graduate School of Education, Cambridge, Massachusetts 02138

RICHARD R. ROSINSKI (137), Interdisciplinary Department of Information Science, Graduate School of Library and Information Sciences, University of Pittsburgh, Pittsburgh, Pennsylvania 15260

HAROLD A. SEDGWICK (33), Department of Behavioral Sciences, College of Optometry, State University of New York, New York, New York 10010

MARGUERITE B. STEVENSON (225), Child and Family Studies, University of Wisconsin—Madison, Madison, Wisconsin 53706

Foreword:
A Prefatory Essay on the Perception of Surfaces versus the Perception of Markings on a Surface

The perception of surfaces, I argue, is radically different from the perception of *markings* on a surface. The former kind of perception is essential to the life of animals, but the latter is not. The former is presupposed when we talk about the latter, and we cannot understand the latter unless we understand the former. But we have been trying to do it the other way around. For many centuries we have assumed that the perception of *forms* is basic to the perception of the *environment*, as forms are all that the eye can deliver to the brain, and depth has to be somehow added to the forms. The perception of forms, however, must be the perception of marks on a surface if it is any kind of perception at all (Gibson, 1951).

The properties of surfaces are not the same as the properties of marks on a surface. I have described those properties of surfaces that are essential to an awareness of what they afford in *The Ecological Approach to Visual Perception* (Gibson, 1979). These properties include what I call *surface layout, object layout, substance,* and *change.* We can distinguish the layout of surfaces in such terms as convexity or concavity, edge or corner, and projected or unprojected at the temporary point of observation. We can distinguish objects, both attached and detached, in relation to the ground or background. We can distinguish the substances beneath the surfaces by means of the texture, color, spottiness, and opacity of the surface. We can distinguish changes in terms of events, mainly the ecological motions and deformations of surfaces, including the living surfaces of animals and men.

The properties of *marks* on a surface, in contrast, are complex and hard to describe. It is not so difficult to distinguish what we call a wall, a wax tablet, a sheet of papyrus, a screen, or a piece of cloth, but the distinguishing properties of the markings are very perplexing. The marks can be deposits, or traces, or lines, or shadows projected on the surface. They are produced by what I call the *graphic act.* This can be finger-tracing, drawing, painting, or engraving, with a tool such as a stylus, brush, or pen, or the marks can be produced with the aid of a simple human device like the ruler or compass, or a complex device such as the printing press, the gadgets of photography, and the projector of lantern slides (Gibson, 1966, Chap. 11). The varieties of *graph* are countless.

The *development* of the graphic act in the human child begins with dabbling and scribbling, the *fundamental* graphic act (Gibson, 1966, Chap. 11); later it differentiates into the manual acts of picturing and writing—with intermediates such as making dots, lines, and circles—and progresses to the technologies of duplicating pictures, lines, and letters. Graphic acts and graphs are little understood. They are *hard* to understand. Depicting and writing are hard enough; but what about diagramming? What about geometrical drawing and curves based on coordinates? What about *decorating* a surface, which seems to be neither picturing nor writing (cf. Gombrich, 1979)? What are the *kinds* of writing? What are ideographs? Numerals? Alphabetic letters? Nonsense syllables? Words?

The properties of surfaces and the properties of the forms and figures produced *on* a surface are different, although psychologists and philosophers have long confused them. I will try to list the differences in more detail.

1. Surfaces have the kind of meanings that I call *affordances,* whereas marks on a surface can have *referential meanings;* that is, the marks refer to something other than the surface itself. A surface does not *stand for* anything. Traces, deposits, or pigments on a surface can. They can be a substitute or surrogate. Referential meanings are not the same as basic perceptual meanings (Gibson, 1966, p. 244). There are volumes on referential meaning, but little on affordance meaning.

2. A surface has a texture but it does not either *represent* or *symbolize* another surface. The pattern *of* a surface and the pattern *on* a surface are different. They can usually be distinguished by the adult human. I am suggesting that the texture, color, parti-coloration, and opacity of a surface are *intrinsic* to it.

3. All animals perceive surfaces, but only human animals make and perceive pictures and symbols so as to communicate.

4. The surface on which a *graph* is produced can be seen underneath the graph, as there is information in the optic array for both. Hence the human child has a dual awareness, of the surface and of the graph at the same time. He may not pay attention to the surface but he is dimly aware of it. I am using "graph" to mean a picture, a script, or anything in between.

5. A "blank" surface can be decorated, regularized, textured, painted, or embellished without producing a graph. The pattern imposed on the surface need not have any referential meaning. The surface is still perceived as such, with what it affords. The beauty of the tool, the orderliness of the pavement, the elegance of the facade can be seen directly. No doubt a sharp division cannot be made between decoration and depiction, but the extremes are distinct.

6. Similarly, surfaces can acquire deposits of dirt or blots of pigment that are not graphic (except by chance). Dirt, like decoration, does not stand for something else. To be sure, a decorated surface is attractive to the human adult, whereas a dirty surface is repellent (skin, clothing, floor, window pane). But the child must learn to see the difference. Gombrich (1979) would probably say that decoration is characterized by *order* and dirt by *disorder*; but I am troubled by the inability of mathematicians to define "order."

7. The various affordances of surfaces, substances, layouts, and events get perceived in the course of development of the young animal by maturation and learning taken together, by *encountering* the surfaces in the habitat, without schooling. On the other hand, the referential meanings of marks on a surface get apprehended by children in ways that differ from the preceding, and also differ from one another. They are different for pictures, drawings, plots, signs, and letters of the alphabet. At one extreme, photographs are independent of cultural conventions. Drawings and diagrams are at least somewhat conventional. Alphabetic writing is wholly conventional. But however different the learning of pictorial reference may be from the learning of linguistic reference (and they *are* very different), they are even more radically different from the learning of what surfaces afford. Encountering these marks is not enough, and the more they vary with the culture to which the growing child belongs, the more this holds true.

8. Surfaces and what they afford are actually perceived. *Pictured* surfaces, objects, places, persons, and events are not actually perceived in the proper meaning of that term. Photographic pictures can at best provide a sort of partial second-hand perception for stay-at-home observers (Gibson, 1954). Chirographic pictures are even less like perceptions; they often provide *imagination* at second hand: of paradise, unicorns, angels, fairies, and monsters. *Described* surfaces, objects, places, animals, and

events, real or fictional, are most certainly not perceived. What one perceives, strictly speaking, is the real environment. The child can see zebras in the zoo, but not unicorns. He can later read zoology or mythology but in either case it is not perceiving. Depiction simulates perception more than description does, but it cannot possibly achieve the level of full perception achieved by ambient vision (looking around) and ambulatory vision (moving around) in my terminology (Gibson, 1979). The motion picture comes even closer to perception than the still picture, but it cannot *become* perception. The so-called "illusion of reality" in viewing pictures only demonstrates that some of the same *kind* of information is made available by a picture as is available in growing up (Gibson, 1971). But the information for the surface of the picture, as much as the information for the surface of the page, is in the light.

Conclusion. A surface of the environment has its own characteristic texture. Rock, sand, wax, plaster, wood, skin, leather, vellum, paper, woven material, canvas, clothing, glass, and house paint can be distinguished. The surface can be *blank* but it always has a certain grain. It may be clean or dirty, plain or decorated, and still be a simple surface, seen as such. But when it is treated so that it displays information about something *other* than a simple surface, the human observer gets a puzzling variety of new experiences. The displayed information can be about a real place or an imaginary one, an existing object somewhere else or a nonexisting object, a living animal or a mythical one, a past, present, or future event, or an impossible event. The information can be about facts of the world conveyed in verbal form, descriptions, or predications; or it can be information conveyed in the form of symbols, loosely so-called, referring to events in the world. Or the information can explicate laws of the world. The advantages of depicting, diagramming, formulating, and writing for the human animal are that they make available to the young of our species what the most discerning of our ancestors have perceived, or imagined, or learned. Knowledge thus accumulates inasmuch as it can be stored in art galleries, museums, and libraries.

ABOUT THIS BOOK

The collection of chapters to which this is a prefatory note is entitled *The Perception of Pictures.* These chapters are not concerned with writing on a surface, diagrams on a surface, histograms on a surface, forms on a surface, blots on a surface, or decorations of a surface, but with *pictures.* The book is not concerned with sculptures, or with statues, models, or toys, all of which seem to be *layouts* of surfaces that stand for *other* layouts. These are produced by derivations of the fundamental *plastic* act instead of the fundamental *graphic* act. The editor was right to exclude them, for the perplexities involved in the understanding of pictures are wide-ranging enough without having to deal with further perplexities like writing and sculpturing.

But nevertheless it is necessary to put pictures into perspective as it were. I have tried in this prefatory essay to relate the psychology of depiction to the psychology of perception, as I understand it, and to suggest how both fit into the general psychology of apprehension.

Perplexities. Is it the case that one can perceive a picture without learning, whereas one has to learn to *read* a script? Or is it the case that one has to learn to read a picture also? Some of the authors in this volume believe the first, but others believe the second. The issue is much debated. But is it a clear issue? Is there more than one kind of learning to perceive? I suggested that, strictly speaking, all we perceive directly are surfaces as such. If so, we should not speak of the *perception* of a picture but of a *nonperceptual* kind of apprehension. But how does it differ from the kind obtained by reading?

What is involved in learning to comprehend medical radiographs, that is, X-ray photographs? They are surely not *read,* but neither are the bones beneath the flesh *perceived,* strictly speaking. Or do they come to be *almost* perceived, after practice?

Here is another perplexity. We speak glibly of a *representation*. What is it exactly? Does it literally re-present to an observer what was present to his visual sense on an earlier occasion? Clearly not. For one reason, the painter can depict something he has never seen, but only dreamed, imagined, or invented, such as a centaur or a winged horse. The term "representation" implies a quite mistaken assumption about optical stimulation.

If so, the meaning of "nonrepresentative" as used is not clear. A caricature, for example, does not re-present to the beholder the same array of light that the person caricatured presents to the beholder. What *does* it present? *Information* about the person? Perhaps, but then what is the difference between that information and the kind made familiar by the modern theory of communication?

A similar confusion arises in connection with our use of the term *image*. It has many different meanings, not one, and we slide from one to another without realizing it when we talk about images. Here are ten different meanings the term can have.

1. A *solid* image. A sculpture, statue, model, or toy, as noted in the preceding.
2. A *pictorial* image. A painting, drawing, engraving, photographic print, projected "slide" or shadow-caster, low relief, or high relief. (I

include reliefs in the category of pictures because they have to be viewed from "in front"; they cannot be viewed from "all sides" as can a solid image. The "back" has no referential meaning. Not everyone will agree with my choice, however.)

3. An *arrested* image. Many would assume that this is the only kind of image, but it is not. What I call the *progressive* image is exemplified by the ancient Chinese shadow-play on a translucent screen, and by the modern cinematograph (Gibson, 1959, Chap. 16). The ordinary sculpture or picture should be thought of not as *still* but as *stopped*.

4. A *mirror* image. The virtual object or scene behind a smooth surface such as an unrippled pool of water or a polished piece of metal that reflects the incident rays "regularly." Incidentally the terms *virtual image* and *real* image as used in geometrical optics are such deceptive misnomers that I think they should be abandoned (Gibson, 1966, p. 227 f.).

5. A *camera* image. The picture formed on the inner surface of a dark chamber with a pinhole (or a lens) on the front wall. We think of it as an arrested image but in fact it may be progressive.

6. A *photographic* camera image. The picture formed on the inner surface of a dark chamber that has actually been arrested by a complicated process involving a *shutter*, an *emulsion*, a *latent* image in the emulsion, a *negative* image on the film, and a *positive* image on another surface. A photographic image has to be fixed while the shutter is open.

7. A *retinal* image. A vague term that covers up the prevalent confusion about vision in physiology and psychology. It can mean either the optical image on the inner surface of the dark chamber of the vertebrate eye, which is not only progressive but is also a sliding sample of the ambient optic array that surrounds the head. This image could, in theory, be observed if one cut out the eye, peeled off the opaque coating, and held it up in front of an eye. Or it can mean a sort of physiological image in the mosaic of photoreceptors of the retina, vaguely taken to be analogous to the latent arrested image of photography. This *snapsnot* image, or features of it, is what supposedly gets "transmitted to the brain." But it *cannot* be literally arrested, as vision is progressive. This image could *not* be observed, even in theory. The comparison of an eye with a camera is false, and the comparison of a retina with a photographic emulsion is even more false. What a muddle!

8. An *afterimage*. Supposedly the aftersensation of overstimulating the photoreceptors, or of prolonged stimulation of them, with a fixated eye. It is often taken as evidence for the valid comparison of a vertebrate retina with a photographic emulsion. But there can be an afterimage of *motion*, which is *not* consistent with the photographic comparison.

9. A *memory* image. Sometimes taken to be the trace of an arrested physiological image that has been transmitted to the brain. But this is

perplexing, as one can remember a motion, and no one can conceive how a progressive image might lay down a trace.

10. A *mental* image. A term for a little-understood kind of experience. Taken literally it implies a little observer, inside the head of the observer, who looks at a picture (or perhaps a sculpture? or a movie?). So it cannot be taken literally. But, if not an image, what is the experience to be called?

Perhaps the deepest of all perplexities connected with pictures is the theory of the cues for depth in a pictorial image and the extension of this to the cues for depth in a *retinal* image. We have assumed that the cues for depth in a picture are the same as the information for layout in the environment. But is it true? What if we have been going about it the wrong way round? If the perception of surfaces is primary and the apprehension of pictorial marks on a surface is secondary, the traditional theory of cues does not apply to life. Most of the authors in this book make the assumption that the cues for depth *do* apply to life. Would some of the puzzles they face be resolved if they rejected it?

One such puzzle concerns perspective. The Renaissance painters who discovered the laws of the projection of a street scene (say) on a transparent picture-plane to a fixed station point called it *artificial* perspective to distinguish it from the *natural* perspective of ordinary perception. There has been endless controversy, for centuries, over the validity of the laws of perspective. The arguments turn up in this book. But have we not forgotten the old distinction when we argue about perspective? Perhaps the laws of pictorial optics are not the same as the laws of environmental optics. This is what I call "ecological" optics. It is emphatically *not* the optics of photons, light-rays, and retinal images.

Do we have to *learn* the cues for depth? Or do we know what they mean *innately*? Both questions are ridiculous. They come from the simpleminded conclusion that because a picture is flat and a retinal image is a picture the deliverances of the retina to the brain are depthless.

Conclusion. The perplexities involved in making and looking at pictures are wide-ranging. They point to unanswered questions in psychology. What is *direct* perception as against mediated knowledge? What is a representation? What exactly should be meant by an image? What is perspective? What are the so-called cues for depth? These are a few of the puzzles that the reader will come up against in reading these chapters.

Most people think they know what a picture is. Anything so familiar must be simple. They are wrong. If the reader thinks he knows what a picture is he will be disillusioned and then aroused, perhaps annoyed, but certainly interested, as he goes through these chapters.

JAMES J. GIBSON
Cornell University

REFERENCES

Gibson, J. J. What is a form? *Psychological Review*, 1951, *58*, 403–412.
Gibson, J. J. A theory of pictorial perception. *Audio-Visual Communication Review*, 1954, *1*, 3–23.
Gibson, J. J. *The senses considered as perceptual systems.* Boston: Houghton-Mifflin, 1966.
Gibson, J. J. The information available in pictures. *Leonardo*, 1971, *4*, 27–35.
Gibson, J. J. *The ecological approach to visual perception.* Boston: Houghton-Mifflin, 1979.
Gombrich, E. H. *The sense of order. A study in the psychology of decorative art.* Cornell University Press, 1979.

Preface

In the last 15 years, there has been a surge of interest in theoretical speculation on the nature of picture making and perception. Gibson, Edgerton, Arnheim, Gombrich, Goodman, Pirenne, and Kennedy, to name only a few, have contributed books to the field reflecting the diverse interests of philosophy, art history, physics, geometry, and psychology in the nature and problems of representational art. In addition, empirical work on the psychology of picture perception has enjoyed of late its own renaissance, which is the first since the observations of the early anthropologists and the developmental catalogues of the child psychologists and art teachers. Recent research has focused on determining the adequacy of pictorial information for Western adult observers, on specifying developmental sequences in children's perception of pictures, on examining the utility of Western pictures for non-Western peoples, on determining the relationship between neurological impairment and pictorial perception, and on testing the ability of animals to use information from pictorial displays.

All of this varied theory and research, although relfecting the diversity of interest in the problem of pictures, has left the student of the field with a wealth of unintegrated and often rather inaccessible information. The present two-volume collection of original chapters on pictorial perception is designed to provide that missing integration. Its purpose is to supply the psychologist, the art historian, the philosopher, the anthropologist, and the geometer with a primary reference and teaching source, which presents a diversity of theoretical viewpoints coupled with integrated reviews of empirical work in the field of picture perception.

Volume I of the collection presents a comprehensive treatment of the traditional projective model of pictorial information. Ralph Norman Haber provides the theoretical foundation of the projective model. Hal Sedgwick undertakes a formal analysis of the character of projective information in perspective pictures. Ernest Lumsden discusses the effects of magnification and minification of projective pictures with special attention to the distortions on distance, slant, shape, and velocity observed under these conditions. Richard Rosinski and James Farber describe the mathematical and perceptual consequences of viewing ordinary pictures from incorrect station points. These chapters thus provide a clear exposition of one of the oldest, and certainly the most familiar, model of "how pictures work," including where, how, and why they occasionally fail. The issues of successful application and failures of the model are further pursued in the chapter by Samuel Edgerton, in which the unique character of perspective information for quantification in pictures is examined, and in the chapter by Sarah Friedman and Marguerite Stevenson on the limits of perspective for the specification of movement in pictures. David Perkins and Margaret Hagen also examine the utility of the projective model in accounting for the perception of caricatures. Lastly, William Mackavey presents several general cases in which the projective model of pictorial information simply fails to account for the appearance of pictures.

Volume II of the collection takes leave of the traditional projective model of pictorial information and presents the reader with several theoretical options for consideration. Margaret Hagen presents critically some of the prevailing alternatives, plus a new synthetic theory of pictures. Julian Hochberg presents an empirically based argument for the critical role of perceptual structures in supplementing the inadequacies of pictorial information, thus giving us a model of picture perception based on mutually supportive characteristics of both organism and stimulus information. Marx Wartofsky goes one step further and presents a model based solely on observer history and characteristics. In the remaining chapters of Volume II, empirical investigations of the applications and limitations of pictorial information are reviewed. Richard Olson, Albert Yonas, and Robert Cooper review the developmental literature; Rebecca Jones and Margaret Hagen, the cross-cultural literature. Hugh Coffman reviews the utilization of pictorial materials in studies and diagnostic evaluations in the neurologically impaired, and John Kennedy examines pictorial production and perception in the blind. Lastly, work examining the sensitivity on nonhuman subjects to pictorial displays is reviewed by Patrick Cabe. Volume II thus provides the reader with the empirical evidence necessary to weight the advantages and disadvantages of the alternative models of pictorial information.

The original idea for such a collection grew out of two conferences on pictorial perception held at the University of Minnesota in the summers of 1976 and 1977, and attended by some of the contributors to the volumes. Thus we wish to express our gratitude to Albert Yonas for instigating the seminars, and to the Center for Research in Human Learning, University of Minnesota, for funding them. In addition, I wish to express my gratitude to the authors for their considerable expenditures of time and effort on their own contributions, and to David Perkins for his generosity in editorial consultation.

Introduction

WHAT, THEN, ARE PICTURES?

All seeing is in the realm of the psychologist, and nobody has ever discussed the process of creating or experiencing art without talking psychology. Rudolf Arnheim (1954) made this observation some 25 years ago, and the purpose of the present collection is to exploit the truth of it. We shall deal with the apparently timeless issues and questions in the area of representational picturing as they occur again and again in diverse fields. What determines the form and appearance of representational pictures? What accounts for the astonishing diversity of artistic styles across cultures and history? How can realistic representation be accomplished at all? Is picture perception an innate ability and is it specifically human? Laborers in the fields of philosophy, art history, and psychology have all attempted in various ways to address these questions. Even within a discipline, or perhaps especially within a discipline, the answers suggested differ wildly and are often directly contradictory. But all of the theorists, and not especially the psychologists, are, in fact, talking psychology. By this, Arnheim meant invoking psychology as the science of the mind. In this collection, talking psychology means invoking a theory of visual perception, explicitly or implicitly, in one's theory of representational art or pictures. For some thinkers, the relationship between visual perception and representational pictures is an intimate and necessary one. For others, the relationship between the two is artificial, unnecessary, and misleading. But even those in the latter group must delineate what they reject, and so find themselves talking psychology if only to show that one need not.

Perceptionists, be they psychologists, philosophers, or art historians, generally seem to offer two sets of mutually contradictory answers to the questions raised about the nature of representational pictures. One set of answers is offered by a group of writers called Constructivists or Conventionalists (depending on who is doing the calling). In a prototypical argument, Nelson Goodman (1968) writes that pictures succeed as representations of objects because they are constructed and read according to an arbitrary but shared code. Thus, realistic portrayal is a matter of habit or cultural convention and not of resemblance between picture and pictured. In a similar vein, Sir Ernst Gombrich (1972a,b) argues that pictures succeed as representations, or look "lifelike," in so far as they are created according to prevailing artistic schemata, and judged by shared social criteria of "convincingness." Going further, Richard Gregory (1970, 1971), the psychologist, argues that a successful picture is an impossible mystery, because it allows of no means for the confirmation or disconfirmation of the object hypotheses it stimulates, as would be the case in ordinary perception.

In quite direct opposition to this general viewpoint is the argument advanced by James Gibson (1950, 1951, 1954, 1960, 1971), Gibson's many disciples and "derivatives" (e.g., Kennedy, Farber, Purdy, Rosinski, Sedgwick, and Hagen), and by Ralph Norman Haber. These theorists argue that a picture succeeds as a representation of ordinary objects and scenes because it contains the same kind of information for determinate perception as is provided by the light reflected from the ordinary environment. Thus the information carried by pictures is both necessary to determinate perception and sufficient without recourse to cultural convention or cognitive constructions.

It is not at all clear that continuation of the armchair debate would end eventually in a consensual resolution of the critical questions about the nature of pictures and their perception. In fact, it is not at all clear that any course of action would have such a happy ending. Nevertheless, a course of action has been chosen in the present collection of original chapters, which promises if not resolution through consensus, at least illumination through exploration. Volume I of the collection has been designed to explore as fully as possible the most elaborated model of the information theory described above: the projective model of pictorial information. This model will be presented both generally and formally, with its applications and limitations explored.

In Part I, the general and formal character of the projective model of pictorial information is comprehensively presented. All of the chapters deal with the consequences of the picture-as-window assumption first presented by Alberti in 1435. He wrote: "First of all, about where I draw. I inscribe a quadrangle of right angles, as large as I wish, which is considered to be an open window through which I see what I want to paint (Spencer's translation, 1966, p. 56)." This model is also familiar to readers through the writings of Leonardo and the woodcuts of Albrecht Dürer. In the first chapter of Volume I, Ralph Norman Haber discusses the picture-as-window assumption within the larger context of ordinary scene perception. He provides a general analysis of optical information with special consideration of the information provided by light reflected from pictures. He considers whether picture perception requires the postulation of special processing or special learning, and concludes that it does not. In Chapter 2, Hal Sedgwick presents a mathematical exposition of the information available in pictures, from the Gibsonian point of view. He concerns himself with demonstrating mathematically that information is available in the light reflected from pictures for the specification of spatial relations among objects or surfaces, for "the distances, sizes, slants, and tilts of things." This formalization of the demonstrated *availability* of pictorial information is an elegant and necessary prerequisite to the exploration of the *utilization* of such information by observers. In Chapters 3 and 4, the special character of the information afforded by pictures is considered as distinct from that provided by the ordinary environment. Lumsden examines the problems of magnification and minification occasioned by different types of pictorial displays, such as those photographed through telescopic lenses. He provides a mathematical explanation of the distortions of distance, slant and shape, and motion frequently observed with such pictures, and refutes the argument that such distortions invalidate perspective. Similarly, Rosinski and Farber consider the special perceptual problems created by the fact that observation of a picture is not limited to correct station-point viewing. They provide a mathematical prediction of which station-point shifts should produce specified distortions and which should not, and consider once again the issue of compensation for station-point shifts.

In Part II, the authors go beyond the formal specification of information, veridical and distorted, provided by pictures, and consider the implications, applications, and limitations of the projective model as a general theory of picture perception. Edgerton, an art historian, examines the intimate connection between the scientific revolution and the artistic revolution that produced Western linear perspective. He argues that Renaissance art had a critical influence on scientific thinking, even a determining influence, because Renaissance art was uniquely capable of mathematical and objective statements producing identical meanings in all viewers. Working from a somewhat opposite point of view, Mackavey considers cases in which the information provided by perspective pictures does not seem objective or veridical, cases in which the compensatory mechanism appears to fail. He examines the situations provided by close viewing, very distant viewing, and trompe-l'oeil pictures. Friedman and Stevenson go on to consider pictures in which the relationship between pictured information and environment seems even more distant. They study still pictures in which movement is depicted. They examine both the informational sources for movement perception in pictures and the responses of different types of viewers to these sources, or indicators, suggesting movement. They argue from an empirical base that movement indicators are on a continuum varying from environmental–perspectival to abstract–arbitrary, and suggest that this also may be true for other types of pictorial information. Perkins and Hagen consider the possibility of extending the projective model, with modifications, to the case of caricature. On examination of the issue, and following a review of the available literature, they argue a compromise case between information and convention. They suggest that selective attention to the information contained within a conventional system, occurring across time, may best characterize the process of caricature recognition.

The projective model of pictorial information is the most elaborated and widely accepted of the theoretical models of picture perception, but it is by no means the only model. Volume II of *The Perception of Pictures* offers several alternative theoretical approaches. Margaret Hagen provides a general overview of several models of picture perception and offers an eclectic model of her own. Julian Hochberg expounds a constructivist model of the process of perceiving pictures with emphasis on the role of mental structures in perception. David Perkins and Robert Cooper revitalize the Gestalt approach to picture perception and, like Hochberg, deal with the problems created by deficient information in the light to the eye. Marx Wartofsky offers the radical alternative of the conventionalist argument that the conceptualization of pictures and their perception is both arbitrary and culturally determined.

Part II of Volume II covers a broad range of empirical investigations regarding the perception of pictorial displays, spanning quite a variety of populations. Richard Olson, Albert Yonas, and Robert Cooper review the developmental literature on picture perception in Western babies and children. Rebecca Jones and Margaret Hagen provide a comprehensive overview of the cross-cultural literature, some of which is carried out within a developmental perspective. Hugh Coffman reviews the literature on pictorial perception in the neurologically impaired, and argues for the utility of a developmental approach to this area of empirical investigation. John Kennedy treats the surprising and thought-provoking topic of pictorial perception among the blind. Patrick Cabe, in a fine methodological review of the animal literature, addresses issues of the fundamental nature of pictorial information and the capacity of various organisms to perceive it.

Together the volumes of *The Perception of Pictures* provide an unprec-
edented organization of a welter of theoretical and empirical work on
pictorial perception. They do not tell the reader that there is only one
viable approach or a single answer to any of the issues and questions on
the nature of pictures and their perception. Rather, these collections
provide a clear exposition of the theoretical alternatives available, and
comprehensive overviews of the empirical work to date. With such tools
in hand, the scholarly pursuit of "the truth about pictures" should be
greatly facilitated. This, at least, is the hope of the contributors to this
work.

MARGARET A. HAGEN

REFERENCES

Arnheim, R. *Art and visual perception: A psychology of the creative eye.* Berkeley: Univ.
    of California Press, 1974. (Originally published in 1954.)
Gibson, J. J. *The perception of the visual world.* Boston: Houghton Mifflin, 1950.
Gibson, J. J. What is a form? *Psychological Review,* 1951, *58,* 403–412.
Gibson, J. J. A theory of pictorial perception. *Audio-Visual Communication Review,* 1954,
    1, 3–23.
Gibson, J. J. Pictures, perspective and perception. *Daedalus,* 1960, *89,* 216–227.
Gibson, J. J. The information available in pictures. *Leonardo,* 1971, *4,* 27–35.
Gombrich, E. H. *Art and illusion: A study in the psychology of pictorial representation.*
    Princeton: Princeton Univ. Press, 1972. (a)
Gombrich, E. H. *The story of art.* London: Phaidon, 1972. (b)
Goodman, N. *Languages of art.* Indianapolis: Bobbs-Merrill, 1968.
Gregory, R. L. *The intelligent eye.* New York: McGraw-Hill, 1970.
Gregory, R. L. *Eye and brain.* New York: McGraw-Hill, 1971.
Spencer, J. R. *Leon Battista Albertia on painting.* New Haven: Yale Univ. Press, 1966.

Contents of Volume II

Dürer's Devices: Beyond the Projective Model of Pictures

Foreword
Rudolf Arnheim

I. Theories of Pictures and Their Perception

Generative Theory: A Descriptively Adequate Perceptual Theory
of Pictorial Representation
Margaret A. Hagen

Pictorial Functions and Perceptual Structures
Julian Hochberg

How the Eye Makes Up What the Light Leaves Out
David N. Perkins and Robert Cooper

Visual Scenarios: The Role of Representation in Visual Perception
Marx W. Wartofsky

II. Empirical Investigation of the Perception of Pictures

Development of Pictorial Perception
Richard Olson, Albert Yonas, and Robert Cooper

A Perspective on Cross-Cultural Picture Perception
Rebecca K. Jones and Margaret A. Hagen

Pictorial Perception: Hemispheric Specialization and Developmental
Regression in the Neurologically Impaired
  Hugh L. Coffman

Blind People Recognizing and Making Haptic Pictures
  John M. Kennedy

Picture Perception in Nonhuman Subjects
  Patrick A. Cabe

GENERAL THEORY AND FORMAL ANALYSIS OF THE PROJECTIVE MODEL OF PICTORIAL INFORMATION

CHAPTER **1** RALPH NORMAN HABER

Perceiving Space from Pictures:
A Theoretical Analysis

Introduction 3
The Geometrical Optics of Scenes—A Stimulus Analysis 4
  Reflectance as a Property of Surfaces 5
  Projection of Light as a Retinal Image—Perspective 6
  Perspective Transformations Produced by Movements and Binocularity 7
  Changes in the Retinal Image When the Eye Rotates in Its Socket 8
  Changes in the Retinal Image When the Head Moves 8
  Changes Produced by Using Two Eyes 9
  Correlation among the Three Scales of Space 9
  Changes Produced by the Optics of the Eye 10
Information about Depth in Light Reflected from Pictures 10
  Motion Information Regarding the Flatness of Pictures 13
  Binocular Disparity Information Regarding the Flatness of Pictures 13
  Summary of the Stimulus Analyses 14
Developmental Aspects of the Dual Reality of Pictures 15
  The Station-Point Controversy 17
Are the Renaissance Rules Capable of Producing Errors in Perception? 21
Do We Have to Learn to Perceive Pictures? 21
Perception of Incomplete Representational Pictures 23
When Will Pictures Create an Illusion 25
Summary 28
References 29

The Perception of Pictures
Volume I

INTRODUCTION

Picture perception, especially those aspects that involve perception of the layout of space, has had a checkered theoretical history. On the one eye, some assume that because pictures are human constructions, it is only through experience and practice with the conventions that we can learn to perceive what pictures represent. On the other eye, others assume that because two dimensions are less than three, it is easier to understand how we perceive pictures than how we perceive natural scenes. This argument is often carried one step further by assuming that the simpler the picture (outline drawings being simpler than photographs), the easier it is to perceive.

Traditional theories of perception when applied to the perception of pictures have generally treated pictures as derived, at least with respect to the perception of scenes. In doing so, these theories have had to add or subtract special processes, special learning, or special experience in their accounts of picture perception. In this chapter such additions or differences are shown to be unnecessary and inappropriate to a proper account of picture perception. (I propose that one perceives pictures by using the same strategies and processes used to perceive three-dimensional scenes.)

There is an obvious parsimony in explaining picture and scene perception by the same processes. The strongest evidence in support of this argument relies on the typical developmental sequence: Infants and children in all cultures have vast amounts of exposure to real scenes before any significant demands are placed on them to process pictures. Even if pictures become a commonplace part of their visual lives, the perception of pictures clearly comes *after* the development of well-practiced procedures for perceiving natural scenes. Therefore, the most reasonable hypothesis is that children, when confronted with pictures, use the same strategies and processes that they use for all other information that impinges on their visual senses. What is not obvious and remains to be demonstrated is that children (and the adults they grow into) can get away with this parsimony. Will it work? Showing how it works is the main goal of this chapter.

THE GEOMETRICAL OPTICS OF SCENES— A STIMULUS ANALYSIS

The task for a visual scientist trying to understand picture or scene perception is twofold. First, he or she has to examine the sources of information, singly and in concert, with respect to accuracy and uniqueness in describing the picture or scene reflecting light to the eye. This examination is a description of the laws governing the relationship between the distal and the proximal stimulus. This lawfulness is of critical importance when we are concerned about the layout of space as the retina has no special receptor for distance (such as we would if, for example, light rays reflected from distant objects were absorbed by more posterior photopigment molecules in each receptor as compared to rays from nearby objects). Therefore, distance—the third dimension of Euclidian space—must be registered in the proximal stimulus in other ways. A stimulus analysis is designed to describe this process. It is basically a task for geometry and for geometrical optics, and does not typically require experiments. It requires consideration of the optics of the eye, however, because the precision of the proximal stimulus representation is determined by those optics. All too often, the stimulus analysis is carried out on a hypothetical projection plane in front of the eye and, as is shown later, the actual projections on the retina are quite different.

The second task of the visual scientist has nothing to do with geometry or optics, but rather is an information-processing analysis. Although geometry can specify the amount, kind, and veracity of information in the proximal stimulus, it can not tell us how that information is used, sampled, or weighted, nor how it is combined with prior information from earlier perceptions or expectancies about the scene. Numerous experiments are required to explain these processes as these questions cannot be answered by logic, speculation, or introspection.

Much of the history of attempts to understand picture and scene perception have foundered upon the inadequacies of one or the other of these analyses, or on a misconception of what these analyses show. This chapter touches briefly on some of the principal attributes of visual stimuli: reflectivity of surfaces, patterning of spectral and luminance discontinuities on the retinal surface as a function of distance and orientation, transformations of these discontinuities with observer movement, and disparities between the patterns on the retinas of the two eyes. This analysis focuses first on the stimulus information from scenes, and then from pictures of scenes.

Reflectance as a Property of Surfaces

Visible light radiates from a light source (e.g., the sun, lightbulbs, or fires), diverging out from the source in all directions. Some of the rays strike surfaces and are either absorbed or are reflected by them. Most surfaces in the natural world reflect light diffusely, so that regardless of the angle of incidence, the light rays diverge in all directions again. In this sense then, such surfaces act as specialized light sources themselves. Some of these reflected rays may happen to impinge on the cornea of an eye, passing through the cornea, the lens, and the optical media inside the eyeball, striking one of the photoreceptors in the retina, and being absorbed by one of its photopigment molecules. Only those particular rays of light finally absorbed by a photopigment molecule have any potential visual significance. All others bound about in the universe unnoticed by human beings and therefore are without visual effect on human beings.

Because humans rarely look directly at light sources, we are concerned primarily with light being reflected from surfaces. When a surface is diffusely reflecting, it is unnecessary to take into account the location of the original light source because every point on the surface is reflecting light in all directions. Only a few of the rays from each point on such a surface are admitted to the eye—the rest are absorbed or reflected by the face or lids and most miss the observer altogether. If the cornea and lens are optically perfect, then all of the divergent rays from each single point on a reflecting surface that reach the cornea are refracted to converge on a single point on the retinal surface at the back of the eye. When refraction is perfect, then the image of light formed on the retinal surface has a one-to-one correspondence with the patterning of the light being reflected from the surface and traveling to the eye.

Surfaces are rarely uniform in reflectance. Rather, some parts of a surface may reflect most of the incident light whereas adjacent parts reflect little. If the scene in front of the eyes has surfaces with varying levels of reflectance then the light reflected from each surface has differing numbers of quanta. Furthermore, although most light sources emit light of all visible wavelengths, surfaces selectively absorb light as a function of wavelength. Such differences in reflectance and light absorption result in corresponding differences in the number of quanta reaching the different parts of the retina. In this way the pattern of reflectances in the scene is reproduced in the pattern of varying numbers of quanta of different wavelengths in the retinal image of that scene.

Projection of Light as a Retinal Image—Perspective

At every moment in time an image is formed on the retina from light reflected from all parts of the scene simultaneously. That image reproduces the variation in reflectances of different parts of the scene itself. Transformations and changes in the pattern of reflectances occur on the retinal image as a function of the distance between the observer's eye and the scene and the viewing angle.

These transformations are described by the principles of geometry dating back to *Euclid's Optics* (ca. 300 B.C.; see Pirenne, 1970). Euclid said that an object of fixed physical size occupies a smaller visual angle if it is far away than if it is near. There is no change in the particular stream of quanta because they do not lose strength with distance, rather the size dimension of the discontinuities of reflectances projected onto the retina change—in perfect correspondence with distance and orientation.

The transformations in the projection of light reflected from surfaces to the eye of an observer is usually called *perspective*. More generally, perspective is concerned with the angles formed by light reflected from objects to the eye. Whenever the observed scene contains variations in distance from the eye, perspective transformations account for differences in the patterns of reflectances from the surface and on the retina.

The relationships between the patterning among the intensity and wavelength variation reflected for different parts of the scene and their projection on the retinal surface provide a major source of information at the retina about the layout of space. Gibson (1950, 1966), Purdy (1960), and Perkins (1975) have described the stimulus analysis in greater detail (see also Sedgwick, Chapter 2, this volume). Haber (1978) and Haber and Hershenson (1980) elaborate this type of analysis by describing the perspective transformation as a *surface scale of space* on the retina. Thus, all visual edges in space that are physically parallel converge to a common vanishing point in the image. If one set of parallel lines is at a different slope from another set, they have a separate vanishing point, with the rate of convergence toward their respective vanishing points being given by their slope away from the observer. Furthermore, surfaces with relatively uniform texture densities are represented as gradients of texture density on the retinal image. The rate of change in the density—the sharpness of the gradient—also defines the rate at which the distance from the observer increases across each of these surfaces.

Such changes in the retinal image form a scale of space because the information is present across the entire retinal image, rather than confined to one part or caused by one particular set of discontinuities in the reflectances. In contrast, interposition is an example of a local depth cue in which the nearer object occludes one farther away. Although this is a powerful source of information about the relative distances of the two objects, it only specifies adjacent discontinuities and does not determine the relationship of those objects to any other nonadjacent objects in the line of sight.

Perspective Transformations Produced by Movements and Binocularity

The preceding discussion and analysis of reflectances of light from distal surfaces to form a retinal image describes the kind of information available from a three-dimensional scene to a stationary eye, equivalent to what an observer would see if he used only one eye and did not move. Of course, in normal perception of scenes or pictures, observers use two eyes and they move both their eyes and their heads extensively. The optical changes that occur between a pattern of reflectances of light from surfaces and the pattern of discontinuity on the retinal image produced by eye movements, by head movements, and by allowing the observer a second eye provide substantial information about the layout of space in the scene.

Changes in the Retinal Image When the Eye Rotates in Its Socket

Two changes of paramount importance occur with eye movements: First, the retinal image is displaced with respect to the retinal surface; and second, the part of the scene viewed with maximum clarity and contrast shifts. The displacement produces no transformation in the pattern of the image—no compression or expansion, nor any transposition among the discontinuities. Of course, the part of the image farthest to the side opposite to the direction of movement no longer falls on any receptive part of the retina and is therefore occluded. Conversely, part of the scene on the other side becomes visible as the eye rotates toward it.

The effects of clarity are different. Although no transformation in the retinal image occurs with eye rotation, the part of the scene represented with sharpest focus shifts because that is always the part in the direct line of sight. Consequently, eye movements are an important component in visual search, as not all of the scene can be seen clearly without eye movements. In addition, eye movements are an important way to build up an integrated perception of an entire scene. However, eye movements without head movements do not provide any direct information about the layout of space.

Changes in the Retinal Image When the Head Moves

These changes are much more complicated because whenever the eye is displaced, the pattern of discontinuities of light on the retinal image undergoes a transformation: Light arising from nearby surfaces is shifted in the retinal image more than light arising from far away surfaces. Thus, in watching the countryside from a moving car, the trees near the road reflect light that sweeps across the retina more quickly than the light reflected from trees in the distance. The relationship between the relative rates of movement of light patterns across the retina is an exact function of the differences in the distances between the objects and the eye. The visual edges created by the physical discontinuities in reflectance are transposed, crossing each other as the observer moves. In this sense then, the relative rates of movement of the patterns of light across the entire retina provide the second *motion scale of space* for the entire scene (see Gibson, 1966; Haber, 1978; Haber & Hershenson, 1980). The ways in which an observer moves within a scene affect the kind of transformation occurring in the retinal image. Each pattern of transformation is unique to each type of movement, and each produces its own kind of complete, retinal, motion scale of space (see also Lee, 1974).

Changes Produced by Using Two Eyes

The preceding discussions have assumed that the observer had an eye patch over one eye. Technically, removing the eye patch produces no changes in the uncovered eye, but the information available about a scene is much more complete when viewed with two eyes than with one be-' cause the visual system of man is capable of comparing the images of the two eyes.

Because the two eyes are slightly separated in the head, and if the scene has variation in depth, the two retinal images of a scene can be slightly different. For example, if one looks at a small part of a scene which has no depth to it, so that all parts are equidistant from the eyes, then the two retinal images correspond exactly over their entire extent. But if there are parts of the scene closer or farther away than the point in the scene on which both eyes are focussed, then the two images do not overlap perfectly and are out of registration. The degree of noncorrespondence or disparity is exactly proportional to the differences in distance (i.e., nearer or farther) from the distance of the object on which the eyes are fixated. If one changes fixation to some other object at a different distance, a new pattern of correspondence and noncorrespondence is created, but again the disparity between the parts of the two images is proportional to the relative distances. In this sense then, the amount and location of the disparities between the two retinal images creates a third *binocular scale of space*. This is the geometric or optical basis for stereopsis or stereoscopic perception.

Correlation among the Three Scales of Space

Three scales of space created by the pattern of light as it is imaged over the retinal surfaces have just been described. As should be obvious from considerations of geometry alone, these three scales are perfectly correlated—that is, they each specify the same depth relationships. This does not mean that they are equally accessible or used by perceivers. The surface scale is always accessible, but the motion scale depends on the observer's motion, and the binocular scale depends on using two eyes. However, showing that the information is available on the retina does not tell us anything about whether or how it is used by perceivers. Furthermore, we know little about the developmental history of the use of these three scales, or of the role of particular experiences or environments in determining their selective use or usefulness.

This chapter has emphasized full, retinal, scales of space in this discussion. There are other visual sources of information about depth that do not arise from a scale of space across the entire retina. Interposition, as already mentioned, is one example. Another example is *adjacency* (see Gogel, 1977), in which areas of the retinal image that share a common contour are seen as being at the same distance from the perceiver. Familiar size or shape may also be a local depth cue—if you know the true size of an object, then its retinal size can be a clue as to how far away it is, and retinal shape can be a clue to orientation or slant.

Changes Produced by the Optics of the Eye

Before proceeding with further stimulus analyses, one important reservation has to be entered—the optical quality of the retinal image. Most stimulus analyses are carried out on a hypothetical plane between the eyes and the scene, on which the reflected light from the scene passes through the plane. In theory, if the plane is perpendicular to the line of sight, the pattern of reflectances from the scene is exactly reproduced on the plane and on the retinal surface (except for the inversion of the latter). However, such a theoretical analysis fails to account for the poor optical properties of the eye. Even with high light intensity, and the smallest possible pupil opening, we have little field depth in human vision. Only the central area of the light pattern projected on the retina is sharply focused. Blur becomes pronounced even a few degrees off center (out of nearly an 80° radius of the visual field). Thus, contrast between adjacent areas of luminance loses sharpness. For example, thin lines are spread out and reduced in contrast against their backgrounds. These facts constitute one important reason why a stimulus analysis can not substitute a projection plane in front of the eyes for the proximal stimulus. Every momentary retinal image is clear and sharp only in its center and progressively more fuzzy the further it is from that center. Therefore, the surface scale of space cannot be completely useful over the entire retinal image without eye movement as a means of integrating the information from the successive glances over a scene.

The preceding discussion represents a brief stimulus analysis of the information that reaches the retina about the layout of space in three-dimensional scenes. The next section contrasts this analysis with the information that comes from pictures—a stimulus analysis of pictures.

INFORMATION ABOUT DEPTH IN LIGHT REFLECTED FROM PICTURES

If you view a flat wall that is perpendicular to the line of sight, all three scales of space indicate the flatness. The surface scale for the viewed contents will be uniform—it contains no perspective changes, no vanishing point, and no texture gradients. The motion scale is also uniform—no matter how you move, no transformations indicating depth occur; rather, all parts of the image of the wall surface move at the same rate. Furthermore, the binocular scale shows no disparity anywhere—both retinal images are the same because no part of the scene is different in distance from any other part. In addition, all the nonscale sources of information about depth indicate flatness. In short, the overwhelming perceptual experience is of a flat surface.

What happens when the flat surface is a photograph or a representational painting of a three-dimensional scene? To analyze this a slight digression to describe a set of perspective rules used to help teach artists how to paint landscape is necessary. These rules help us to compare the retinal images from such a picture to those from the scene itself.

Beginning in the fifteenth century, many Renaissance painters devised rules and procedures to create paintings that would provide the same perspective transformation to the eye as would light reflected from the scene itself. Among the earliest of these were Alberti in 1434 (Grayson, 1972), followed by Dürer (1471–1528) (Panofsky, 1948), and Leonardo da Vinci near the end of fifteenth century. These rules do not tell painters how they should paint but are designed to aid them in learning some of the skills of representative art. Once the rules are mastered, the artist can violate or elaborate on them as his art dictates.

These perspective rules are quite simple in principle. They instruct a landscape painter to choose a vantage point from which to paint his picture. Then the artist should place a sheet of glass between his eye and the scene so that he is looking through the glass at the scene. Then the artist should trace the scene he sees through the glass onto the glass. Thus, nearby objects occupy large areas on the glass, generally near the bottom of the glass, painted in more saturated colors with sharper boundaries, coarser texture, and so forth. Far objects are sketched higher up on the glass plane, and are smaller, paler, and finer textured. Parallel lines stretching away from the painter are drawn as converging upward on the glass, toward a vanishing point.

After the artist completes the sketch on the glass, he then reproduces it onto canvas. The result is an accurate two-dimensional representation of the three-dimensional scene. It is accurate in the sense that the surface scale of space on the glass, entered by variations in perspective, texture, and the like, exactly reproduce the luminance and spectral discontinuities on the retinal pattern (except for blurring toward the edges which was unknown at the time of the Renaissance).

The painter's rules do not end with the geometry of perspective. Filling in the texture, and especially the colors when the sketch on the glass is transferred to the canvas, is not a simple process. Pirenne (1970) and

Hochberg (1978) note, for example, that the scene reflects a far greater range of contrasts than can any set of pigments on a canvas. This has led to other rules involving reduced colors, juxtaposition of shadows, and even taking into account the lateral inhibitory processes of the visual system to define edges (Ratliff, 1965). However, the principles are the same—geometry, color mixing, shadowing, and induction processes— all are used to produce a two-dimensional pattern that can produce the same retinal patterns as that reflected from the three-dimensional scene when viewed from the correct position.

A modern camera using a 50-mm focal length lens produces a print that also meets painters' rules, at least with respect to all of its visual edges. The print has far greater restrictions of intensity and spectral contrast than the scene itself (though some film emulsions and development processes do a better job than others). Except for trick photography or special lenses, photographs are the same as representational paintings (see Lumsden, Chapter 3 of this volume for a discussion of telephoto effects).

If the only sources of information in a picture about spatial layout come from the perspective transformations of the depicted visual edges, then it is easy to see how a picture of a scene conveys correct information about the space in the scene itself. Yet there are other sources of information, some from other aspects of the surface of the picture, some from motion perspective, and some from binocular disparity perspective. As we shall see, pictures present conflicting information: They convey information about a scene in depth while telling us we are looking at a flat two-dimensional surface hung on a wall. This conflict creates what is called the dual reality of pictures. Having shown that the Renaissance painters' rules provide a method of relating information about space through pictures, the following discussion will briefly consider the sources of information that make pictures look flat.

The surround of a picture—its frame and the flat wall on which it is hung—provide strong indications that the picture is flat as all of the surface information from the frame and wall are perfectly correlated with the information from the picture surface itself. (If you view a picture from an angle, the texture and disparity gradients exactly match that of the wall surface.) The picture surface contributes massive information about flatness. We can usually see the texture of the canvas or photographic paper, which projects a zero gradient over the surface if you stand directly in front of the picture. (The effect of flatness from texture can be minimized if viewing is sufficiently far so that the textural surface is below acuity threshold.) In addition, to the extent that the construction of the picture fails to mimic the pattern and ranges of light reflections from the scene it represents, it may look flat. Typically, the range of color saturations, and the range of intensity contrast are much narrower in the light reflected from pictures than from the scene. This tends to flatten the picture and reduce the impact of depth—an effect that occurs in almost all paintings and photographs.

Motion Information Regarding the Flatness of Pictures

Three very different changes occur when the head moves causing the location of the eyes in space to be shifted. First, if the two eyes remain fixated on the same point in a picture but are moved in space (e.g., when one walks past a picture while still looking at a particular part), the area of maximum clarity remains the same, but the pattern of luminance and spectral discontinuities over the retina expand on the side toward which the head moved and contract on the other side. Such expansion and contraction is exactly proportional to the changes in the distance of each point on the picture surface to the eyes. Even so, no transpositional changes in luminance and spectral discontinuities occur—each discontinuity remains in the same relation to each other one. Thus, the absence of relative changes in the luminance and spectral discontinuities when the head moves is a powerful source of information that the scene is flat. This is probably our most powerful source of such information.

Second, if one walks past a picture but does not hold fixation constant, then not only is there an expansion and contraction as the pattern is shifted along the retina, but also a shift of maximal clarity. There still is no relative change in the position of the discontinuities on the pattern because there is no "in front of" or "behind" in the scene—hence, information that the picture is flat.

Third, a change on the retina occurs if you move closer or farther from a picture. This causes the entire pattern to expand or contract, with a maximum change occurring in the part of the pattern reflected from the nearest part of the picture. As with each of the other motion-produced changes, no relative transpositional changes occur in the retinal pattern with radial motion. Thus, every variety of observer motion before a flat picture reveals its flatness. There is no way in which moving can lead to information that a flat picture is a window opening into a scene.

Binocular Disparity Information Regarding the Flatness of Pictures

Here the story is quite like that for motion. When looking at a small, flat picture straight on, there is no disparity between the two retinal images corresponding to any part of the picture. As this is a circumstance that arises only when all parts of the scene are equidistant from the two eyes, the picture must be flat.

If the picture is large relative to the viewing distance, then the edges of the picture are farther away from the eyes than the center, and there is a slight difference in the distances of the center and the edge. This produces a disparity between the two images regardless of where the observer is fixating on the picture surface. However, this disparity is exactly consistent with the disparity of the wall and the frame—hence the surface of the picture and the surface of the wall are seen as flush. Furthermore, there are no local disparities over the picture surface (i.e., no part of the picture is farther away or closer than any of its neighboring parts, only a continuously uniform gradient of disparity indicating a flat though extended surface. The same is true if the picture is viewed from an angle as this produces a gradient of disparity indicative of the slant, but without any local disparities. Therefore, the picture still must be a flat surface.

Summary of the Stimulus Analyses

We have considered the stimulus information being reflected to the eye from three-dimensional scenes and from pictures. If the observer moves or uses both eyes there is no way a flat picture can conceal its flatness. If the observer holds his head stationary and uses only one eye, then there is both flatness and three-dimensional information available: flatness from the wall and frame, from the surface texture of the picture, and from the potential limitations of the painters' rules to properly reflect the intensity and spectral contrasts from a picture surface. On the other hand, the luminance and spectral discontinuities that represent visual edges are capable of reflecting virtually the same pattern as does the scene it represents, so that all the sources of depth arising from local depth cues and the surface scale of space are present and can, in theory, be used to perceive the three-dimensional layout of the pictures. This combination of information about depth and flatness coexisting in the retinal projection from pictures accounts for their dual reality.

No claim is made that a picture of a scene and the scene itself will be confused. However, if all that you see is the picture surface itself, with nothing of the surrounding wall or frame visible, and if you use only one eye, do not move, and stand in the correct place to view the picture, then in theory, you should have trouble determining whether you are looking at a picture of a scene or the scene itself. The degree of confusion should be determined by the adequacy of the picture or photograph to duplicate the range of intensity and spectral contrasts. Hochberg (1972) tested this by restricting viewers of real scenes to one eye through an immobile peephole in which a piece of cellophane was placed between the viewer and the scene. He found viewers could not tell whether they were looking at a real scene or at a picture of a scene. Hagen, Glick, and Morse (1978) obtained the same result, using a slightly different, though comparable, procedure.

DEVELOPMENTAL ASPECTS OF THE DUAL REALITY OF PICTURES

As the preceding stimulus analysis makes clear, pictures have a dual reality. They can be perceived as flat objects in their own right, with certain shapes, brightnesses, contours, and colors, often a frame around them, etc. They also can be representative of some three-dimensional reality in which the flatness and frame are ignored and the contours and colors are perceived quite differently. Perceivers can apparently extract either of these realities of pictures and go back and forth between the two easily. The dual reality of pictures is clearest for so-called representational pictures, especially photographs of natural scenes. Adult perceivers have little difficulty recognizing or matching such two-dimensional representations to the natural scenes that gave rise to them. Additionally, they have little trouble correctly interpreting the object information and the spatial layout in such pictures. However, we should expect that these two realities interact with each other. Does seeing that the picture surface is flat affect our perception of the scene depicted? Does seeing the depicted scene affect our perception of the flat picture surface? The answer to all of these questions is clearly yes; and our understanding of this interaction is critical to the understanding of how we perceive the layout of space from pictures. Some of the answers are more apparent when considering the development of each of these realities. If the perception of depth and flatness in pictures follows the same processes as those for perceiving the depth or flatness in real scenes, then presumably this aspect of perception develops and improves with age and experience, in parallel with perceiving real scenes. If the abilities to determine depth and flatness develop together, then children at all ages have access to the dual reality of pictures. But if one develops sooner than the other, something quite different may happen.

For example, if children do not perceive the flatness of pictures until relatively late, then they would treat pictures and real scenes in the same way. Such equivalence leads to quite predictable types of errors in perceiving pictures. On the other hand, regardless of how children perceive depth in real scenes, if they are sensitive to the flatness information in pictures, then they should have trouble seeing the depth information in pictures. During the years that this is true, pictures would be perceived as flat surfaces only, and would not convey a layout of space.

Thus, the possible outcomes of the relative rates of development of perceiving depth in pictures and perceiving the flatness of pictures lead to quite different predictions about picture perception. Fortunately, data suggest one of these alternatives is correct: Flatness information becomes available later.

Cooper (1975), as noted in Hagen (1976), studied the ability of children to compensate for perspective distortion in pictures viewed obliquely. He found that 3 year olds treated the projections on the retina from pictures as if they had come from real objects and not pictured objects. Thus, the children's responses indicate a direct perception of three-dimensionality in a scene without the recognition that the scenes were only two-dimensional. Similarly, Benson and Yonas (1973) investigated the development of the utilization of direction of illumination as a source of information about depth in pictures. They found that adults assume that illumination is always from the top of the picture regardless of picture orientation, but young children (3 year olds) apparently assume that illumination is overhead regardless of the picture orientation. Young children made many errors in distinguishing convexity from concavity whenever the picture was turned on its side, but not when it was oriented properly. Benson and Yonas interpreted these data as showing that the ability to see a picture as a flat object in its own right develops later than the ability to perceive the depth relationships in pictures (or in real scenes).

Hagen (1976) also found a developmental improvement from ages 5 to 20 in the utilization of shadow information in pictures to determine the direction of the source of illumination. As Piaget and Inhelder (1967) showed that this process was fully developed for scenes in real space by ages 7–8, Hagen argued that there was a lag in perceiving the surface information in pictures beyond that of perceiving the depth information in pictures.

These studies all suggest that young children, even at ages when they can perceive the depth information in pictures, are not as good at perceiving the surface information—particularly that the picture is a flat object in its own right. In this case, pictures do not have a dual reality and contain only the reality of a window opening into space.

The nature of this development is not clear in these experiments. Young children must have access to the sources of information about flatness because these same sources define depth. However, it appears as if they do not apply such cues to pictures, but prefer to treat all projections on the retina as if they came from three-dimensional scenes. In doing so, young children make the kinds of mistakes in their perception described previously.

Another series of developmental experiments manipulated the effects of flat surface information on the perception of depth relationships in pictures. These studies demonstrated the importance of flatness information in correctly perceiving pictures. Yonas and Hagen (1973) attempted to remove flatness information from pictures by eliminating motion parallax and using rear-projected slides. When flatness information was removed, perceivers at all ages (3, 7, and 20 years) improved in their ability to perceive the depth relationships in pictures. Accuracy did not reach the level found in real scene controls, presumably because the experiment cound not remove all of the cues for flatness.

Conversely, Hochberg (1962) tried to make real scenes look like pictures by placing cellophane with a frame around it between the viewer and the scene. He found that when this kind of flatness information was provided, viewers could not distinguish the picture from the real scene it represented. Even more critically, Hagen, Glick, and Morse (1978) showed that if you make a viewer think he is looking at a picture by adding irrelevant cues of flatness (e.g., a plate of glass placed between the viewer and the scene), the perceiver treats the new scene as if it were a picture of the scene and makes the same type of errors that are made in looking at an actual print of the scene. Thus, not only does the perceiver confuse the modified scene with its picture (Hochberg's findings), but he or she perceives the depth relationships in the modified scene and its picture in the same way.

This line of evidence suggests that children develop the ability to perceive the three-dimensional relationships in real scenes and in pictures before they perceive the surface qualities, especially the flatness of pictures. Apparently, for some period in normal development, pictures do not have a dual reality for children. This does not mean that pictures look more vivid or are seen in "plastic depth" (to use Schlosberg's term, 1941). Rather, being less sensitive to the surface quality and the flatness of pictures leads to qualitatively different perceptions from pictures. The differences produce substantial errors when pictures are viewed from the wrong station point—that is, from a position in space other than the one where the painter or camera stood.

If it were not for the relevance of the station-point requirement, failure to distinguish the dual reality of pictures would have few theoretical consequences. But the station point is critical, sufficiently so to have sunk previous attempts to expound a theory of the type proposed here. The following section therefore considers the issue.

The Station-Point Controversy

The Renaissance painters' rules depend upon a critical Picture–Observer interaction. Even if a painter follows the rules correctly, and the observer uses only one motionless eye, the observer must still stand in the same place as the artist did when he sketched on glass. Failure to view from the proper station point results in a pattern on the retinal surface (ignoring blur for a moment) that is no longer isomorphic with the one on the hypothetical plate of glass. Therefore, it does not contain the proper surface scale of space and the local cues for the correct three-dimensional scene. Accordingly, failure of the observers to have their eyes where the painter had his (or where the camera's lens was for a photograph) should lead to errors in perception of the layout of the three-dimensionality perceived from the picture.

However, Hagen and Elliott (1976) and Hagen and Jones (1978) have demonstrated experimentally that observing from the correct station point is irrelevant for adults but critical for children when matching pictures to the three-dimensional objects depicted, and when rating pictures for their naturalness or their pleasantness. Farber and Rosinski (1978) and Rosinki and Farber (Chapter 4, this volume) review most of the available evidence on the perceptual effects of viewing from various incorrect station points. Their evidence suggests that whenever the viewer is restricted to a static monocular view, what is seen depends entirely on the geometrical distortions created by the incorrect station point. However, whenever the viewer can use two eyes, or move, then the resulting perception often seems to be independent of the station point, and cannot be predicted by the geometrical distortions at all.

The discrepancy between geometry and appearance has been a traditional stumbling block for the type of theory presented here, as in Kennedy and Ostry's (1976) criticism of Gibson (1951, 1971). If the correct perception of the third dimension in a picture depends upon the picture projecting the same pattern of light as did the scene represented by the picture, why is it irrelevant when the pattern of projected light changes with the viewer's position or orientation?

The most developed answer to this problem comes from Pirenne (1970). He argues that as long as the viewer can register the dual reality of a picture then he or she can determine what should be the correct station point and compensate for any distortions on the retina produced by an incorrect station point. Consequently, although the flatness of pictures might, in theory, detract from the perception of depth, the ability to perceive such flatness, according to Pirenne, allows the viewer to align himself before pictures properly and see the depth correctly. Pirenne's argument coincides closely with the pattern of results reviewed by Farber and Rosinski (1978), though they neither acknowledge Pirenne nor his position. However, the dual reality of pictures is perceived only under free binocular viewing, yet under such conditions incorrect station-point distortions seem irrelevant to the perception of both children and adults.

Hagen (1976) reports a study that was designed to test Pirenne's explanation by testing its corollary: Reducing the information for flatness should make surface information less useful and therefore less informative about depth. In the study, subjects viewed a picture of two objects of differing size, one placed nearer than the other. They had to point to the larger object. A correct response required correct perception of the depth relationships. Viewing was monocular through a peephole, either from the correct station point or obliquely from 40° to the side. To manipulate surface information, Hagen used photographic prints that had low surface information. The subjects were 4 years old, 7 years old, and adults. She tested children on the assumption that the compensatory mechanisms required experience and practice with viewing pictures and so should be less developed in children as they appear to be less sensitive to the surface information in pictures from which to base a compensatory process.

The results are consistent with the Pirenne hypothesis. Adults scored better when viewing slides versus prints at the correct station point, but not at the wrong one. When the viewing pointed shifted, the slides provide little surface information, and so did not help the perceiver to compensate. For the 4 year olds (who overall were much poorer), accuracy was not affected by station point on the slides, but they did much worse on prints at the wrong station point, presumably because children cannot compensate for the distortion. Here, then, is some evidence that adults use surface information to compensate for the wrong station point in order to correctly perceive the depth relationships in pictures. When that surface information is removed, as when viewing transparencies, then depth is distorted when viewed from the wrong station point. Furthermore, the ability to use such surface information for compensation is not available to children, so viewing from the wrong station point reduces the accuracy of their depth perception.

Hagen's experiment gives subjects little surface information about flatness—only the surface scale of space is available. The motion scale is probably the most powerful one both for depth in scenes and for flatness in pictures. If she had not used a peephole, but permitted free head movements, then even the 4-year olds should have been able to compensate for the oblique view of the print. Children, even younger than 4 years old, have substantial perceptual stability (Bower, 1974; Cohen & Salapatek, 1975), so Hagen's experiment gives an underestimate of the developmental rate. In addition, it should be noted that Hagen's response measure was a relative size judgment, which should have been unaffected by the oblique view transformation. However, her subjects were apparently judging relative areas, rather than linear extent, a judgment dependent on the shapes of the objects and, therefore, affected by the oblique transformation. Nevertheless, the indirect nature of such a "shape" judgment undoubtedly underestimated the degree of disruption and compensation taking place in this study.

What is lacking from Pirenne's hypothesis is the compensatory mechanism itself. What aspects of the surface are used to perceive depth correctly? We can answer this by considering the more general, perceptual compensation tasks routinely performed by perceivers. One can move around while looking at any scene without the scene appearing to change, even though each successive retinal pattern undergoes massive changes. Perceivers must have ways to attend only to the commonalities of the successive patterns over time and different perspectives, and to ignore the particular retinal pattern of any instant in time. The representations constructed of a scene or picture are not tied to, nor do they resemble, any one of the momentary retinal patterns projected from that scene or picture.

To understand the station point problem, one must broaden the focus of picture viewing to beyond the single glance. Although the painters' rules apply to a one-eyed stationary observer, they do not require that his eyeball be still. The visual system is capable of powerful compensatory processes as a result of eye movements. One does not perceive movement in the environment when the eyes are moved, even though that movement produces a massive sweep of information across the retinal surface. Furthermore, the position of a target presented during a saccadic movement is accurately located in space even though the eye is moving rapidly (Matin, 1972). The same is true during pursuit movements (White, 1976). All of these must imply that humans have ways of ignoring the displacments occuring across the retina when they are caused by eye movements. Said another way, the specific location of the pattern of stimulation on the retina is not used in our processing. Although the relationships within the patterns are critical, where the pattern is located over the retina at any one instance does not seem to matter.

The same evidence and conclusions apply when head movements are considered. The visual world remains quite stationary despite our head or whole body movements. This is true whether the eyes also move, and whether they hold fixation on some position in space. Furthermore, the head and eyes are very precisely coordinated during locomotion through space so that the whold world remains stable and stationary. Finally, the visual world remains stationary when the motion of the body is toward or away from the scene or picture being viewed. The retinal changes of compression or expansion of the pattern on the retina under these circumstances is never attributed to the world moving toward or away from the viewer.

In summary, neither the absolute location of stimulation on the retina during each instant in time, nor the various transformations of the retinal pattern are directly perceived. This is not to say that the visual system is inattentive to such translations or transformations. Whatever the explanation for how these compensations are accomplished, it involves a processing of such changes, but that processing is designed to preserve a stability or constancy of perception.

Regarding station points, the preceding arguments suggest that neither the precise location of a pattern on the retina, nor the particular transformation of the pattern over time enter directly into our perceptions of scenes or pictures. The perceiver is not dependent upon a particular place from which to view a scene, anymore than he or she should see the scene differently if moving past it, in and out of it, or remaining stationary.

Because these compensatory processes are more general than picture processing, it seems most unlikely that specific experience with pictures is necessary for compensation to be carried out.

Although painters' rules require painters to specify their location in order to define any particular pattern on the canvas, both the painter and the viewer are free to move about. If the painter moves, the pattern on the canvas will be different but still resemble the information in the scene. If the viewer moves, the momentary retinal patterns will be changed, but that only defines where he stood and where his eyes were pointing, not how the scene or painting looks.

ARE THE RENAISSANCE RULES CAPABLE OF PRODUCING ERRORS IN PERCEPTION?

Is a painting produced by painters' rules unique to the scene it represents? Could a painting or photograph be made of a three-dimensional scene that would match some other three-dimensional scene just as well? From the analysis already presented, it follows that for a stationary, one-eyed observer, standing in the proper place, the retinal pattern arising from light reflected from a Leonardo-inspired painting or photograph and the retinal pattern arising from a three-dimensional scene would be close to identical. Any differences primarily result from the painter's inability to represent the range of color tones, shadings, and shadowings contained in the scene. Given the restriction on monocularity, movement, and viewer position, picture and scene perception must follow the same rules, whatever those rules are. Therefore, perceptions occurring from viewing a scene should match those arising from viewing a properly painted or photographed view of that scene so that a perceiver should never misperceive the picture of a scene as being representative of some other scene.

This is not to say that perceivers never misperceive (Several instances of misperception will be discussed). Rather, the previous analysis suggests that principles accounting for misperceptions are not unique to pictured scenes, but are determined by the information processing of light from scenes and pictures alike. What needs to be learned and the methods developed to handle inadequate or ambiguous information are the same for pictures of scenes as for scenes themselves.

DO WE HAVE TO LEARN TO PERCEIVE PICTURES?

Because pictures and other two-dimensional representations are invented or constructed by human beings (perhaps with the exception of shadows cast by objects), theorists have assumed that perceivers are unable to perceive the layout of space or recognize the objects portrayed in pictures without prior visual training or experience with pictures. However, I am arguing here that perception of pictures follows the same rules and processes as the perception of three-dimensional scenes. In addition, it is my position that perception of the three-dimensional scenes develops first. Therefore, those aspects to be learned in the perception of scenes by implication, must also be learned in picture perception.

If scene perception develops first, then as soon as one aspect of scene perception can be accomplished (whether with or without the need of experience) that same aspect can be applied to pictures without further experience. Thus, the classic study by Hochberg and Brooks (1962) is open to two interpretations. They tested a 19-month-old child who had never been exposed to any two-dimensional representations. Despite this, the child was equally accurate in identifying familiar objects from pictures of the objects as from seeing the objects themselves. Hochberg and Brooks did not report data about the perception of the layout of space in pictures, but at least with respect to object identification, no prior experience *with pictures* seemed necessary. This is a powerful result, perhaps even an instance in which we can generalize from one American child to all children for all time.

This result does not rule out the possibility that object identification in three-dimensional scenes is learned (scenes a 19 month old has already had extensive experience with over his entire life). No attempt was made to control this in the Hochberg and Brooks study. Therefore (playing the devil's advocate for the moment) if object identification from scenes is learned and pictures are perceived using the same processes used for scenes, then it follows that being able to perceive objects in pictures is also learned—a conclusion quite contrary to the one offered by Hochberg and Brooks.

Such logic can also be applied to the cross-cultural literature on picture perception (see Hagen & Jones, 1978, for recent reviews). Although there are cultural groups who do not produce or utilize two-dimensional representations, finding that aspects of their picture perception are accurate, even upon first exposure, does not specify the acquisition process. On the other hand, finding differences in picture perception between people with no experience and those with lots of experience does implicate an experiential variable.

Unfortunately, the choice of stimuli (e.g., Hudson, 1960) used in the cross-cultural research has been poor enough to weaken most reasonable conclusions. Although the evidence for naming objects from such pictures is generally consistent with the conclusions of Hochberg and Brooks, the data suggests that many people who had never seen pictures before had trouble extracting the layout of space from Hudson's pictures. This has been true both for African subjects and for Westerners. Hagen and Jones (1978) examined some of the stimuli in detail, and then used them to test subjects who were thoroughly familiar with pictures. They found that many of the pictures used in the cross-cultural research did not produce reliable responses from such subjects.

Specifically, they found that some of the sources of information about the layout of space in the picture did not follow rules of perspective. If the picture does not reflect luminance and spectral discontinuity to the eye that correspond with those from the appropriate real scene, there is no way to attribute a perceiver's erroneous responses to a failure to understand and use rules of perspective. Erroneous responses could be merely due to a confusion in the face of conflicting rules—rules that are perfectly well understood. No problems would have existed here if properly made photographs were used as stimuli. However, nearly all of the work reported to date uses outline drawings—all of which delete some of Leonardo's rules and most of which treat others inconsistently.

According to the thesis presented here, it is my opinion that being able to perceive the layout of space from pictures does not require specific training or experience. However, given the dual reality of pictures, it is critical that perceivers unfamiliar with pictures understand that they are being asked about the depth reality, not the flat reality. Otherwise, the perceiver could simply say that he perceives all parts of the picture equidistant from him because it is flat. To my knowledge, cross-cultural research does not control for this possibility. Until we have better data, I am very hesitant to interpret any of the reported research as supportive of a learned component of picture perception and certainly not supportive of a learned process independent of space perception in general.

PERCEPTION OF INCOMPLETE REPRESENTATIONAL PICTURES

Although recent civilization has vastly increased the number of pictures that lack complete perspective information, very little is known about how we perceive the layout of space from an outline drawing, a cartoon, a sketch, or a caricature. Of course, creators of such pictures are usually not interested in conveying information about the layout of space, nor do they care if what is conveyed is correctly perceived, as long as the viewer recognizes the objects portrayed.

There are outline drawings in which depth information is being communicated, and viewers seem to have little trouble perceiving their three-dimensionality. The only formal attempt to explain the perception of outline pictures—that of Gibson (1951)—argues that light reflected from an outline drawing projects sufficient information to the retina related to all three-dimensions so that such drawings can be perceived correctly. This perception, according to Gibson, is not based upon convention or prior experience with such pictures, but is possible because of the formal similarity of the depth information available from three-dimensional scenes and from outline pictures representing such scenes.

Kennedy (1974) and Kennedy and Ospty (1976) examined Gibson's assertion and other attempts to explain the perception of spatial layout in incompletely drawn representational pictures. Although they make a number of telling criticisms of all such explanations, nearly all of their criticisms are concerned with object identification and not with spatial layout. Object identification is not a trivial problem. A number of writers have properly noted that it is often easier to recognize an object portrayed in a cartoon or caricature than from a high fidelity photograph of it (see Ryan & Schwartz, 1956, for a test). Hochberg (1972) talks about an object having a *canonical* form—the form that best displays its characteristic features—what might be called a prototype. This would delete all ambiguous features, all features that the form shares with other forms and so are not definitional or distinctive, and all features which are irrelevant or noninformative. Outline drawings or cartoons provide typical examples of this when their purpose is to use pictures to promote identification or recognition of a specific object quickly.

Perkins (1975) and Goldman and Hagen (1978) have empirically addressed the problem of feature variation in caricatures. With such drawings, recognizability is essential, so the selection of features to distort cannot be haphazard. Goldman and Hagen analyzed 100 caricatures of Richard Nixon, created by 17 different artists. They found great consistency in the features selected for exaggeration (especially jowls, box-like jaw, length of nose), consistent with and between artists and times. Different public figures obviously have different features exaggerated, but for Mr. Nixon, these features must be part of his canonical form.

How is the layout of space conveyed by outline drawings that so obviously do not contain all of the information of a photograph, and often contain incorrect information as in the deliberate distortion of a cartoon or caricature? One answer is that they do not convey spatial information. A caricature is almost, by definition, of an object or person, and not of a scene. Consequently, neither the artist nor the viewer cares very much if the scene containing the caricatured person looks a little flat or funny. Additionally it is possible that there is canonical depth in pictures for the layout of space. Perceivers undoubtedly do not use all of Leonardo's rules, or weight them equally to perceive a three-dimensional layout from its two-dimensional picture. If the goal of picturing is to convey as rapidly or specifically as possible the layout of space, then the unnecessary, lowly weighted or uninformative elements of a picture could be deleted to achieve an economical three-dimensionality. For most scenes, outline perspective, followed by interposition and adjacency, would seem to be the most powerful cues, with shadowing and aerial perspective among the least pervasive.

The existence of canonical form and canonical depth does not in and of itself demand that the perception of outline pictures is learned. What is required is a research program on procedures that make pictures more effective with respect to some goal, while using fewer features. When we know some of the rules of feature deletion in the service of faster or more accurate recognition of objects or of the layout of space, then we can determine whether the application of such rules depends upon special learning or experiences. This discovery requires first a new stimulus analysis of the kind described earlier. Once the elements of canonical depth of form are described, then we can relate them to a fully articulated picture or scene from which they are taken. This will permit us to determine whether the elements of canonical depth are a subset of all of the sources of information for depth, or if some of them are emergent elements not found in fully articulated pictures or photographs. I cannot predict the outcome of this analysis, but whatever the particular rules that allow identification of depth prove to be, they probably will apply equally to natural scenes, representational pictures, and outline drawings.

WHEN WILL PICTURES CREATE AN ILLUSION?

Outline drawings that create visual illusions have delighted both viewers and theorists for several centuries, although the theorists have not always been clear about why these drawings produce the effects they do. As illusion-producing drawings must, in some sense, function this way because of the operation of normal principles of perception applied to unusual drawings or situations, they have been sought out as demonstrations to help elucidate those normal principles.

A perception is called an *illusion* when what the perceiver describes does not agree with some physical measurement of the distal stimulus (Coren & Girgus, 1977). Based upon the prior discussion, such a circumstance should rarely, if ever, occur when the distal stimulus is a visually rich, three-dimensional scene. However, this definition of illusion, as Coren and Girgus emphasize, does not make sense when applied to any two-dimensional picture, photograph, or even a line drawing.

Consider, first, problems with respect to fully representational paintings or photographs. Such pictures already have undergone the perspective transformation from the three-dimensional scene they represent to a two-dimensional picture surface. To the extent that a viewer perceives the three-dimensional scene represented in the picture, there must be a mismatch between the distal *picture* surface and his perception. Thus, a photograph of a receding railroad track contains vastly *unequal* line lengths of the various railway ties (as measured with a ruler on the distal picture surface), but these are all perceived *as equal.* In fact, every aspect, feature, or element of the distal picture surface produces an illusory perception if illusions are defined in this way.

However, no one calls such mismatches illusions! Rather the mismatches result from an appropriate application of constancy scaling in which the perceiver uses the information in the picture to construct a correct representation of the three-dimensional scene—the proper layout of space. Perceivers might be aware or might be made aware of the picture being flat and that the railway ties are of all different sizes on the picture surface. If that occurs, then the perceiver has two different perceptions, the two realities of pictures. However, as the three-dimensionality of representational pictures and photographs is so powerful, even the cues to flatness are not sufficient to prevent the construction of the three-dimensional layout of space with its attendant constancy scaling.

In the experimental literature, the term "illusion" is reserved not for these instances of representational pictures of photographs, but for certain kinds of line drawings. In this case, mismatch between the distal features in the drawing and our perception of these features is called an illusion. For this not to be whimsy on the part of the illusion-theorists, there must be some critical difference between such drawings and all other two-dimensional stimuli. There are two such critical differences. First, the drawings are not intended by their creators to be representative of three-dimensional scenes. Second, the balance between the dual realities of the pictures has swung so far toward flatness that is is difficult to perceive the three-dimensionality, even though there is some potential information about three-dimensional space. So, perceivers act as if they are looking at a flat drawing, but they still perceive enough of its depth reality as if it were a representation of a three-dimensional scene. Because the artist had no intention of drawing a three-dimensional scene, such drawings are said to produce a misapplication or innapropriate constancy scaling.

This explanation of line drawn illusions was first porposed by Thiery (1896), but is more typically identified with Gregory (1966, 1970). The theory states that perceivers use the two-dimensional information in outline drawings to construct a representation of a three-dimensional scene in the same way that they can construct three-dimensional space from fully representational pictures or photographs. It is a misapplication of constancy only because there is no three-dimensional scene supposedly being denoted by the illusion producing drawings. That is, we, as theorists, insist the drawing should be treated as flat, whereas we, as perceivers, treat it like any other picture and construct a perception of it as if it represented a scene.

One problem with this theory is that perceivers often do not report perceiving the apparent depth relationships that this theory says are responsible for the apparent size changes. Thus, for the Muller–Lyer illusion, viewers should perceive the apparently longer line as farther away than the apparently shorter line in order to account for why one sees the size difference. Yet many observers, even those with strong illusions of size, see the distances as equal or even occasionally the longer line as closer (Worrall, 1974).

It is easy to see why this might happen at least with respect to the vast majority of two-dimensional line illusions. The drawings are so impoverished that they appear flat, with no depth in them at all. The two-dimensional information that specifies three-dimensionality may be registered, but it is not perceived as such because it is at variance with the clear flatness of the picture given by other sources of information. The registration, or taking into account, is sufficient to produce the apparent size (or shape or directionality) changes, but it itself is not perceived. Epstein (1973) and Rock (1975) provide a fuller discussion of the registered-but-not-perceived distinction. Gregory (1966, 1970) has shown that if the cues of flatness are reduced in the drawing, then not only is the illusory effect greatly increased, but the depth becomes apparent to the perceiver as well.

It should be noted that nature does provide a few three-dimensional illusions directly, the most famous being the size illuision of the moon at various orientations in the sky. The moon illusion can be explained by misappropriate constancy scaling (Rock & Kaufman, 1962). The relative absence of depth information from such far away objects in the sky leads the zenith moon to be interpreted as nearer than the horizon moon, which is seen as behind the horizon terrain. As the visual angle of the moon is constant regardless of its elevation, the registered difference in distance results in a perceived difference in size.

Coren (1974) discusses a set of illusory drawings that create subjective contours. These are illusory because most perceivers report seeing a contour when no intensity or wavelength discontinuity exists in either the proximal or distal stimulus drawing. Coren considers the edges as being perceived in stereoscopically viewed random dot stereograms, the edges defining objects when only the shadows cast by the objects are drawn, and the edges of an unshown object seen overlapping a more articulate one. Coren argues that, in all three instances, the subjective contour is perceived because there is depth information in the drawings that leads perceivers to structure the entire configuration on several depth levels. Even if no contour is drawn to separate the different levels, one is perceived because a part of the figure is seen in front of another part. In support of his argument, he presents data about each of the three types of subjective contour examples to show that perceivers do see them in depth. Furthermore, when they are redrawn so as to eliminate the depth information, the subjective contours also disappear.

It is not my contention that the dual reality of pictures accounts for all subjective contours, of for all of the so-called visual illusions. There can be other factors besides stratification in depth that induce contours in perception where none existed in the luminance discontinuities. Most of the Gestalt laws of organization are predictions about perceptual structure even in the absence of physical structure. Although some of these laws concern depth, others do not. For example, the law of closure is most explicitly a statement of when subjective contours connecting physically unconnected elements occur. Ware and Kennedy (1977) report a subjective contour demonstration that is much more akin to closure than to induced stratification. However, it is my contention that pictures, because of their dual reality, are interpretable in two ways. When clever people draw their pictures carefully, they can pit those two interpretations against each other so that we perceive the picture in atypical ways.

The interpretation of visual illusions is basically the same as that proposed here for all picture perception. Perceivers treat all luminance and spectral discontinuities on the retina as representations of a three-dimensional scene if there is any source of information conducive to that construction. In this way all features of the retinal pattern are interpreted as if they were reflected from a three-dimensional scene, even when the perceiver has other information to tell him that it was only a two-dimensional picture. The dual reality of pictures holds—the picture is still seen as flat (hence, no depth in the picture plane), but the perceiver can also construct the three-dimensional scene the picture represents. It is the latter process that makes all picture perception illusionary.

As mentioned earlier, one should not have illusory perceptions when looking at visually rich three-dimensional scenes. The moon illusion occurs because the sky is so devoid of information about true distances (i.e., motion perspective, binocular disparity, and a continous surface texture all are absent). The relative motion illusion of the moon racing through the clouds disappears as soon as a perceptual anchor is added to the visual scene (e.g., try to get the illusion if you view the moon through tree branches or through a small window).

SUMMARY

The ability to perceive the three-dimensional layout of space in a flat two-dimensional picture is commonplace, but not always clearly understood. The thesis presented here is that perceivers use the same perceptual processes when looking at pictures as when looking at natural scenes. This implies that with normal viewing, pictures, unlike scenes, have a dual reality: They are perceived as flat surfaces because head movements and binocular disparity produce retinal patterns indicative of flatness, and they are perceived as representative of three-dimensional scenes because the momentary retinal pattern to either eye alone is the same as that reflected from the actual scene being represented by the picture.

The Renaissance painters worked out the procedures by which artists could create canvasses that project the same pattern of light to the eye as the scene being painted. This chapter has examined the stimulus basis for these rules in some detail. It has also explored the problems apparently requiring a common station point for viewing a scene and a picture of a scene. Surprisingly, the actual position of the viewer rarely seems to matter. Although Pirenne has argued that viewers have to learn through experience with pictures how to compensate for their incorrect station points, it is suggested here that this type of compensation is but one subclass of all the compensations perceivers have to make for their own orientation and movements. Such compensations have little to do with the experience of looking at pictures. The implications of this thesis are examined within the context of brief discussions of the role of experience in perceiving pictures: the possibilities and causes of misperception of pictures; how perceivers approach and perceive incompletely drawn representational pictures, outline drawings, cartoons and caricatures; and finally why all picture-looking is illusory.

REFERENCES

Benson, C. W., & Yonas, A. Development of sensitivity to static pictorial depth information. *Perception & Psychophysics*, 1973, *13*, 361–366.

Bower, T. G. R. *Development in infancy*. San Francisco: Freeman, 1974.

Cohen, L. B., & Salapatek, P. *Infant perception: From sensation to cognition* (2 vols.). New York: Academic Press, 1975.

Cooper, R. *The development of recursion in pictorial perception*. Paper given at Conference on Picture Perception, Center for Research on Human Learning, University of Minnesota, July, 1975.

Coren, S. Subjective contours and apparent depth. *Psychological Review*, 1974, *79*, 339–367.

Coren, S. & Girgus, J. S. Illusions and constancies. In W. Epstein (Ed.), *Statibility and constancy in visual perception*. New York: Wiley, 1977. Pp. 255–284.

Epstein, W. The process of "taking into account" in visual perception. *Perception*, 1973, *2*, 267–285.

Farber, J., & Rosinski, R. R. Geometric transformation of pictured space. *Perception*, 1978, *7*, 269–282.

Gibson, J. J. *The perception of the visual world*. Boston: Houghton-Mifflin, 1950.

Gibson, J. J. A theory of pictorial perception. *Audio-Visual Communication Review,* 1951, *1,* 1–23.

Gibson, J. J. *The senses considered as perceptual systems.* Boston: Houghton-Mifflin, 1966.

Gibson, J. J. The information available in pictures. *Leonardo, 1971, 4,* 27–35.

Gogel, W. C. The metric of visual space. In W. Epstein (Ed.), *Stability and constancy in visual perception.* New York: Wiley, 1977. Pp. 129–182.

Goldman, M., & Hagen, M. A. The forms of caricature: Physiognomy and political bias. *Studies in the Anthropology of Visual Communication,* 1978, *8,* 30–36.

Grayson, C. L. B. *Aberti, on painting and on sculpture.* Translated from the Latin, 1434. London: Phaidon Press, 1972.

Gregory, R. L. Visual illusions. In B. Foss (Ed.), *New horizons in psychology.* Baltimore: Penguin, 1966.

Gregory, R. L. *The intelligent eye.* London: Weidenfeld & Nicholson, 1970.

Haber, R. N. Visual Perception. In M. R. Rosenweig (Ed.), *The annual review of psychology* (Vol. 29). 1978. Pp. 31–59.

Haber, R. N., & Hershenson, M. *The psychology of visual perception* (2nd ed.). New York: Holt, 1980.

Hagen, M. A. The development of sensitivity to cast and attached shadows in pictures as information for the direction of the source of illumination. *Perception and Psychophysics,* 1976, *20,* 25–28.

Hagen, M. A. Influence of picture surface and station point on the ability to compensate for oblique view in pictorial perception. *Developmental Psychology,* 1976, *12,* 57–63.

Hagen, M. A. Picture perception; toward a theoretical model. *Psychological Bulletin,* 1976, *81,* 471–497.

Hagen, M. A. Problems with picture perception: A reply to Rosinski, *Psychological Bulletin,* 1976, *83,* 1176–1178.

Hagen, M. A., & Elliott, H. B. An investigation of the relationship between viewing condition and preference for true and modified linear perspective in adults. *Journal of Experimental Psychology: Human Perception and Performance,* 1976, *2,* 429–490.

Hagen, M. A., Glick, R., & Morse, B. The role of two-dimensional surface characteristics in pictured depth perception. *Perceptual and Motor Skills, 1978, 46,* 875–881.

Hagen, M. A., & Jones, R. K. Cultural effects on pictorial perception: How many words is one picture really worth? In R. Walk & H. Pick (Eds.), *Perception and experience.* New York: Plenum, 1978, Pp. 171–212.

Hagen, M. A., & Jones, R. K. Differential patterns of preference for modified linear perspective in children and adults. *Journal of Experimental Child Psychology,* 1978, *26,* 205–215.

Hochberg, J. E. Art and perception. In E. C. Carterette & H. Friedman (Eds.), *Handbook of perception* (Vol. 10). New York: Academic Press, 1978.

Hochberg, J. E. The representation of things and people. In E. H. Gombrich, J. Hochberg, & M. Black (Eds.), *Art, perception, and reality.* Baltimore: Johns Hopkins Press, 1972. Pp. 47–94.

Hochberg, J. E. The psychophysics of pictorial perception. *Audio-Visual Communication Review.* 1962, *10,* 22–54.

Hochberg, J. E., & Brooks, V. Pictorial recognition as an unlearned ability. A study of one child's performance. *American Journal of Psychology,* 1962, *75,* 624–628.

Hudson, W. Pictorial depth perception in subcultural groups in Africa. *Journal of Social Psychology,* 1960, *52,* 183–208.

Kennedy, J. M. *A psychology of picture perception: Information and images.* San Francisco: Jossey-Bass, 1974.

Kennedy, J. M., & Ostry, D. J. Approaches to picture perception: Perceptual experience and ecological optics. *Canadian Journal of Psychology,* 1976, *30,* 90–98.

Matin, L. Eye movements and perceived visual direction. In D. Jameson & L. M. Hurvich (Eds.), *Handbook of sensory physiology* (Vol. 7). *Berlin:* Heidelberg & Springer-Verlag, 1972.

Panofsky, E. *Albrect Dürer* (Vol. 1). Princeton, New Jersey: Princeton Univ. Press, 1948.

Perkins, D. N. Compensating for distortion in viewing pictures obliquely. *Perception and Psychophysics.* 1973, *14,* 13–19.

Perkins, D. N. A definition of caricature. *Studies in the Anthropology of Visual Communication,* 1975, *2* (1).

Piaget, J., & Inhelder, B. *The child's conception of space.* New York: Norton, 1967.

Pirenne, M. H. *Optics, painting, and photography.* New York: Cambridge Univ. Press, 1970.

Purdy, W. C. The hypothesis of psychophysical correspondence in space perception. *General Electric Technical Information Series.* 1960, (No. R 60EL C 56).

Ratliff, F. *Mach bands: Quantitative studies on neural networks in the retina.* San Francisco: Holden-Day, 1965.

Richter, J. P. *The notebooks of Leonardo di Vinci* (Vol. 1). New York: Dover Press, 1970.

Rock, I. *An introduction to perception.* New York: MacMillan, 1975.

Rock, I., & Kaufman, L. The moon illusion II. *Science,* 1962, *136,* 1023–1031.

Rosinski, R. R. Picture perception and monocular vision: A reply to Hagen. *Psychological Bulletin,* 1976, *83,* 1175.

Ryan, T. A., & Schwartz, C. Speed perception as a function of mode of presentation. *American Journal of Psychology.* 1956, *69,* 60–69.

Schlosberg, H. Stereoscopic depth from single pictures. *American Journal of Psychology,* 1941, *54,* 601–605.

Thiery, A Uber, Geometrisch-optische Tauschungen. *Philosophische Studiern,* 1896, *12,* 67–126.

Ware, C., & Kennedy, J. M. Illusory line linking solid rods. *Perception,* 1977, 6, 601–602.

White, C. W. Visual Masking during pursuit eye movements. *Journal of Experimental Psychology: Human Perception and Performance.* 1976, *2,* 469–478.

Worrall, N. A test of Gregory's Theory of primary constancy scaling. *American Journal of Psychology,* 1974, *84,* 505–510.

Yonas, A., & Hagen, M. A. Effects of static and Kinetic depth information on the perception of size by children and adults. *Journal of Experimental Child Psychology,* 1973, 15, 254–265.

The Geometry of Spatial Layout in Pictorial Representation

Fundamental Concepts 34
   The Information in Light 34
   The Projective Model of Vision 35
   The Picture Plane 38
   The Station Point 40
Orthographic Projection 41
   The Plan and the Elevation 41
   Constructing a Picture from an Orthographic Projection 45
   The Apparent Ambiguity of Pictorial Representation 48
Perspective Constructions 48
   Constructing Pictures Directly in the Picture Plane 48
   The Horizon and the Trace 50
   The Grid 52
   Projective Heights 59
   Other Planes, Other Horizons 59
   Scale 61
Geometrical Information for Spatial Relations 62
   Pictorial Invariants 62
   Redundancy of Information 66
   Finding the Station Point 66
   Scale 71
   Occlusion 71
   Optical Contact 72
   Texture 73
   Gradients 76
   The Horizon 82
   Height in the Picture Plane 86
   Other Information, Other Invariants 87

33

The Perception of Pictures
Volume I

FUNDAMENTAL CONCEPTS

The Information in Light

One of the functions that pictures serve is to show us how things look. J. J. Gibson has argued (1971) that pictures do this by structuring the light that they reflect so that it conveys information to our eyes that is similar, in certain essential respects, to that which we receive from the actual scenes. If pictures were able to exactly duplicate the light from the scenes they represent, then the process of perceiving a picture would be identical to the process of directly perceiving the scene it represented, and there would be no separable subject of investigation which we could identify as "pictorial" perception. But a picture cannot duplicate the light from a real scene. The flat and pigmented surface of a picture produces a distribution of reflected light that, if measured by some device for recording luminous energy, would be found, almost without exception, to differ radically in amount, spectral composition, and spatial distribution from the reflected light coming from the scene the picture represents. The essential similarity between the ways in which the scene and a picture of it act on the light reaching our eyes is an intellectual puzzle, posed in the Renaissance, whose solution is still a subject of debate today.

Gibson, extending previous theoretical and empirical advances, formulated a broad solution to this puzzle. He (1961, 1966) asserts that the surfaces and textures of the environment give structure to the light reflected from them. This structure is a set of complex invariant relations that exist, over time, between the light intensities coming from different surfaces or facets of the environment; although the intensities themselves may change radically over time some aspects of the relations between them will remain invariant. For example, when two surfaces meet at an angle, as adjacent walls of a room do, almost any source of illumination will light them unequally. As a result, the distribution of light intensities coming from the surfaces to an observer will have a discontinuity corresponding to their line of intersection. The intensity of light coming from either of these surfaces may vary enormously depending on the intensity and location of their source of illumination, but except in unusual or contrived circumstances the discontinuity corresponding to their intersection will always be there. It is an invariant structure in the light.

The structure in the light from an environment is mathematically related to the structure of the environment itself. This makes it possible, at least in principle, for an observer to visually register the structure in the light and to extract information about the structure of the environment from it. Visual perception, according to Gibson, is just such a process.

This new conception of visual perception enables Gibson to propose that a picture shows us how something looks by providing us with an array of light whose structure is similar to that in the array of light from the scene itself, even though the actual intensities of light making up the two arrays may be very different. As Gibson (1971) puts it:

> It is possible to suggest a new theory of pictorial perception only because a new theory of visual perception has been formulated. The latter is based on the radical assumption that light can convey information about the world. . . . This assumption, in turn, depends on a new conception of light in terms of the array at a point of observation—light considered not merely as a stimulus but also as a structure [p. 34].

Gibson (1961) uses the term *optic array* to refer to the structured array of light coming from the environment to a point in space where an eye might be placed. By creating the concept of the optic array, Gibson helped to clarify the distinction between the structure of the environment and the structure of the light coming to the eye from the environment. The two structures—that of the environment and that of the optic array—are mathematically related but not identical. This distinction allows Gibson (1971) to formally define a picture as "a surface so treated that a delimited optic array to a point of observation is made available that contains the same kind of information that is found in the ambient optic arrays of an ordinary environment (p. 31)."

The purpose of this chapter is to investigate and to flesh out this definition by investigating from a mathematical standpoint the information contained in the structured light reflected from pictures. Our concern is with this essentially mathematical question of what information is available, rather than with the empirical question of how well people are able to use such information. Our investigation is restricted to information about spatial layout—the distances, sizes, slants, and tilts of things—both because it is there that the puzzle of pictorial representation has often seemed most difficult and because we are there on the firmest ground mathematically. Let us begin by looking at the geometrical basis on which pictures are constructed. In doing so, we approach the question of what information is present in pictures by asking how information is put into them.

The Projective Model of Vision

The geometrical analysis of pictorial information given here is based on what will be referred to as the *projective model of vision*. This model entails a number of simplifications that make the analysis a great deal more tractable, while retaining much of the structure, both in the environment and in the light, that we need to consider.

The behavior of light in a natural environment is extremely complex. The various environmental sources of light, natural and artificial, each emit light of different and sometimes varying spectral composition and energy level. Light is absorbed, reflected, and refracted by the atmosphere through which it travels, and is then multiply absorbed, reflected, and refracted in a myriad of complicated ways by the textured surfaces of objects that it strikes. Light that enters the eye is refracted at four surfaces, two of which (the front and back of the lens) are of variable curvature, passes through an aperture of variable size, and is subjected to scatter by two ocular media. Consequently, it should not be surprising that, except for the very simplest cases, it is not practical to attempt to calculate the actual distribution of light reaching the retina.

Some form of the projective model of vision has been widely used since the time of Euclid. By idealizing reality, this model makes possible the precise, though limited, analysis of complicated visual situations. There are three aspects to this simplification. First, the environment is idealized. Abstract geometrical forms composed of planes, lines, and points are substituted for all the differently textured and imperfectly formed objects in the environment; complex or irregular forms are approximated by aggregations of simpler ones. Second, the nature of light is idealized. All considerations of spectral composition and energy, of wavefronts and particles, are dropped, and light is abstracted to a single one of its characteristics—that of traveling in straight lines, or rays. Finally, all of the labyrinthine complications of image formation within the eye are neglected and the eye is simply treated as an abstract point in space. In this way all the complexities of natural vision are given a geometrical description in which geometrical forms (the surfaces of objects) are projected by straight lines to a point in space (the eye). For each surface this projection forms a *visual pyramid,* with the eye as its apex and the geometrical surface as its base (see Figure 2.1).

In this context the optic array is an array of solid visual angles, each visual angle being subtended by a surface in the environment. Because

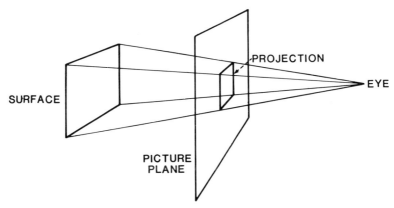

FIGURE 2.1. The visual pyramid and the picture plane. In this perspective view, the surface is the base of a "pyramid" whose apex is at the eye. The intersection of the visual pyramid with a portion of the picture plane is also shown.

of the complexity and richness of the environment, in which each object is made up of many surfaces that are divisible into smaller surfaces or facets, the optic array can be described as a nested set of solid visual angles corresponding to the hierarchically organized surfaces and facets of the environment (see Figure 2.2; also, see Gibson, 1966, pp. 192–194).

The projective model may be extended somewhat by describing the rays of light as continuing through the point of the eye and striking the curved retina behind it, thus forming an inverted "image" of each surface on the retina. Although this extension can be very helpful in conceptualizing how the brain actually registers visual information, it is not essential to the projective model of vision, which is concerned with describing the relation between the environment and the light coming to the eye. The projective model of vision was used productively long before the function of the lens and retina was accurately described by Kepler in 1604. Euclid described many projective properties in his *Optics* (c. 300 B.C.), such as the diminution of visual angle with increasing distance, and in 1436, Alberti (1972) wrote a detailed description, based on a projective model, of how to construct pictures in accurate perspective.

The limitations of the projective model of vision should be recognized. Clearly, many important features of the environment such as colors, textural qualities, and the complexities of curved or irregular surfaces cannot

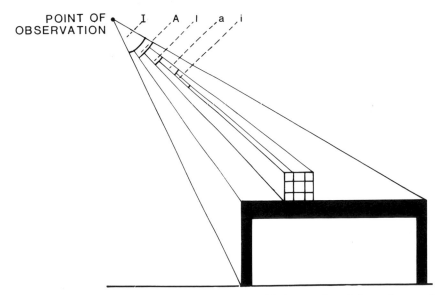

FIGURE 2.2. Nested solid angles in the optic array. This is a portion of the optic array from an environment containing a table with a box on it. The labeled angles are a sample of the hierarchical organization of nested visual angles that fill the optic array. *I* is subtended by the entire table, *A* by the table top, *1* by the box, *a* by the top of the box, and *i* by a texture element of the box's top.

be treated by this model. Effects of illumination, such as shading and brightness or of the optical system of the eye, such as its limited depth of field, likewise must be analyzed by other, more complicated models. Also, Gibson (1971) has pointed out that pictorial representations need not follow the laws of projection in order to be informative.[1] Gibson uses the example of caricature, because even though a caricature drawing of a man does not give a faithful projection of his features it may reproduce higher order features or relations that are of greater importance to perception. As Gibson (1971) says: "The caricature may be faithful to those features of the man that distinguish him from all other men and thus may truly represent him in a higher sense of the term. It may correspond to him in the sense of being uniquely specific to him—more so than a projective drawing or a photographic portrait would be (p. 29)."

These limitations make it clear that a complete description of the information available in the light coming to the eye cannot be provided by a projective model of vision. Nevertheless, that model does seem appropriate for the present undertaking. This chapter is concerned with the pictorial information that specifies spatial layout, and it can be argued that most of that information is encompassed within the projective model.[2] Pictorial representations, such as caricatures, that depart from projective accuracy have little concern for the accurate rendering of distance, sizes, slants, and tilts. On the other hand, the classical techniques of perspective construction, directed almost exclusively, and with considerable success, to the problem of accurate representation of spatial layout, *are* based on the projective model. Therefore, the projective model is well suited to the limited aims of this investigation. Using that model we shall first see how the geometrical scaffolding of a picture is constructed and then examine that scaffolding to see how it supports the observer's perception of spatial relations in the completed picture.

The Picture Plane

Any geometrical plane placed between an object and the eye will intersect the visual pyramid (or the nested set of visual pyramids) projecting from the object to the eye. That intersection defines a geometrical shape in the plane that can be said to be projectively equivalent to the original

---

[1] Gibson's (1971) criticism is directed toward "the point-projection theory of pictorial information." The projective model described here is closer to Gibson's own alternative formulation in that it describes the environment as a hierarchically organized arrangement of surfaces, rather than as an assemblage of points or spots of color. It is worth noting that although perspective theorists may subscribe, as Gibson observes, to a point-projection theory, the actual practice of perspective construction generally has been directed mainly toward the projection of surfaces.

[2] Much of the information for spatial layout available to a binocular observer or a moving observer can also be analyzed within the projective model.

object, seen from this particular location. In other words, this geometrical form lies precisely within the same visual rays and consequently has precisely the same structure in the optic array as the object itself. Thus, the two-dimensional geometrical shape in the plane is a visual substitute for the original object. It is a pictorial *re-presentation* of the object. This plane is referred to as the *picture plane*. It can be placed at any distance between the eye and the object (or even behind the object, in which case the object is projected onto it by an extension of the visual pyramid away from the eye until it is intercepted by the picture plane). The picture plane can also be placed at any angle. Every different location of the picture plane will intersect the visual pyramid differently and therefore produce a different picture.

The picture plane, being an abstract geometrical entity, is thought of as extending endlessly in all directions. A proper picture, however, has a definite shape and is of limited extent. It is necessary in constructing a picture not only to choose the location of the picture plane but also to choose the boundaries framing the picture. When the object of the picture is an extended scene, then the choice of the frame determines what portion of the scene will be represented in the picture. For simplicity the analysis in this chapter is restricted to the most common choice of picture plane and frame. The picture plane is taken to be vertical and located between the object and the eye. The picture's frame is taken to be rectangular, with the sides vertical and the top and bottom horizontal, and to be positioned so as to include the portion of the picture plane that is directly in front on the observer's eye.[3]

There is a one-to-one relation between structures in the picture plane and structures in the half of the optic array that the picture plane fills; to every line segment in the picture plane there corresponds a visual angle in the optic array. Equal line segments in the picture plane do not necessarily subtend equal visual angles in the optic array, however. The picture plane is closest to the eye at the point where it is intersected by the visual ray perpendicular to it. This point is called the center of the picture plane. Visual rays intersecting the picture plane farther and farther from its center are increasingly long and make increasingly acute angles with the picture plane (see Figure 2.3). As a result, the greater the distance between a line segment in the picture and the center of the picture plane, the smaller the visual angle it subtends in the optic array. The relation between distances in the picture plane and visual angles in the optic array is a trigonometric one, where the distance from a point in the picture plane to its center is proportional to the *tangent* of the visual angle that

---

[3] These restrictions comprehend the vast majority of pictorial representations but exclude several interesting classes of pictures such as anamorphic paintings (Baltrušaitis, 1969; Gilman, 1978; Leeman, 1976) and paintings that are incorporated into architectural structures (Mastai, 1975; Pirenne, 1970, pp. 79–94).

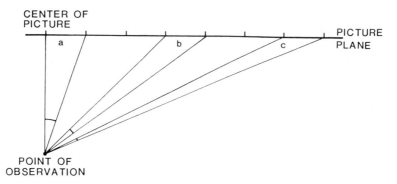

FIGURE 2.3. The picture plane and the optic array. Equal extents in the picture plane, such as *a*, *b*, and *c*, may subtend unequal angles in the optic array. The farther the extent is from the center of the picture, the smaller the visual angle is that it subtends.

this distance subtends in the optic array. The transformation between the picture plane and the optic array is thus quite simple. It has nevertheless been the source of considerable confusion among some writers on perspective who have held that "artificial perspective" (meaning projection onto the picture plane) is a distortion of "natural perspective" (meaning the visual angles subtended at the eye) and consequently gives an inaccurate representation of the environment if the boundaries of the picture are placed too far from the center of the picture plane (see Pirenne, 1970 or Ware, 1900 for a full and careful discussion of this confusion).[4]

The Station Point

The *station point* of a picture is the point in space at which the eye is placed when the picture is constructed—the point to which the scene is projected. For a given scene, the location of the picture plane and of the station point jointly determine the form of the picture. If a different station point is chosen, a different picture will generally result. Alberti, in the earliest treatise on perspective construction, compares the picture frame to an open window through which the scene to be represented is viewed (Alberti, 1972, p. 55). This analogy is helpful in visualizing the effects of changes in the position of the station point. As we approach

[4] Confusion about the "distortions" accompanying artificial perspective continues to be common, even in books on perspective (see, for example, Coulin, 1966, p. 66; Doblin, 1956; Lawson, 1943, pp. 205–207; and Walters and Bromham, 1970, pp. 32–33). This is not to say that there are not real and important differences between artificial and natural perspective. The former samples only a limited subset of an optic array at a fixed location, whereas the latter encompasses the entire optic array and implies the possibility of a moving point of observation (see Gibson, 1979, pp. 69–71).

a window we see more of the scene; as we move to the left, a portion of the scene on the left side becomes hidden by the window frame while more is revealed on the right, etc. Somewhat more subtle changes, involving shifts in projective relations, also occur when we move. For example, a steeple in the distance may have been directly in line with a tree in the foreground, but after we move it no longer is. Each different station point results in a different view or picture. Once a picture has been constructed, however, it is no longer responsive to our movements; it is like a view frozen onto a window. When we move away from the station point from which a picture was constructed, that picture no longer corresponds to our new view through the window, and therefore no longer accurately represents that view to us. The nature of the inaccuracies produced by viewing a picture from a point of observation other than its station point and the effects of these inaccuracies on our perception are questions of great interest, but as they are taken up elsewhere in this volume, we shall not consider them in this chapter. A companion question, which is addressed in this chapter, is what information is available to the observer of a picture to indicate how to find the correct station point from which to view the picture. We shall return to this question after considering some of the principal methods by which information about the spatial relations in a three-dimensional scene is frozen onto the two-dimensional surface of a picture.

ORTHOGRAPHIC PROJECTION

The Plan and the Elevation

Anyone who has casually leafed through a manual on perspective, glancing at the complex diagrams that always abound in such works, is apt to have formed the impression that perspective construction is a very complicated business. In truth, the accurate construction of a pictorial representation of a scene that is at all complicated can require a great deal of skill and care, but the basic rules underlying such constructions are really quite simple. The complexity arises from the use of secondary, and even tertiary, rules which have been introduced as practical aids in the process of construction. Although it is possible in principle to make a perspective representation of any scene through the use of only a few very simple rules, the task is generally easier if a more complex set of rules is used. We shall begin, though, with the simple rules.

These rules can be expressed either geometrically or algebraically. We shall consider both forms of expression together. Initially a system for indicating where things are located in space is needed. We shall use a three-dimensional Cartesian coordinate system, in which every point in space is localized by its position relative to three mutually perpendicular axes, referred to as the X axis, the Y axis, and the Z axis (see Figure 2.4). For convenience, we shall take the station point as the origin, or point of intersection, of the three axes. The X axis is taken to be horizontal, and the Y axis to be vertical. The vertical plane that contains these two axes is called the X–Y plane. The system of axes is oriented in space so that the X–Y plane is parallel to the picture plane, which is also vertical. The Z axis is then horizontal and is perpendicular to both the X–Y plane and the picture plane. The point at which the Z axis intersects the picture plane is the center of the picture. The location of the picture plane relative to the station point is simply given by the distance along the Z axis from the station point to the center of the picture. We shall refer to this value as d. The location of any point, P, in space can be specified by a trio of values (x,y,z), which stand for distances along the X, Y, and Z axes, respectively. A visual ray from P to the station point will intersect the picture plane at another point, which we shall call P'. P' is, thus, the representation of P. The location of P' can also be specified by a trio of values: (x',y',z'). If we can find either a method of geometrical construction or a series of algebraic equations that will enable us to find x', y', and z'

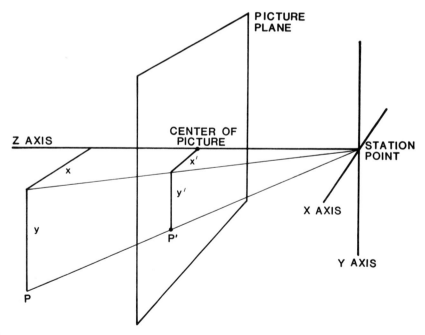

FIGURE 2.4. The X-Y-Z coordinate system. This is a perspective view of the three axes of the coordinate system. The picture plane, a point, P, in space, and its projection, P', onto the picture plane are also shown. The extents x and y give the position of P relative to the X and Y axes; the extents x' and y' give the position of P' relative to those two axes.

when we know x, y, and z, then we shall have a completely general solution to the problem of pictorial representation. We shall have, in other
words, a method for finding the representation in the picture plane of
any point in space.

The value of z' is given to us immediately because we know d, the
distance along the Z axis of the picture plane from the station point.
Because the picture plane is perpendicular to the Z axis, every point in
the picture plane has the same Z axis value, which is simply d. Thus, for
our first equation we can write

$$z' = d.$$

Let us now consider how to find x' and y'. We can simplify this problem
by reducing it from one problem in three-dimensional space to two problems in two-dimensional space. The method that uses this approach is
known as *orthographic projection* and is commonly used in architectural
and mechanical drawing.[5] In orthographic projection the three-dimensional information concerning the object or scene is divided into two
two-dimensional drawings: the plan and the elevation. The plan, sometimes called a top view, is drawn entirely in the horizontal plane containing the Z axis and the X axis, and it shows the relation of every point
in the scene to these two axes. The plan contains no information about
any point's vertical position (i.e., its relation to the Y axis). It is as though
we were viewing the scene from above and the entire scene had been
flattened into the horizontal X–Z plane (see Figure 2.5). In the plan the
station point lies at the intersection of the X and Z axes; the picture plane,
because it is a vertical plane being viewed from above, appears as a single
horizontal line that is parallel to the X axis and that intersects the Z axis
at a distance d from the station point.

The elevation, sometimes called a side view, is drawn entirely in the
vertical plane containing the Z axis and the Y axis, and it shows the relation
of every point in the scene to these two axes. The elevation contains no
information about the lateral position of any point. Here it is as though
we were viewing the scene from the side, and the entire scene had been
compressed into the vertical Y–Z plane (see Figure 2.6). In the elevation
the station point lies at the intersection of the Y and Z axes, and the
picture plane, because it is now a vertical plane being seen from the side,
appears as a single vertical line that is parallel to the Y axis and that
intersects the Z axis at a distance d from the station point.

The plan and the elevation contain between them all of the information
about the three-dimensional location of every point in the object or

[5] More detailed discussions of orthographic projection and its uses can be found in French
and Vierck (1978) or Bethune (1977).

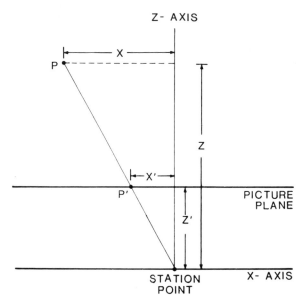

FIGURE 2.5. The plan. This is an orthographic projection of the three-dimensional scene onto the horizontal plane through the station point. The plan shows the station point, the picture plane, and the *x* and *z* coordinates of all points, such as *P*, and of their projections, such as *P'*, onto the picture plane.

scene. The positions in the picture plane of the corresponding projections of these points can be found either geometrically or algebraically by using the plan and the elevation. The plan is used to determine the lateral position (*x'*) of each point and the elevation is used to determine the vertical position (*y'*).

Let us first consider how the plan is used. If we draw the visual ray from the station point to *P*, whose coordinates in the plan are *x* and *z*, it intersects the picture plane at *P'*, whose coordinates in the plan are *x'* and *z'*. The plan thus allows us immediately to determine *x'* geometrically. We can also readily derive an algebraic equation for *x'*. By dropping perpendiculars from *P* and *P'* to the Z-axis, we create two right triangles, one smaller than the other, but both having the same shape (see Figure 2.5). Thus *P* and *P'* are related by being the corresponding vertices of proportional right triangles. The two sides of the right triangle having *P* as a vertex are *x* and *z*, while the two sides of the right triangle having *P'* as a vertex are *x'* and *z'*. Because the two right triangles are proportional, it follows that $x'/x = z'/z$. We already know that $z' = d$, so we can now solve for *x'* to obtain

$$x' = x\,(d/z).$$

Now let us consider the elevation. If we draw the visual ray from the station point to P, whose coordinates in the elevation are y and z, it intersects the picture plane at P', whose coordinates there are y' and z'. The elevation thus allows us to immediately determine y' geometrically. We can also derive an algebraic equation for y' by using a procedure exactly analogous to that which we used with the plan to derive the equation for x'. Again using proportional triangles we find that $y'/y = z'/z$, and hence

$$y' = y\,(d/z).$$

Thus, all of perspective reduces to the simple series of proportions: $x'/x = y'/y = z'/z$. On this basis we can find the pictorial representation of any point in space either by simple geometrical constructions based on a plan and an elevation or by equally simple algebraic equations.

Constructing a Picture from an Orthographic Projection

The use of orthographic projections in constructing pictorial representations typically relies on geometrical rather than numerical methods. Both the plan and the elevation of the object are first drawn in the picture plane; then the perspective representation of the object is geometrically derived from them (see Figure 2.7). The plan and the elevation are so

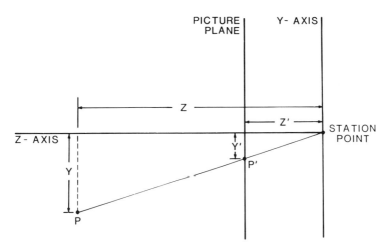

FIGURE 2.6. The elevation. This is an orthographic projection of the three-dimensional scene onto the vertical plane that contains the Y and Z axes. The elevation shows the station point, the picture plane, and the y and z coordinates of all points, such as P, and of their projections, such as P', onto the picture plane.

drawn in the picture plane that both the station point of the plan and the station point of the elevation coincide with the center of the picture.[6] As was shown above, in the plan the visual ray from each point on the object to the station point intersects the horizontal line of the plan's picture plane (see Figure 2.5) at a location having the x' coordinate of that point's representation. If a vertical line is passed through that intersection, every point along that vertical line will have the same x' coordinate. Similarly, in the elevation the visual ray from each point on the object to the station point intersects the vertical line of the elevation's picture plane (see Figure 2.6) at a location having the y' coordinate of that point's representation. If a horizontal line is passed through that intersection, every point along that horizontal line will have the same y' coordinate. It follows that the location in the picture plane of the representation, P', of each point on the object can be found geometrically by determining where the vertical line passing through the point's x' coordinate in the plan intersects the horizontal line passing through the point's y' coordinate in the elevation. That intersection has the coordinates x' and y', and is thus the location of P'. With rectilinear objects only the representation of the endpoints of each straight line segment need to determined in this way. The rest of the representation can then be found by appropriately connecting the representations of the endpoints.

The three algebraic equations just discussed are derived geometrically, but once they are known, they allow a picture to be made purely on the basis of numerical calculations whose results are then plotted directly on the picture plane without any intervening geometrical constructions at all. To do this it would be necessary to assign numerical coordinates to every important point on each object (e.g., to all endpoints of line segments) and then calculate x' and y' for each of these points (z' is always the same). This would not be difficult, but it could be tedious. It is a solution better adapted to a computer than to an artist or draftsman.

An important hitch to such a purely automatic numerical procedure arises, however, with the problem of occlusion. Not every point on a solid three-dimensional object can be seen from every point of view; surfaces of the object that are closer to the station point often hide, or occlude, some of its other surfaces. In complex scenes one object may occlude all or part of another object. Unless the pictorial representation is to ignore occlusion by treating everything as though it is transparent, some

[6] It is a fundamental but not uncommon misconception to take the center of the picture in a picture constructed from orthographic projections as being a vanishing point of the picture, analogous to the vanishing point in parallel perspective (see pp. 53–57). The "center of projection" does indicate where a perpendicular from the station point intersects the picture plane, but orthographic projection does not include the concept of vanishing points and makes no use of them.

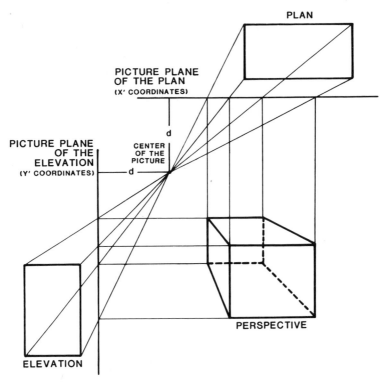

FIGURE 2.7. Constructing a perspective representation from orthographic projections. There are four steps in the construction illustrated here. (a) The plan and elevation are drawn on the picture plane. (b) Projection lines are drawn from the plan and elevation to the center of the picture. Their intersections with the horizontal and vertical projections of the picture plane determine the x' and y' coordinates of the perspective. (c) Vertical lines are passed through the x' coordinates and horizontal lines through the y' coordinates. Their intersections determine the corners of the object in perspective. (d) The corner points are connected appropriately, giving a perspective representation of the object. (Note: The perspective view in this figure is constructed to be viewed with the eye at a distance d (less than 1 in.) above the center of the picture. Because the reader's eye is actually much farther than that from the page, considerable distortion is introduced into the apparent shape of the object in perspective.)

points (those that are occluded) must be eliminated from the picture. This is usually not a hard job for an artist or draftsman, who can examine the picture by eye and rely on knowledge of what the picture should look like to choose which points should be eliminated. It is a major problem, however, for the completely automated, computer-calculated solutions these equations otherwise lend themselves to. Much of the sophistication of current computer graphics programs is directed toward attempts to deal with this problem.

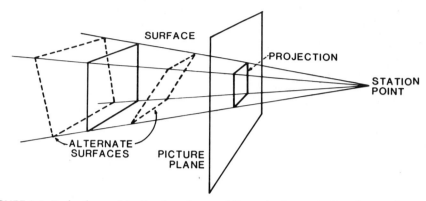

FIGURE 2.8. Projective ambiguity. A surface and its projection onto the picture plane are shown here in perspective. This same projection would be produced by any alternate surface whose contours fit precisely within the same visual pyramid. Only two such alternate surfaces are shown, but an infinite number are possible.

The Apparent Ambiguity of Pictorial Representation

Although orthgraphic projection is a universally applicable method from which a perspective representation of any object or scene may theoretically be formed, its use is conceptually centered on the projections of isolated points in space. What this atomistic approach suggests—a suggestion that dominated perceptual theory for hundreds of years—is the infinite ambiguity of pictorial representation. A given point (x', y', z') on the picture plane could be the representation of any point in space whose coordinates (x, y, z) have the same proportional relation, and there is an infinite number of such points (see Figure 2.8). That would suggest, as many have concluded, that although "experience" may lead us to make the correct "interpretation" of a picture, there is little actual information available in the picture to compel that interpretation. As we shall see in the following sections, however, just as an attention to the invariant properties of normal environments has led artists to develop more complex and more powerful ways of constructing pictorial representations, so it is that these same invariant properties can be shown, given certain constraints, to make available to the observer abundant information for the perception of the spatial relations represented in pictures.

PERSPECTIVE CONSTRUCTIONS

Constructing Pictures Directly in the Picture Plane

Although orthographic projection in principle provides a universal method for constructing pictorial representations, it has several serious technical limitations. First, it is rather tedious because it requires three detailed drawings—the plan, the elevation, and the perspective representation itself. More fundamentally, it is a procedure based on measurement rather than visual inspection. Neither the plan nor the elevation, both of which must be produced before the perspective representation, looks much like the object or scene. Both are abstract geometrical constructions that, although together they contain all of the spatial information about the object, do not put that information together in a visually coherent way. This method can work well for the engineer wishing to design a machine but is rarely appropriate for an artist wishing to capture the visual appearance of a scene. Finally, orthographic projection is better suited to the representation of a single object or cluster of objects than to an extended scene such as a landscape. When there are large distances between objects, the uniform scales of the plan and elevation may render them impractical (e.g., consider attempting to make a plan and an elevation for a picture showing a country house in the foreground, a village in the midground, and a range of mountains in the distant background).

These limitations are avoided by a family of methods that are referred to as *perspective constructions.*[7] These methods construct the pictorial representation directly on the picture plane, without the use of intermediate drawings such as the plan and elevation. In doing this they rely on a geometrical model of the environment that incorporates certain invariant properties of normal environments. Although these methods are capable of being extended universally, they are conceptually directed toward, and are most easily applied to, the representation of scenes that conform to that model. In examining these methods here we shall omit numerous subtleties and ramifications, and limit ourselves to considering

---

[7] It seems probable that the use of orthographic projections to produce accurate pictorial representations of spatial layout historically preceded the use of the perspective construction techniques that are described in this section, but not all art historians would agree with this position. It is generally accepted that the first modern description of perspective construction techniques was published by Alberti around 1435. It is also generally accepted that Brunelleschi produced at least two paintings (now lost) in accurate perspective some time earlier (around 1413 by recent estimates; see Kemp, 1978). What remains in doubt is the method by which Brunelleschi produced his paintings. Kemp (1978) argues persuasively that the available evidence is simply not adequate to support any firm conclusions. Nevertheless, some of the suggested theories seem clearly more plausible than others (for a recent example of an ingenious but rather implausible account of Brunelleschi's discovery see Edgerton, 1975). The most plausible hypothesis (Krautheimer, 1956, pp. 234–245; J. White, 1967, pp. 124–126) is that Brunelleschi's experience and concerns as an architect led him to the idea of geometrically combining the plan and the elevation of a building to obtain a single, three-dimensional view. This hypothesis is consistent with the analysis of one existing painting that appears to have been strongly influenced by Brunelleschi (see Janson, 1967), and is supported by Kemp's recent demonstration (1978) that Brunelleschi was probably acquainted with surveying techniques that would have allowed him to make the measurements necessary to produce an accurate plan and elevation.

the broad outlines of the procedures by which these methods succeed in representing the spatial relations of a scene on the picture plane.[8]

The geometrical model on which perspective constructions are based conceptualizes the natural environment as an extended ground plane on which the buildings, people, vegetation, and even the geographical features of the environment rest. Based on this conceptualization, a representation is constructed on the picture plane in three steps. First, a projection of the ground plane, which is idealized as being perfectly flat and horizontal and extending endlessly in all directions, is constructed on the picture plane. Second, the ground plane is thought of as being overlaid with a lined grid of squares, having a suitable size and orientation to the picture plane. Perspective techniques are then used to construct the projected representation of such a grid (or of as much of it as is needed) on the picture plane. This ground plane grid is then used as a kind of coordinate system by means of which the floor plans of buildings, the positions of people, etc. are laid out directly on the picture plane. Third, perspective techniques are then used to determine how the heights of all of the features indicated on the ground plane should be represented on the picture plane. This completes the representation of the basic three-dimensional geometrical structure of the scene. Details and elaborations (such as shadows or reflections), not considered here, can now be added to the picture. We shall look at the geometry of each of these steps in turn.

The Horizon and the Trace

A flat, horizontal ground plane extending to infinity can be represented on the picture plane by two horizontal lines. The first is the line in which the ground plane intersects the vertical picture plane; this line will be referred to as the *trace line* of the ground plane. The second is the *horizon line* of the ground plane. The horizon line is the projective limit of the ground plane. Any visual ray from the station point that passes through the picture plane below the horizon line eventually intersects the ground plane; any visual ray that passes through the picture plane above the horizon line increasingly diverges from the ground plane; and any visual ray that passes through the picture plane at the horizon line remains parallel to the ground plane, intersecting it only at infinity (i.e., at the horizon [see Figure 2.9]). Therefore, the horizon marks the far limit of the visible ground plane but this limit is infinitely far away. The horizon of the ground plane is conceptually rather different from the actual ho-

---

[8] An excellent detailed account of perspective techniques is given in Ware, 1900. A more readily available but much less rigorous work on the subject is by G. White, 1968.

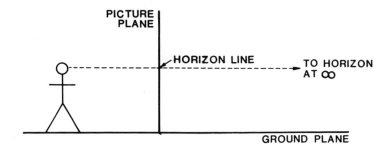

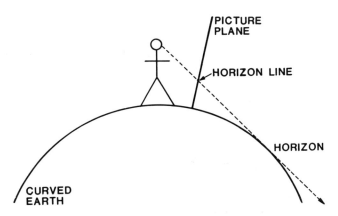

FIGURE 2.9. The horizon line. The upper drawing shows the horizon line of the ground plane. The lower drawing shows the horizon line of the Earth. The curvature of the Earth's surface is greatly exaggerated here; if it were drawn to scale there would be no perceptible difference between the two drawings.

rizon of the Earth, which is a line of tangency marking a definite location on the Earth's curved surface beyond which the surface is not projected to the station point (Figure 2.9). Nevertheless, the radius of curvature of the Earth is large enough that the portion of its surface included in most pictorial representations is a close geometrical approximation of a flat plane.

Because the visual rays from the station point to the horizon are parallel to the ground plane, the line in which they intersect the picture is necessarily at the same height above the ground plane as is the station point. Consequently, the horizon line is always at "eye level." If the station point is raised or lowered, the location of the horizon line on the picture plane rises and falls correspondingly. In contrast, the location of the trace line of the ground plane, because it is an actual line of intersection with the picture plane rather than a projection to it, is unaffected by the position of the station point (see Figure 2.10).

The Grid

The square grid superimposed on the ground plane can be thought of as consisting of two perpendicular sets or systems of equally spaced parallel lines. The problem of constructing a perspective representation of such a grid thus reduces to the problem of constructing the perspective representation of a system of parallel lines of any chosen orientation and spacing.

Although each of the line segments making up a scene is finite in length, each line segment is considered, in the geometry of perspective, to be only a segment of a line that is unbounded, extending forever in both directions. Much of the power of perspective techniques is derived from the properties of such abstract, unbounded lines. Any unbounded line

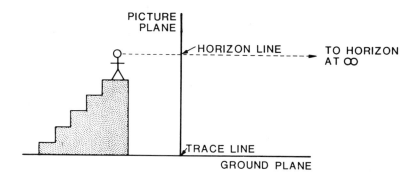

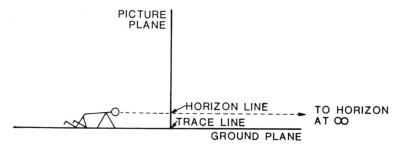

FIGURE 2.10. The horizon line rises and falls with the station point. The horizon line of the ground plane is always at eye level. The position of the trace line on the picture plane is not affected by the position of the station point.

in the ground plane that is not parallel to the picture plane must eventually intersect it in one direction, and in the other direction, must reach to infinity. The projection of such a line of course lies in the picture plane and extends upward at some angle from the point where it intersects the trace line of the ground plane to the point where it intersects the horizon line. Although the line itself is horizontal, its projection is not.

The projections of any system of parallel lines that are not parallel to the picture plane converge to a single point on the horizon line. This point is referred to as the *vanishing point* of the system (see Figure 2.11). This convergence occurs because although the actual separation between any two such lines remains constant along their entire length, the visual angle subtended by that separation approaches zero as its distance from the station point approaches infinity. The projection of a system of evenly spaced parallel lines thus looks like an inverted fan whose lines spread out from their vanishing point on the horizon line to intersect the trace line at equally spaced intervals. Each different system of parallel lines has a different vanishing point on the horizon line.

To construct the projections corresponding to a particular system of parallel lines, it is necessary to locate the proper vanishing point for those lines. The principle for finding such a vanishing point is quite simple. For

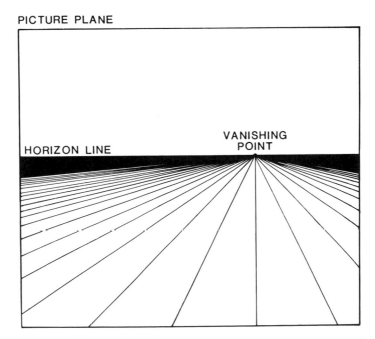

FIGURE 2.11. Projective convergence of parallel lines to a vanishing point.

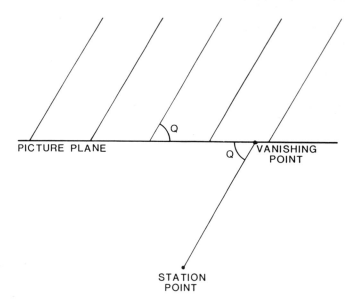

FIGURE 2.12. Finding a vanishing point. A system of parallel lines on the ground plane is shown from above. The horizontal line through the station point that is parallel to those lines intersects the picture plane at the lines' vanishing point.

every system of parallel lines in the ground plane there exists in the space above the ground plane one parallel line that, if extended into the space in front of the picture plane, passes through the station point (see Figure 2.12). This line through the station point intersects the picture plane on the horizon line and at the vanishing point of the system of lines to which it is parallel. This implies that in order to find the vanishing point for a system of parallel lines that make a given angle (e.g., 60°) with the picture plane, all that is necessary is to pass through the station point a single horizontal line that intersects the picture plane in that particular angle. That point of intersection will be on the horizon line and will be the vanishing point of the system.

   Having found the vanishing point of a system of parallel lines, we need to determine where each of the lines in the system intersects the trace line of the ground plane.[9] Once this has been done, the representation of the system can be constructed simply by connecting the set of points on the trace line with the vanishing point on the horizon. If a system of parallel lines is evenly spaced, then the lines will necessarily intersect the picture plane at equal intervals. Unless the lines intersect the picture

---

[9] In practice secondary lines closer to the horizon are commonly used to supplement the trace line (see Ware, 1900, pp. 101–102).

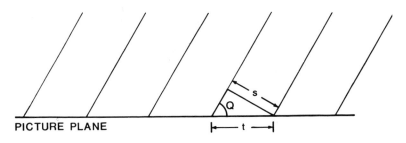

PICTURE PLANE

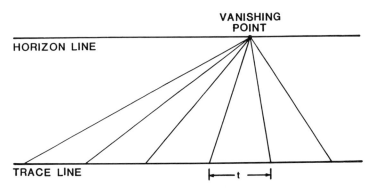

VANISHING
POINT

HORIZON LINE

TRACE LINE

FIGURE 2.13. Finding how parallel lines intersect the trace line. The upper drawing is a plan view of parallel lines making an angle Q with the picture plane. The perpendicular spacing (s) between the lines is less then the spacing (t) with which they intersect the picture plane. The lower drawing is a perspective view of the same parallel lines. The spacing (t) is the same as in the upper drawing because the trace line is the actual intersection of the ground plane with the picture plane.

plane at right angles, these intervals will be greater than the perpendicular spacing between the lines (see Figure 2.13). Once we have chosen the perpendicular spacing between the lines (call it s) and the angle (call it Q) that the lines make with the picture plane, the appropriate spacing (call it t) for the points of intersection with the trace line is easy to find. The interval t is the hypoteneuse of a right triangle, one of whose sides is s and one of whose angles is Q. Thus, t can be found either by measurement in a auxiliary drawing of this triangle (such as Figure 2.13) or by calculation from the equivalent trigonometric expression

$$t = s/\sin Q.$$

Once t has been found, a set of evenly spaced points of intersection can be laid out along the trace line of the ground plane, and the lines making up the pictorial representation of the system of parallel lines can be drawn in.[10]

The perspective representation of the second and perpendicular system of parallel lines making up the grid of squares is constructed in just the same way. We need only note here that the vanishing point of this system is found by passing a second horizontal line, at right angles to the first, through the station point and that a second value for t, the spacing of intersections with the trace line, must be found. It is necessary to find a second value for t because although the perpendicular spacing, s, between lines in the second system of parallel lines is the same as that in the first system, the angle, Q, at which the lines intersect the picture plane will generally be different.

In the square grid whose construction has just been described neither set of parallel lines is parallel to the picture plane. A perspective construction based on such a grid is referred to as *angular perspective*. If, alternatively, the grid is chosen so as to include one system of parallel lines that *is* parallel to the picture plane, the resulting perspective construction is referred to as *parallel perspective*. If every orientation of the grid to the picture plane were used equally often in constructing pictures, then parallel perspective constructions would be very infrequent. Parallel perspective, however, is often deliberately chosen, in part because it is simpler to understand and can be produced by a somewhat simpler construction than that used for angular perspective.

The construction of a ground plane grid in parallel perspective differs from the procedure for angular perspective in several ways. Because, in parallel perspective, one system of lines is parallel to the picture plane, it follows that the other system of lines must be perpendicular to it. The vanishing point of the perpendicular system of lines is found simply by dropping a perpendicular from the station point to the picture plane.

---

[10] The method given here of determining the intersections of a system of parallel lines with the trace line was chosen for its conceptual simplicity, but it does require either an auxiliary drawing or a trigonometric calculation. The method in common use is somewhat more complicated, but has the advantage of being a geometrical construction that is done entirely on the picture plane. This commonly used method involves the use of a *distance point* (sometimes called a measuring point). Except for the system of lines parallel to the picture plane, every system of parallel lines has two distance points. A distance point of a system of parallel lines is the vanishing point of another system of parallel lines. This second system of parallel lines is chosen to be at such an angle to the first system that when any line from the second system intersects any line from the first system the two lines together form the base and one side of an isosceles triangle whose other side is the trace line of the ground plane. Because the two sides of an isoceles triangle are always equal, lines from the trace line to a distance point of a system of lines can be used to accurately transfer distances from the trace line to any line in that system. In this way, distance points can be used more generally than just in the construction of the ground plane grid. For descriptions of how to find and use distance points see Ware, 1900, pp. 68–76 or G. White, 1968, pp. 26–33.

Additionally, these perpendicular lines intersect the trace line with a spacing (t) equal to their perpendicular spacing (s). Thus, the projection onto the picture plane of a system of lines that are perpendicular to it is particularly easy to construct. The system of lines parallel to the picture plane does not have a vanishing point because the projections of its lines are all parallel to the horizon line (parallel perspective is sometimes called *one-point perspective* for this reason, whereas angular perspective is called *two-point perspective*). Similarly, these lines are all parallel to the trace line and so do not intersect it either. Consequently, determining the spacing of the projections of these lines requires a technique different from that used in angular perspective.

The projective representation of a system of evenly spaced lines parallel to the picture plane is a system of horizontal lines that are compressed progressively closer together higher in the picture plane, finally reaching an infinite density at the horizon line (see Figure 2.14). The amount of this compression can be found by considering a side view (see Figure 2.15). Here the picture plane appears as a vertical line and the system of parallel lines appears as a series of evenly spaced points. The points at which the picture plane is intersected by the visual rays from the parallel system of lines can be seen to grow closer together as the lines become farther from the picture plane. In constructing a representation in parallel

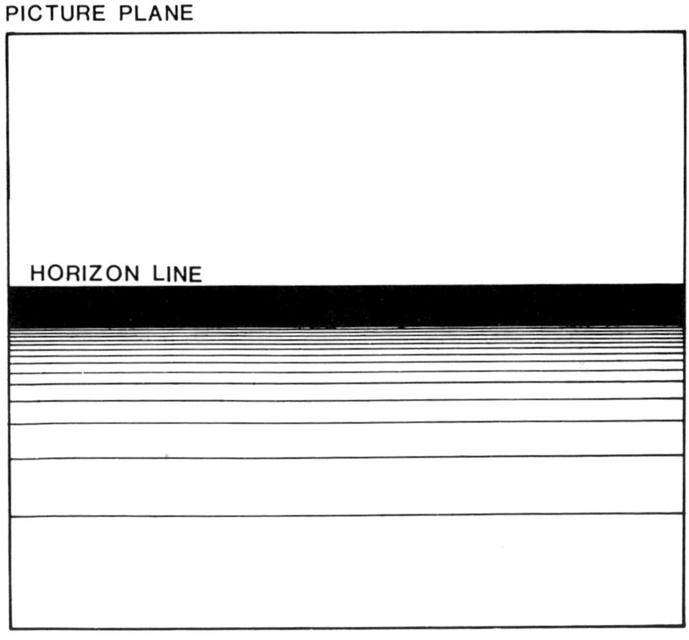

FIGURE 2.14. Projective compression of lines parallel to the picture plane.

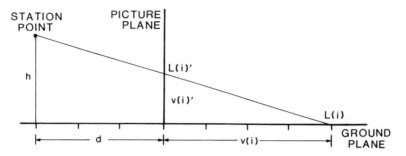

FIGURE 2.15. Finding the compression in parallel perspective. In this side view of the ground plane the system of lines parallel to the picture plane appear as evenly spaced dots. $L(i)$ is the ith line from the picture plane and $L(i)'$ is its projection onto the picture plane. The distance of $L(i)$ from the picture plane is $v(i)$, and the height of $L(i)'$ in the picture plane is $v(i)'$. The station point's distance from the picture plane is d and its height above the ground plane is h.

perspective, these intervals can either be transferred directly from such an auxiliary drawing or can be calculated from the simple proportion

$$v'/h = v/z$$

where v is the distance from the picture plane to any one of the parallel lines on the ground, v' is the projective distance in the picture plane from the trace line of the ground plane to the projection of that line, and h is the height of the point of observation above the ground plane.[11]

---

[11] There is an equivalent form of this equation that is sometimes more convenient to use in constructing the representation of a system of evenly spaced lines parallel to the picture plane. For this equivalent form to be usable, the parallel lines on the ground must be placed so that one of them exactly coincides with the intersection of the ground plane and the picture plane. Consider each line (L) in the system to be given a number (i), starting at the picture plane, so that $L(0)$ is at the intersection of the ground plane with the picture plane and $L(i)$ is the ith line away from the picture plane. Let the spacing between the lines be s; then $v(i) = is$, where $v(i)$ is the distance of the ith line from the picture plane. In this construction the distance, d, of the station point from the picture plane must be chosen to be an integral multiple of s (as in Figure 2.15). If we refer to this mutiple as m, then $d = ms$. Noting that $z(i) = v(i) + d$, we may make substitutions into the original equation to obtain $v'(i)/h = is/(is + ms)$. The term s drops out leaving $v'(i)/h = i/(i + m)$. For any given construction, m is a constant, and each successive value of $v'(i)$ can be found simply by increasing i by 1 in the equation.

This construction can also be done geometrically by using a distance point (see Footnote 10) of the system of lines perpendicular to the picture plane. The distance point construction is somewhat simplified in this case because the distance points of this system of lines are identical to the vanishing points of the diagonals of the squares making up the grid.

Projective Heights

Once the representation of the grid covering the ground plane has been constructed on the picture plane, either in angular or parallel perspective, the floor plans, locations, etc. of objects to be represented can then be laid out directly on the picture plane. What then remains is to correctly represent on the picture plane the heights of the various features of the scene. This can be done using a rule referred to here as the *horizon-ratio relation.*[12] For simplicity let us use as an example a vertical pole of a given height standing at a specified place on the ground plane. Whatever the distance of this pole from the station point is, the visual ray from the station point to the horizon that intersects this pole will do so at a distance above the ground plane that is equal to the height of the station point (see Figure 2.16). This is necessarily so because all of the visual rays to the horizon are parallel to the ground plane and thus are the same height above it along their entire length. It follows that, in the projection of the pole onto the picture plane, the horizon line will intersect the pole at a known height—the height of the station point. The length of the pole's projection from the ground to where it crosses the horizon line thus provides a kind of scale against which the correct projective height of the entire pole can be determined by proportions. For instance, if the pole is intended to be $1\frac{1}{2}$ times the height of the station point, the projection of the part of the pole above the horizon line should be half the length of the pole's projection below the horizon line. Alternatively, if the pole is intended to be only half the height of the station point, its projection should extend only half way from the ground to the horizon line. This rule of proportions is the horizon-ratio relation referred to above. Using the horizon-ratio relation, the correct projection of the height of any object located on the ground plane grid can readily be constructed.

Other Planes, Other Horizons

This completes our presentation of the basic components of perspective constructions. It should be pointed out, however, (as Ware, 1900, stresses) that the ground plane is unique only from an ecological or practical point of view, not from a mathematical point of view. *Any* plane, however it may be tilted or slanted, can be projected onto the picture plane with its own trace line and horizon line and its own set of vanishing points. The use of planes other than the ground plane sometimes is nec-

[12] This rule was first described by Alberti in 1436 (Alberti, 1972, p. 71). See Edgerton (1975, pp. 26, 184) for an interesting discussion of a related post-Brunelleschian rule that Edgerton refers to as "horizon line isocephaly."

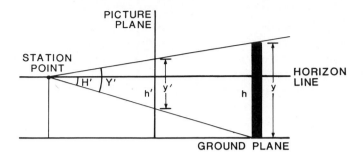

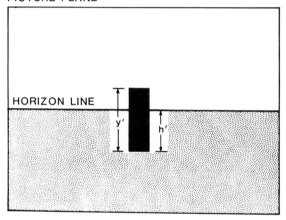

FIGURE 2.16. The horizon-ratio relation. The upper drawing is a side view of an object standing on the ground plane. The lower drawing is a perspective view of the same object. The intersection of the horizon line with the object provides a scale marker equal to the height of the point of observation. The height of the object (y) relative to the height of the point of observation (h) is given by the projective height of the object (y') relative to this scale marker (h'): $y/h = y'/h'$.

essary in more complex pictorial representations. For instance, a cube standing on one of its corners will have none of its edges parallel to either the ground plane or the picture plane. Constructing the perspective representation of such a cube requires the use of auxiliary planes that run parallel to the sides of the cube and of three vanishing points (one for each set of parallel edges) that lie in the horizon lines of these auxiliary planes rather than in the horizon line of the ground plane (such a construction is referred to as *oblique perspective* or *three-point perspective*).

Scale

So far, our discussion of perspective constructions has implicitly assumed that the pictorial representation was being constructed on the basis of a full-scale scene. For such a scene, the ground plane of the scene is conceived as being continuous with the ground plane of the observer, and all heights, widths, etc. of objects in the scene are the same as those of similar objects in the real world of the observer. In practice, such a procedure is very cumbersome because of the required size of the working surface. For instance, if the height of the station point is five feet, this would require that the trace line and the horizon line be vertically separated by five feet on the surface that is being used as the picture plane. Even though the intended frame of the picture may be much smaller than this, so that the trace line will not be included within the representation when it is completed, the trace line is nevertheless necessary, as was seen above, during the construction of the representation. To avoid this difficulty and for other comparable reasons of convenience, it is common to mathematically scale down the scene before constructing its pictorial representation.

This scaling down is accomplished by taking the station point as the center of the scene and then shrinking the scene by having every point in the scene move centripetally toward this center by a fixed proportion of its original distance from the center (see Figure 2.17). The distance from the station point to the picture plane is left unchanged. A little reflection will show that, because each point in the scene is moving along its own visual ray toward the station point, such a procedure changes

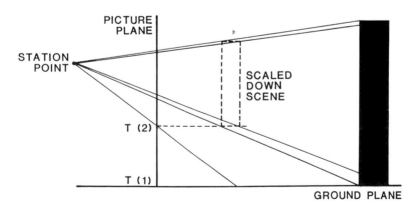

FIGURE 2.17. Scaling down the scene. The scaled down scene, indicated by dotted lines, maintains the same projective relations as the original scene. $T(2)$, the trace line of the scaled down ground plane, is higher on the picture plane than $T(1)$, the trace line of the original ground plane.

none of the angular relations in the optic array at the station point. Consequently, the projection of this scaled down scene onto the picture plane is completely identical to what would have been obtained from the full-scale scene.

Reverting for a moment to the algebraic equations derived earlier (see pp. 44–45), we can see that the possibility of scaling results from perspective being based on proportional relations. If we take k to be the factor by which the entire scene is scaled down, we can use the algebraic expressions for lateral (x') and vertical (y') extents in the picture plane to show that multiplying all of the coordinates of the scene by k leaves every x' and y' unchanged:

$$x' = kx(d/kz) = x(d/z) \text{ and}$$

$$y' = ky(d/kz) = y(d/z).$$

Although no projection to the picture plane is changed by this scaling procedure, there *is* a change in the trace line, which is not a projection but is rather the actual line of intersection of the ground plane with the picture plane. Because the distance of the picture plane is left unchanged as the scene is scaled down, the intersection of the ground plane with the picture plane changes. As a result the vertical distance in the picture plane between the trace line and the horizon line is reduced proportionally to the scale factor. For example, if the scale factor is 1/10 and the height of the station point is 5 ft, the scaled down separation between the trace line and the horizon line on the picture plane would be 6 in. One convenient way of constructing a picture is to choose a scale factor such that the trace line of the ground plane in the scaled down scene coincides with the desired bottom edge of the picture's frame (see Figure 2.17).

GEOMETRICAL INFORMATION FOR SPATIAL RELATIONS

Pictorial Invariants

Now that we have seen how the geometrical framework, or skeleton, of a pictorial representation is constructed, we are in a position to consider the question that is of central concern in this chapter: what geometrical information is available in a picture concerning the spatial relations that exist in the scene which it represents? As we shall see, the perspective constructions, which depend for their usefulness on geometrical regularities within the normal environment, serve to incorporate within the picture geometrical structures that contain a wealth of potentially useable information about the three-dimensional scene. In particular, information concerning spatial relations such as the distance, size, orientation, and slant of each visible surface of an object is available pictorially in the geometrical relations that exist between the object and the ground plane.

Our approach, guided by J. J. Gibson's definition of a picture (see p. 35), is to compare the optic array made available by a pictorial representation with the optic array made available by the actual environment and to ask which of the structures carrying information about the spatial layout that are present in the latter are also present in the former. In principle, then, this attempt presupposes a knowledge of the information for spatial layout that is available to direct perception. In fact, such knowledge is still incomplete, although it has increased considerably in the past few decades. The incompleteness of our knowledge of direct perception necessarily limits our analysis of pictorial perception, but it also introduces the possibility that in analyzing pictorial representation we may extend and clarify our knowledge of the information that is available for direct perception.

What is immediately apparent when we compare the optic arrays of direct perception with those of pictorial perception is how much more limited is the information available in pictorial perception. Two powerful classes of information available for direct perception but not produced by pictures are the information available only to a binocular observer and the information available only to a moving observer. Binocular information has traditionally been analyzed into convergence information and stereoscopic information. Convergence information arises because the amount that the two eyes must converge to fixate a given point is related, by an easily specified trigonometric function, to the distance of the point (Descartes, 1965). Stereoscopic information refers to the residual disparities existing, for a given convergence angle, between the visual angles subtended at the two eyes between points that are at different distances (Wheatstone, 1838). A suggestion has recently been made for a new analysis of binocular information in terms of the disparity between the structures of the two optic arrays that are available to the two eyes of the observer (Barrand, 1979; Gibson, 1979). However it is analyzed, though, the binocular information available to the observer of a picture specifies only the picture's flatness; this information specifies nothing about the scene represented by the picture.

The information conveyed by motion has traditionally been referred to as "motion parallax" and analyzed in terms of the differential angular velocities of two points at different distances from a moving observer (e.g., Ittleson, 1960). Gibson and his students have shown, however, that the information available to a moving observer is much more extensive and more powerful than the traditional analysis implies. Movement of the observer produces complex flow fields in the optic arrays from textured surfaces (Gibson, Olum, & Rosenblatt, 1955; Purdy, 1960; Warren, 1976), projective transformations in the solid angles subtended in the optic array by plane surfaces (Gibson, 1957; Hay, 1966), and the progressive deletion (or accretion) from the optic array of the projections of objects that are being occluded (or disoccluded) (Gibson, Kaplan, Reynolds, & Wheeler, 1969; Kaplan, 1969). For each kind of change that movement produces in the optic array, however, some mathematical structure of the optic array remains invariant. Each of these invariant structures mathematically specifies some spatial relation in the environment (see Gibson, 1979, for a detailed discussion of these invariants). What is important here is that such changes, with their accompanying invariants, cannot occur in pictorial representations in the way that they occur in direct perception. To the moving observer of a picture these invariants specify the flat surface of the picture, not the scene represented.[13]

Gibson's formulation of direct perception as the registration of information carried by invariant structures in the optic array has done much to increase our understanding of how unambiguous and veridical perception is normally possible, but it has at the same time given new emphasis to the problem of understanding picture perception by showing how relatively impoverished is the information available from a pictorial representation.

The ambiguity of pictorial representations, considered as geometrical projections, has been noted earlier in this chapter (see p. 48). Various theoretical approaches have been offered to reconcile this mathematical fact with the empirical observation that many pictures yield a single unequivocal perception of spatial layout (see, for example, Hochberg, 1962, 1972). The approach Gibson has taken is to extend the concept of invariants to include pictorial representations. In 1971 Gibson suggested that

> an *informative* picture contains the same kind of timeless invariants that a sequence of perspectives contains. If it does not provide the eye with these invariants, it is not a good picture of the object (for example, if it is not depicted from a favorable point of view) . . . . The timeless invariants become more obvious over time, it is true, in a motion picture as compared with a still picture but some of them at least are still present in the latter [p. 31].

Gibson is not more explicit here about what he intends but he seems to be pointing to a class of *pictorial invariants* that correspond to the invariants under change that exist in the optic array from a real scene.

---

[13] Gibson (1971) suggests that the sophisticated adult viewer can go back and forth between attending to the information that specifies the picture surface and attending to the information that specifies the things represented in the picture.

In Gibson's most recent discussion of pictures (Gibson, 1979), he offers some examples of how the registering of invariants in direct perception could be transferred to pictorial perception:

> [W]hen the young child sees the family cat at play, the front view, side view, rear view, top view, and so on are not seen, and what gets perceived is the *invariant* cat . . . . Hence, when the child first sees a picture of a cat he is prepared to pick up the invariants, and he pays no attention to the frozen perspective of the picture, drawing, photograph, or cartoon . . . . When he sees the cat half-hidden by the chair, he perceives a partly hidden cat, not a half-cat, and therefore he is prepared to see the same thing in a drawing [pp. 271–272].

This example suggests that, because the optic array at any moment of direct perception is always in the process of revealing invariants through change, the optic array from a pictorial representation can be taken as an arrested optic array, frozen in the process of revealing its invariants. We might say, in other words, that pictorial invariants are structures in the static optic array from a picture that *would* remain invariant *if* the optic array were from a real scene and were being transformed by a movement of the observer.

Let us consider one very simple example that might fit this concept of pictorial invariants. One of the most fundamental spatial relations is continuity. A line, a contour, or an edge is physically continuous when it is not broken by gaps or dislocations. An edge or contour that is continuous will generally project as a continuous line in the optic array. Such *optical continuity* does not always specify *physical continuity*, however, because it is possible, either by accident or by contrivance, for two discontinuous physical edges to be arranged in space so that they are projected as one continuous line in the optic array to some particular point of observation.[14] In such a situation, however, any slight movement of the point of observation will disrupt the optical continuity; only when the edge is actually physically continuous will its projection still be a continuous line in the optic array when the point of observation moves. Thus, we can say that *invariant optical continuity* under the changes in the optic array that are produced by motion of the observer does specify physical continuity.

In the static optic array of a pictorial representation, optical continuity could be taken as pictorial invariant that specifies physical continuity in the scene represented. This means that *if* the optic array were from a real scene, then the optical continuity *would* remain invariant when the point of observation moved. Although there is no mathematical guarantee that such a condition holds for every picture, we could say, using Gibson's

---

[14] Two physically discontinuous line segments will project as a continuous line in the optic array if the two edges are parallel and a line connecting their two adjacent endpoints can be extended to pass through the station point.

phrase, that a picture for which this was not true—a picture whose station point was chosen so that two physically discontinuous edges were projected as one continuous line—would not be a "good picture." Rather than being informative, the picture would misinform us.

Redundancy of Information

Gibson has pointed out that the structured light coming from a normal environment is rich in information. Different structures in the optic array carry the same or overlapping information about the spatial layout of the environment. The information is thus redundant, enabling an organism to accurately register spatial layout even if its visual system can sample only some of the available information. Although this redundancy is richest for direct perception, it also exists in the optic array made available by pictorial representations. As will be seen below, information about size, distance, and other characteristics of spatial layout can be carried by a number of redundant structures in the optic arrays from pictures. This redundancy is all the more necessary in pictures because the individual forms of information, relying as they do on pictorial invariants, are more subject to qualification than their corresponding forms in direct perception. A given structure or configuration in a picture might, taken in isolation, be ambiguous (see Kennedy's discussion, 1974, chapters 7 and 8, of the multiple uses of line in pictorial representations). Within the context of a picture that is, in Gibson's sense, a good picture, however, the redundant information may be expected to function in a mutually supporting way to eliminate multiple alternatives and thus remove ambiguity. Such complex interdependencies may be at the heart of successful pictorial representations, but nevertheless, to examine them here would take us over too arduous, lengthy, and uncertain a path. Instead, we shall examine each of the principal forms of layout information more or less in isolation, leaving to a later and more detailed exposition the task of more completely analyzing the underlying pictorial invariants and of showing that these different forms of information support each other in the way that has been suggested here. Not all of the information that we shall discuss is available in every picture. What information is available in a particular picture depends not only on how the picture is constructed but also on how much of the framework is left visible in the completed picture.

Finding the Station Point

An observer viewing a picture is free, circumstances permitting, to look at it from any distance and at any angle. No matter what point of view is adopted, we can meaningfully ask what the picture, seen from that point of view, geometrically represents. In other words, what three-dimensional scene in what location would present essentially the same structure of light to the observer's eye as that picture, seen from that point of view, does? In general, every different point of view produces a different answer. For a given picture, these answers are the same in many respects. If a picture represents two trees and a house when seen from one point of view, it will represent two trees and a house from any point of view. The spatial arrangements of the trees and house, their sizes, and even their shapes will differ, however, from one point of view to the next. In general, only from one point of view (i.e., the station point from which the pictorial representation was constructed) does the picture represent exactly the scene that the artist saw, or had in mind, when constructing it. The scenes that the picture represents to other points of view are generally referred to as "distortions" of this original scene. The nature of those distortions is not our concern here; rather we must consider the implication that an observer wishing to obtain a geometricallly undistorted view of the scene must find the correct station point of the picture and place her or his eye there. Very occasionally the artist will take care of this for the observer by some contrivance such as placing the picture in a box so that it can only be seen through a single peephole located at the station point.[15] Much more frequently, however, it is left up to the observer to find the station point.[16]

Once the observer is at the station point, the processes of picking up information about the scene are likely to be similar to, although more restricted than, some of those used in viewing real scenes. The task of *finding* the station point, however, is unique to pictorial perception and has no counterpart in the viewing of real scenes. It would thus be of considerable interest to know how well observers are actually able to perform this task. We shall not consider this empirical question here as our chief concern is with *available* information. We shall confine ourselves instead to the logically prior question of how, and how well, an ideal observer could *potentially* perform this task. In other words, what geometrical information is available in a pictorial representation to specify where its station point is? The specific answer to this question can differ with the content of each particular picture, but a fairly general idea of

[15] Although rarely enforced by the artist, the requirement of a single fixed point of view has been essential to the concept of perspective representation from its inception. The first known example of an exact perspective representation in the Renaissance (by Brunelleschi, see Footnote 7) was constructed so that the observer had to view it through a fixed peephole (see Manetti's account, translated in White, 1967, p. 116).

[16] Many artists, including some of the earliest users of perspective, have adapted their constructions to reduce the geometrical distortions that occur if the observer does not find the correct station point. (For discussions of the various strategies they have used, see Jones and Hagen, 1978; Pirenne, 1970, pp. 116–135; & Ware, 1900, pp. 160–172.)

the nature of the available information can be obtained even if we restrict ourselves to considering a picture containing the basic perspective frame-work: the representation of an infinitely extended ground plane covered with a grid of lined squares at some angle to the picture plane.

Even an ideal observer cannot progress toward finding the station point without some information about the represented spatial layout that does not depend on already being at the correct station point. Such infor-mation, which we might refer to loosely as "contextual," is apt to be complex and specific to the particular picture (e.g., the ground plane in the picture may be specified as being horizontal by being represented as functioning as a stable surface of support). With such station-point-independent information about layout, the observer can then search for a station point from which that layout is geometrically specified. In the example we are considering, the observer must have information iden-tifying the line in the picture that represents the horizon of the ground plane and must also have information that the two systems of lines con-verging to the horizon represent a grid of squares covering the ground plane.

Because the horizon of the ground plane is always at eye level, the height of the station point is easy for an observer to find; it is the same as that of the horizon line of the picture. Thus the observer's search for the correct station point can be confined to an imaginary horizontal plane stretching out in space in front of the picture and intersecting the picture in the horizon line.[17]

Let us now turn our attention to the grid of lined squares covering the ground plane. This grid is made up of two sets of evenly spaced parallel lines at right angles to each other. The perspective representations of each of these two sets of lines will, if sufficiently extended, converge to a vanishing point on the horizon. The two vanishing points thus deter-mined will often lie on a portion of the horizon line outside the frame of the actual picture, but here, as usual, we must consider the abstract plane of the picture as extending indefinitely beyond the borders set by the frame. As we have seen above, a line extending from the station point to one of the vanishing points must be parallel to all those parallel lines whose perspective representations converge on that vanishing point. Thus, because the two systems of parallel lines are at right angles, the station point must be located in such a way that lines drawn from it to the two vanishing points make a right angle with each other. This geo-

[17] In working with perspective constructions, it is common practice to imagine the hor-izontal plane containing the station point to be rotated downward by 90°, using the horizon line as an axis, so that the station point lies in the picture plane. This maneuver has no theoretical significance but has the practical effect that construction lines involving the station point can be drawn in the picture plane; the results are the same.

metrical fact places a sharp restriction on the locations in the horizontal plane through the horizon line that could be the correct station point. It is a general theorem of geometry that if the hypoteneuse of any right triangle is taken as the diameter of a circle then the right-angled vertex opposite the hypoteneuse will lie on the circumference of the circle (see Figure 2.18). Therefore, the station point must lie somewhere along the horizontal semicircle that can be drawn between the two vanishing points in the space in front of the picture plane. If the observer chooses a point of observation that is not on this semicircle, then the two systems of parallel lines on the ground plane will not be represented as being at right angles to each other.

Only one point on the horizontal semicircle connecting the vanishing points is the correct station point, but from any other point on the semicircle the pictured grid still represents two systems of evenly spaced parallel lines at right angles to each other. The difference is that from the correct station point the elements of the grid represent squares, whereas from any other point on the semicircle they represent rectangles having one side longer than the other. This suggests a way of finding out where on the semicircle the correct station point is located. Implicit in any grid of squares or rectangles is another grid—the grid composed of their diagonals. These diagonals also form two systems of parallel lines and, consequently, their perspective representations also converge to two vanishing points on the horizon. The diagonals of squares differ from the diagonals of all other rectangles, however, in being at right angles to one another. As a result, the correct station point of the square grid must lie on the horizontal semicircle connecting the two vanishing points of its

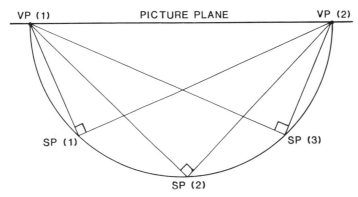

FIGURE 2.18. Station points for perpendicular systems of lines. The horizontal plane through the horizon line is here seen from above. *VP*(1) and *VP*(2) are the vanishing points of two systems of parallel lines. As the lines connecting *SP*(1), *SP*(2), and *SP*(3) to the vanishing points illustrate, for any station point on the semicircle between *VP*(1) and *VP*(2) the two systems of parallel lines are represented as being at right angles to each other.

implicit diagonals. The unique position of the correct station point is thus given by the intersection of two horizontal semicircles, one connecting the two vanishing points of the square grid, the other connecting the two vanishing points of its implicit diagonals (see Figure 2.19).

An entire grid of squares on the ground plane is not actually necessary for locating the station point, as the perspective representation of a single square in the ground plane will do just as well for finding the four vanishing points of its sides and diagonals. Once again, though, there must be some contextual information in the picture to specify to the observer that this pictorial form is the pictorial representation of a square. We can conclude then that visual information for finding the correct station point may be available, even in fairly minimal perspective constructions, as long as certain station-point-independent information about what the constructions represent is also present. Whether observers are actually able to use this information is another question. For the remainder of this

30°/60° GROUND PLANE GRID

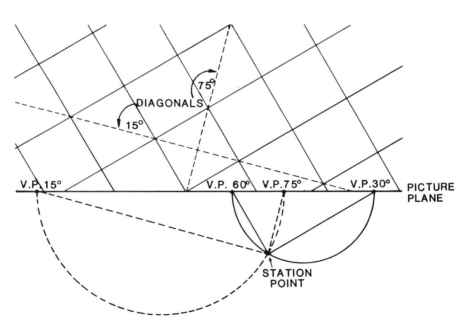

FIGURE 2.19. Finding the station point at the intersection of two semicircles. This is a view from above of a ground plane grid whose lines are angled at either 30° or 60° to the picture plane. The diagonals of this grid, indicated by dotted lines, are angled at either 15° or 75° to the picture plane. VP 30°, VP 60°, VP 15°, and VP 75° are the vanishing points of these four systems of parallel lines. The station point lies where the semicircle connecting VP 30° and VP 60° intersects the semicircle connecting VP 15° and VP 75°.

analysis, however, we shall assume that the observer has succeeded in placing her or his eye at the correct station point.

Scale

As we have already observed, the construction of a pictorial representation of a scene can be based on a scaled-down model of the scene if that is more convenient. As long as the actual distance from the picture plane to the station point is not changed and the station point maintains the same relative position in the scaled-down model as it had in the original scene, the resulting representation will be identical to one based on the actual, full-scale scene. It necessarily follows that an observer looking at a pictorial representation has absolutely no way of telling whether it is a representation based on a full-sized or scaled-down (or scaled-up) scene. In other words, a pictorial representation provides no geometrical information about the overall scale of the scene that it represents. In this fundamental way a picture differs from an actual open window through which we always see the actual full-scale world and for which, consequently, there is no question of scale. In the remainder of this analysis, it is assumed that a picture always *represents* a full-scale scene, such as might be seen through an actual window, even when the picture is *constructed* on the basis of a scaled-down model. This is the most convenient approach to take and we shall presume it to be in accord with the intentions of the person who constructed the picture. Whether the visual system actually responds to pictures in this way is an empirical question. When a picture is presented so as to "fool the eye," appearing to be an actual scene rather than a picture of one, then we might expect the scene to be perceived as being full-scale. It is far more common, however, for it to be clearly visible to the observer that the picture is, in fact, only a picture. When this is the case, we cannot simply take it for granted that the represented scene is perceived as being full-scale. Whether pictures might not sometimes be perceived as representing scaled-down, miniature worlds or enormous, larger-than-life worlds is a question for empirical investigation (see Hochberg, 1962, p. 41).

Occlusion

When one surface partially occludes another in a pictorial representation, the occluding surface is necessarily closer to the observer than is the occluded surface. This is rather limited information about spatial layout, but in a crowded scene it can help to set up ordinal scales of distance among the objects in the environment.

Although the spatial information that occlusion specifies is straightforward, the information that specifies occlusion in a picture is complex.

In direct perception, occlusion is specified to a moving observer when an edge of the occluding surface progressively hides or reveals the occluded surface (see Gibson, 1979, for a more detailed discussion). This information, which is another form of invariance under change, cannot be reproduced in the static array of a pictorial representation. A number of attempts from a variety of theoretical orientations have been made to explain how occlusion is represented pictorially.[18] Each of these approaches probably points to some type of information concerning occlusion that may be present in the optic array from a picture, but a comprehensive analysis of such information has yet to be made.

Optical Contact

As has already been stated, the model of the environment underlying perspective constructions consists of an extended ground plane on which are laid out all the buildings, shrubbery, inhabitants, and other elements of the scene. This extended ground plane visually unites all the elements of the scene, providing a visible framework in relation to which the spatial layout of these elements is precisely specified geometrically. Each object in a picture is first related to the ground plane and then, through its relation to the ground plane, is related to other objects in the picture. Therefore, to correctly register the represented position of an object, an observer needs information about that object's point of contact with the ground plane. This information is provided by optical contact, by which is meant contiguity in the picture plane between the projection of the bottom edge of the object and the projection of the ground plane (see Figure 2.20). As Gibson pointed out (1950, pp. 178–180), if an object is floating above the surface of the ground or is held above it by some hidden support, then its optical contact with the ground is deceptive, because the projection is the same as if the object were resting on a more distant portion of the ground (see Figure 2.20). In viewing a real scene, which is far richer in visual information than a picture, instances in which optical contact is not accompanied by actual physical contact can be geometrically specified by binocular stereopsis or by motion parallax; in pictures, which lack these forms of information, these instances still can be specified in a variety of ways, such as by cast shadows (see Figure 2.21). Even when such confirming information is completely absent, how-

[18] One recent approach to the problem of specifying the information for occlusion in pictures that has had considerable success is scene analysis. In particular, Waltz's analysis (1975) of line drawings of scenes with shadows has shown by computer simulation that, in the two-dimensional projection of a complicated jumble of differently shaped blocks, the three-dimensional layout of the blocks is usually unambiguously specified by the pattern of intersections of the projected contours. This approach is closely related to Gibson's theories, but appears to have developed independently of them.

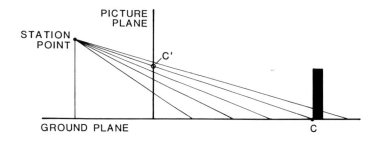

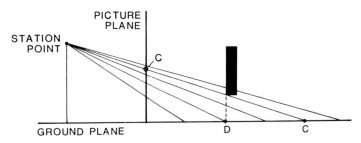

FIGURE 2.20. Optical contact. In the upper drawing projective contiguity at *C′* corresponds to physical contact between the object and ground at *C*. In the lower drawing projective contiguity at *C′* is deceptive because the object is floating in the air above *D*.

ever, optical contact with the ground plane can be thought of as another pictorial invariant (i.e., in a good picture the scene represented is such that optical contact would remain invariant, and thus would specify physical contact, if a moving observer were to view the actual scene).

Texture

Gibson has pointed out that the texture of the ground provides information for spatial relations between objects by covering the ground with a homogeneous scale of reference (Gibson, 1959). In perspective constructions the lined grid of squares that overlays the ground plane is analogous to the textured ground of the real environment. The analogy is not perfect because the perspective grid is more regular and less dense than natural texture and also because the grid is often concealed in the finished picture. Nevertheless, this grid can provide a form of "texture" information for size and distance in some pictures.

Gibson (1959) states that "the size of an object is given by the size of its projection relative to the size of the elements of texture or structure

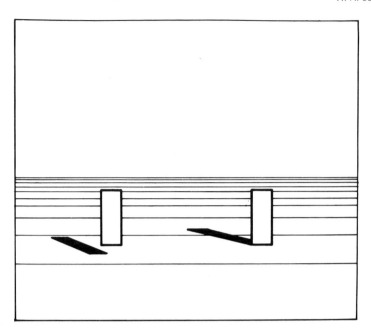

FIGURE 2.21. Contact with ground specified by cast shadows. The object on the left is suspended in the air as is shown by the gap between the projections of it and of its shadow on the ground. In contrast, the contiguity between the projection of the object on the right and the projection of its cast shadows shows this object to be in contact with the ground.

in the adjacent optical array (p. 479)." More specifically, the length of any edge that is resting on the ground plane is indicated by the amount of texture (i.e., number of grid squares) that it covers projectively (see Figure 2.22). Because the projective sizes of both the object and the grid on which it rests are reduced proportionally with increased distance, the relation between them remains invariant with distance (e.g., if the squares of the grid are 1 ft. on a side, a yardstick resting on the ground will be three squares long no matter what distance it is seen from). This relation is true for any orientation of the yardstick (with respect to the picture plane) *as long as it is resting on the ground.* If the yardstick is tilted up from the ground (e.g., to the vertical) then its projection in the picture plane covers more than three squares because the yardstick is no longer undergoing the same amount of projective compression as is the ground it occludes.

The distance between objects is also geometricallly specified in the same way (i.e., by the number of grid squares, in whatever direction, separating their points of contact with the ground plane). The distance from the observer to the object would also be specified in this way if the picture actually showed the whole extent of the ground plane between

FIGURE 2.22. Size and distance specified by the texture of the ground plane. In this perspective view the relation between each of the two objects and the grid covering the ground plane specifies that the objects both have the same ground plane dimensions (three by two squares) and are separated by a distance of two squares.

the object and the feet of the observer, but the bottom frame of the picture generally occludes some of the ground plane nearest to the observer.

The sizes and distances geometrically specified by this texture information are all relative to the size of the grid (e.g., an object may be projectively specified as two squares deep and three squares wide).[19] Absolute dimensions, in some known metric, are not specified unless the

[19] Because of increasing compression the farther portions of each square in a grid in angular perspective will project into smaller visual angles than the nearer portions. With such a grid, if an object does not cover an integral number of grid squares, its exact dimensions cannot be arrived at by linear interpolation between lines of the projected grid. For a grid in parallel perspective, on the other hand, each line parallel to the picture plane is uniformly compressed along its entire length. In this case, fractional frontal dimensions of objects (e.g., 2.5 squares) can be exactly determined by interpolation within squares of the projected grid.

size of the grid elements is somehow evident from the context of the picture or is geometrically specified. There are several optic array structures that do specify the grid size, relative to the height of the station point; we shall consider these structures next.

Gradients

In his early analysis of the ways in which spatial layout is specified by objects' relations to the ground plane, Gibson (1950) placed considerable emphasis on various gradients, such as the gradient of increasing density in the projection of the ground plane as it recedes from the observer. This increasing compression toward the horizon, which was mentioned in our discussion of parallel perspective, was postulated by Gibson as geometrically specifying a level ground plane receding from the observer. W. C. Purdy, a student of Gibson's, has carried out a detailed mathematical study of gradients in which he extends Gibson's hypotheses and gives mathematical formulations of a wide range of potential gradient information (Purdy, 1960). Although Purdy's analysis is concerned with direct perception, much of the information he discusses is available, at least approximately, from pictorial representations. It is that pictorially available information that we shall consider here.

OPTICAL SLANT

In his discussion of gradients Purdy makes use of Gibson's concept of optical slant (Gibson & Cornsweet, 1952). The optical slant of a particular location on a surface is defined as the angle (R) at which a visual ray from the station point intersects the surface at that location (see Figure 2.23). Let us for concreteness focus our discussion on the optical slants of locations along the ground, although much of what we say could be applied to any surface. The optical slants of locations along the ground vary with

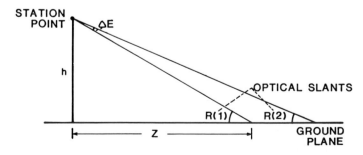

FIGURE 2.23. Optical slant. *R*(1) and *R*(2) are the optical slants of two locations on the ground plane.

their distance from the station point; the farther from the station point a location is, the smaller is the optical slant (R) at that location. Because distance and optical slant vary together, it follows that any structure in the optic array that provides information about the optical slant of a location on the ground will also provide information about that location's distance from the station point. The gradients identified by Gibson and mathematically analyzed by Purdy do just that.

Expanding somewhat on Gibson's description, Purdy defines five separate gradients, each of which reflects a different aspect of the optic array projection of the ground. These are the gradient of texture size, the gradient of texture density, the gradient of texture compression, the gradient of texture foreshortening, and the gradient of linear perspective. Mathematically, Purdy's analyses of these gradients are all very similar; for the purpose of showing how a gradient can specify optical slant, the gradient of texture size may be taken as a sufficiently representative example.

GRADIENT OF TEXTURE SIZE

The size of an element of texture is given by its area, referred to here as a. If texture is conceptualized as a square grid covering the ground, then $a = s^2$, where s is the length of the side of an individual square element of texture. Each element of texture projects into a solid visual angle in the optic array. We shall refer to the area of that visual angle as A. Let us now consider the optic array projections of the succession of texture elements along any line stretching directly away from the station point (see Figure 2.24). Purdy assumes that the texture itself is uniform, that is, that every texture element has the same size.[20] The projections of these elements change in two ways, however, as elements farther and farther away are considered. First, the solid visual angle (A) subtended by each successive element is smaller than that subtended by the preceding, closer element; we shall express the difference in visual angle size between any two successive elements as ΔA. Second, each successive element projects to a somewhat higher location in the optic array; the angular difference between the optic array heights of any two successive texture elements (measured from their centers) will be referred to as ΔE. We can form a ratio $\Delta A/\Delta E$ that expresses the rate at which projected texture size changes as height in the optic array changes for any two successive texture elements. The value of $\Delta A/\Delta E$ at any location depends

---

[20] Purdy (1960) describes the possibility of extending his analysis to include a type of surface texture, which he refers to as "stochastically regular," in which the texture "is composed of elements whose parameters (length, width, area, shape) vary randomly according to some frequency density function which is the *same throughout the extent of the surface* (p. 12)." Purdy does not attempt any mathematical analysis of the gradients produced by stochastically regular textures.

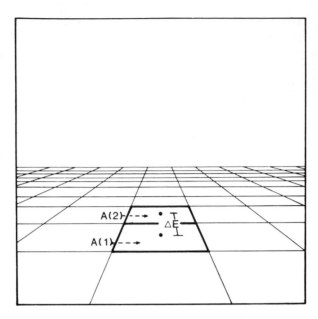

FIGURE 2.24. The gradient of texture size. In this perspective view of the ground plane two successive grid squares ("texture elements") are indicated with heavy lines. $A(1)$ and $A(2)$ indicate the solid visual angles projected by those two squares; $\Delta A = A(1) - A(2)$. The angular difference between their optic array heights is given by ΔE.

upon the coarseness of the texture grid. By dividing this ratio by the projected size of the texture element at that location, however, we can obtain a more complex ratio, $(\Delta A/\Delta E)\ /A$, that is independent of the coarseness of the texture grid. This complex ratio can be taken as an expression of the gradient of texture size at that location, which Purdy (1960) defines as "the relative rate of change of the solid angle subtended by successive texture elements as the line of regard is swept along a radial direction (p. 7)."

For pairs of successive elements farther and farther from the station point each of the terms of the ratio $(\Delta A/\Delta E)\ /A$ decreases, but the three terms decrease at different rates so that the overall value of the ratio is continually changing. As a result, each successively farther location has a unique value of the gradient of texture size associated with it.

The ratio $(\Delta A/\Delta E)\ /A$ must be mathematically manipulated in two ways before we shall arrive at the expression Purdy uses for the gradient of texture size. The first manipulation is to substitute ΔR, which is the change in optical slant between two successive texture elements, for ΔE, which is the change in optic array height between those same two elements. The equivalence of ΔR and ΔE is due to a general theorem of geometry that states that the sum of two interior angles of a triangle (ΔE and R (2)

in Figure 2.23) is equal to the remaining exterior angle (R(1) in Figure 2.23). That is, $\Delta E + R(2) = R(1)$; hence $\Delta E = R(1) - R(2) = \Delta R$. This substitution is critical in relating the gradient of texture size, which is an optic array structure, to optical slant. Thus, we can express the gradient of texture size by the ratio $(\Delta A/\Delta R)/A$.

The second manipulation we must perform is to consider what happens to the expression for the gradient of texture size as the grid of texture elements covering the ground is made finer and finer until, at the limit, the grid becomes infinitely dense. This manipulation allows Purdy to use calculus to find the relation between optical slant and the gradient for texture size. The expression dA/dR, which can be thought of as referring to the change that occurs in A for an infinitesimal change in R, is thus substituted for $\Delta A/\Delta R$. This gives Purdy's expression for the gradient of texture size, which he refers to as Gs:

$$Gs = (dA/dR)/A.$$

Purdy's derivations of the relation between texture gradients and optical slant are idealizations in that the use of calculus in them assumes that the texture is infinitely dense and the differences between adjacent texture elements are arbitrarily small. One can argue, as Purdy does, that in real scenes this is not an unrealistic approximation because any unit of texture is divisible into smaller subunits of texture. The assumption is not as well satisfied by perspective representations. The perspective grid covering the ground plane has a finite density that is determined by the size chosen for the individual squares. It is possible to derive relations analogous to Purdy's, but based on the finite differences between texture elements (see Sedgwick, 1973). Such finite difference approximations, however, have not been systematically explored. Therefore, this chapter follows Purdy's analysis and assumes that its results would generalize reasonably well to the description of the optic array characteristics of a grid of finite density.

Using calculus,[21] Purdy is able to show that

$$Gs/3 = 1/\tan R.$$

Thus, the gradient of texture size projected from a particular location on the ground specifies the optical slant, R, at that location by means of a simple trigonometric relation. On the basis of this invariant relation, Purdy derives optic array relations in which the distances and frontal

---

[21] Briefly, Purdy's derivation is as follows (for details, see Purdy, 1960, pp. 5–8). The solid visual angle, A, subtended by an element of texture is closely approximated by the equation $A = (a/h^2) \sin^3 R$ as long as the angular dimensions of A are small with respect to R (all terms here are used as they are defined in the text). This equation is differentiated to obtain $dA/dR = (a/h^2) 3 \sin^2 R \cos R$. The gradient of texture size (Gs) can then be quickly calculated. $Gs = (dA/dR)/A = (a/h^2) 3 \sin^2 R \cos R/(a/h^2) \sin^3 R = 3 \cot R$. Thus, $Gs/3 = 1/\tan R$.

dimensions of surfaces in contact with the ground plane are specified relative to the height of the station point.

DISTANCE

Let us consider first how the distance of some location on the ground plane is specified by the gradient for texture size. The perpendicular distance, h, from the station point to the point on the ground directly beneath it and z, the distance along the ground to the given location, are the two legs of a right triangle (see Figure 2.23). The optical slant, R, at that location, is one angle of that triangle. There is thus a simple trigonometric relation between R, z, and h:

$$1/\tan R = z/h.$$

Combining this relation with the relation between optical slant and the gradient of texture size given above, Purdy immediately obtains a relation specifying the distance of an object, relative to the height of the point of observation, in terms of the gradient of texture size at the location on the ground plane where the object makes contact:

$$z/h = Gs/3.$$

SIZE

Having found a gradient relation specifying distance, Purdy derives a gradient relation specifying size. The visual angle subtended by an object decreases regularly as the object's distance from the station point increases; visual angle and distance together thus mathematically specify size. The exact relation connecting these three variables is trigonometric, but if the size of the object is fairly small relative to its distance, a good approximation is given by the relation

$$f = zF,$$

where f is a dimension of the object in the plane perpendicular to the line of regard, F is the visual angle (expressed in radians) that it subtends, and z is the object's distance along the ground from the station point. Combining this relation with the relation that was just derived between distance and the gradient of texture size yields

$$f/h = FGs/3.$$

Therefore, an object's size relative to the height of the station point is also specified by a simple optic array relation involving the gradient of texture size.

GEOGRAPHICAL SLANT

Gibson refers to the slant of a surface relative to some other reference surface, such as the horizontal ground, as *geographical slant* to distinguish it from optical slant (Gibson & Cornsweet, 1952). Unlike optical slant, which decreases for locations on the surface that are farther from the station point, the geographical slant of a surface is the same everywhere and is independent of the location of the station point. The optical slant at some location on the surface, therefore, cannot by itself specify the geographical slant of the surface. Purdy (1960) points out, however, that "the geographical slant of [a] surface, say with respect to the horizontal, is given by the difference between the optical slant of the surface at any point and the angular distance of this point from the horizontal (p. 18)." Expressed algebraically, if *S* is the geographical slant of the surface, if *R* is the optical slant of the surface at some point, and if *U* is the angular distance of that point from the horizontal, then

$$S = R - U.$$

The basis for this equation can be seen from examining the geometrical relation between these three angles (see Figure 2.25). *S* and *U* are two interior angles of a triangle whose remaining exterior angle is *R*; it follows from a general theorem of geometry that we have already mentioned (see pp. 78–79) that $S + U = R$; thus $S = R - U$. The optical slant, *R*, is specified, as we have already seen, by gradients such as the gradient of texture size. As for the angle *U*, Purdy (1960) notes that "the horizontal reference may be defined by a horizontal ground or floor, by the observer's vestibular sense, or by any equivalent source (p. 18)." We may further note that in

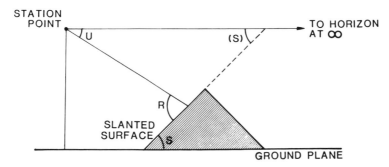

FIGURE 2.25. Geographical slant, optical slant, and the horizon. A surface slanted up from the ground plane is here seen from the side. *S* is the geographical slant of the surface. The dotted line shows that the surface would make the same angle, (*S*), if extended to meet the visual ray to the horizon. *R* is the optical slant of an arbitrarily chosen location on the surface, and *U* is the projective angle between that location and the horizon.

pictorial representations the horizontal reference may be specified by the horizon line of the ground plane. The analysis of the perspective structures relating texture gradients to geographical slant thus introduces a familiar pictorial feature—the horizon line—into our consideration of the information available in pictures.

The Horizon

The sizes, distances, directions, and slants of the surfaces of objects that are resting on the ground can all be specified by optic array relations between those surfaces and the horizon line of the ground plane. I have described and analyzed some of these relations in detail elsewhere (Sedgwick, 1973) with reference to direct perception.[22] Here we shall consider how these relations might enter into the perception of pictorial representations. The horizon relations described in this section are commonly available in pictures because the horizon line is an essential element in the construction of perspective representations.

SIZE

Let us consider first how size is specified by this form of geometrical relation. The lengths of edges that are parallel to the picture plane are specified by the *horizon-ratio relation,* already discussed in connection with the perspective representation of height. The horizon line intersects every object on the ground plane at the same height, and because projection is based on proportions, the following ratio exists:

$$y/h = y'/h',$$

where y is the height of an object, y' is its projective height in the picture plane, h is the height of the station point, and h' is the distance in the picture plane between the object's intersection with the horizon line and the object's point of contact with the ground plane (see Figure 2.16). This relation between extents in the picture plane can also be expressed as a relation between visual angles in the optic array:

$$y/h = \tan Y'/\tan H',$$

where Y' and H' are the visual angles subtended by y' and h', respectively. When the angles Y' and H' are fairly small, which will be the case whenever y is small relative to z, the object's distance from the station point,

---

[22] Hay (1974) discusses the information that is potentially available in the optic array relations among an object's vanishing points, which he refers to as the object's ghost image. His analysis is closely related mathematically to, although different in emphasis from, the analysis of horizon information for directions and slants given here.

their tangents can be approximated by the angles themselves:

$$y/h \approx Y'/H'.$$

Although the horizon-ratio relation is used in perspective constructions to obtain the projective heights of objects, it can be applied to any dimension that is parallel to the picture plane. For instance, if x is the width of the object and x' is its projective width, then $x/h = x'/h'$. In each case the dimension in question is specified relative to the height, h, of the station point (e.g., if $x/h = 3$, then the width, x, is three times the height of the station point).

Absolute dimensions (i.e., lengths in some known metric) are not available from the horizon-ratio relation unless the height of the station point is somehow known or specified in that metric. The sizes of objects relative to each other are specified, however, by the horizon-ratio relation even when the height of the station point is not known. For example, if $y(1)/h = 3$ and $y(2)/h = 2$, then $y(1) = 1.5\ y(2)$ (see Figure 2.26).

DISTANCE

It should be noted that the specification of an object's size by the horizon-ratio relation does not depend upon the specification of its distance. The horizon ratio relations of objects are invariant with distance because the visual ray to the horizon is parallel to the ground plane and conse-

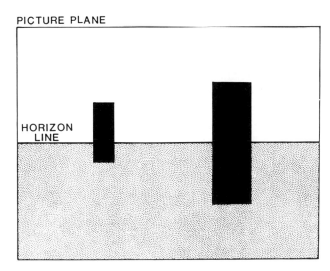

FIGURE 2.26. Horizon-ratio relation for relative height. The object on the left is 3 times the height of the point of observation. The object on the right is twice the height of the point of observation. Thus, the object on the left is 1.5 times the height of the object on the right.

quently its height above the ground plane does not vary with distance. The distance of an object resting on the ground is, however, also specified by its projective relation to the horizon line. The angle, H', between the horizon line and the object's point of contact with the ground decreases regularly as the object's distance from the station point increases (see Figure 2.16). A simple trigonometric relation exists in which z, the object's distance along the ground from the station point, is given by

$$z/h = 1/\tan H'.$$

This distance relation is similar to the horizon-ratio relation in that its specification of distance, rather than being absolute, is relative to the height of the station point or else specifies the relative distances of two objects as expressed in the relation

$$z(1)/z(2) = \tan H'(2)/\tan H'(1).$$

For distances that are at least a few times larger than the height of the station point, the angle H' is small enough so that it can be taken as a good approximation of its tangent.

DIRECTION

If an object is resting on the ground plane, its bottom edges that are in contact with the ground will be horizontal. The projection of any such edge will not be horizontal, however, unless that edge is parallel to the picture plane. Other horizontal edges have projections that make some angle with the horizontal in the picture plane. In principle, any angle of projection in the picture plane can be produced by any direction of horizontal line segment on the ground plane. This is apparent in the inverted fan of lines converging to a vanishing point that any system of parallel lines, whatever their direction, produces (see Figure 2.11). The direction of an edge is thus not specified directly by the angle of its projection. Its direction is specified, however, by the relation between its projection, the station point, and the horizon line.

If the line segment that is the projection of the edge is extended until it intersects the horizon, the point of intersection is the vanishing point of the line. Now let us consider the imaginary horizontal line in front of the picture plane that passes through the station point and has the same direction as (i.e., is parallel to) the edge. This line, as was shown in our discussion of the construction of the perspective grid, intersects the picture plane at the vanishing point of the system of parallel lines to which the edge belongs. Thus, the direction of an edge resting on the ground plane is specified by the direction from the station point to the vanishing point of the edge's projection in the picture plane. In other words, the direction of the edge is given by the direction in which an observer must look to see its vanishing point on the horizon.[23]

GEOGRAPHICAL SLANT

Although the preceding discussion has focused on how horizon-related information specifies the direction of edges lying in the ground plane, its conclusion has more general applicability. Any edge, whether in the ground plane or not, has its direction specified by the direction of its vanishing point. For the vanishing point of the edge to be locatable, either the horizon line of the plane in which the edge lies must be indicated in the perspective construction or two parallel edges must be present so that their vanishing point is specified by their intersection. An instance of this latter situation that is of particular interest is the information specifying the geographical slant of a rectangular surface. If the rectangular surface of an object is slanted directly up from the horizontal, so that its bottom edge remains parallel to the picture plane, then the receding parallel edges of the surface will intersect at a vanishing point on the horizon line of the slanted plane in which the surface lies. Because this plane is slanted directly up from the ground plane, its horizon line is parallel to but higher than the horizon line of the ground plane. (If the plane were slanted directly down, its horizon line would be parallel to but lower than the horizon line of the ground plane.) The slant of the surface is specified by the direction of its vanishing point from the station point. Hence, its angle of slant relative to the horizontal is equal to the angular elevation, subtended at the station point, of its horizon line above the horizon line of the ground plane (see Figure 2.27). For example, if the distance of the station point from the picture plane is one meter and the horizon line of the plane is one meter above the horizon line of the ground plane, then the plane must be slanted up from the horizontal at a 45° angle.

DISTORTIONS

Although the distortions that are geometrically specified when the eye is not at the station point are not the subject of this chapter, it may be

---

[23] In perspective constructions, vanishing points can be used to determine the directions of lines, and distance points (see Footnote 10) can be used to determine their lengths and distances. Similarly, just as there is an horizon relation that involves the vanishing point and that specifies direction, there is also an horizon relation that involves the distance point (and the trace line) and that specifies length and distance. This latter horizon relation involves such complicated extrapolations, however, that its utility to the visual system is questionable.

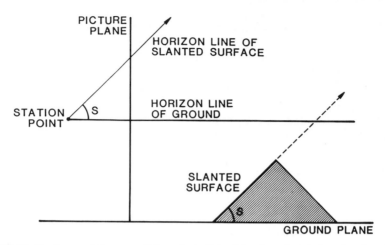

FIGURE 2.27. Horizon relation specifying slant. This side view shows that the visual angle between the horizon of a slanted surface and the horizon of the ground is equal to the geographical slant of the surface.

noted that the analysis of horizon relations given here is readily extendable to an analysis of distortions. For example, it follows directly from the horizon relations discussed above that the geometrically specified direction of a line segment lying in the ground plane rotates clockwise (seen from above) in a precisely determined way as the eye moves from right to left in front of the picture plane. In addition, the geometrically specified slant of a surface grows steeper as the eye approaches the picture plane. Other examples of such an analysis are discussed elsewhere in more detail (see Sedgwick, 1973).[24]

Height in the Picture Plane

The discussion of horizon relations that specify various aspects of spatial layout has been predicated on the horizon line of the ground plane's being specified in the representation, either directly by a line on the picture plane or, in a few cases, indirectly by the implicit convergence of the projections of parallel lines. Because the horizon line is always at the same height as the station point, however, it is also possible to specify the horizon line simply as that imaginary horizontal line in the picture plane that is at "eye-level." Therefore, it is possible to specify where the horizon line should be in any perspective representation, even when there is no perspective construction in the picture plane to indicate the position of the horizon line. Such an imaginary, eye-level, horizon line

---

[24] Also see Farber and Rosinski, 1978, and Chapter 4 of this volume.

is capable, in principle, of supporting all of the horizon relations described in the previous section. Whether the visual system is capable of registering eye-level on the picture plane with sufficient accuracy to make this form of information useful is an empirical question whose answer may vary considerably, depending on the particular horizon relation in question. For instance, it can be calculated from the horizon relations already discussed that an error of one degree in locating the horizon line of the ground plane would produce only a one degree error in the registration of the slant of a surface but would produce an error of approximately 20% in the registration of the height of an object whose distance from the station point was ten times the height of the station point.

The ubiquitous presence of an implicit horizon line is the basis of the statement that height in the picture is a cue to distance (e.g., Brunswik, 1956). On the one hand, this statement is too narrow because it does not include size, direction, and slant, all of which are also specified by projective relations involving the implicit eye-level horizon. On the other hand, it is too broad because the relation of increasing distance to increasing projective height on the picture plane only holds true geometrically for objects resting on the ground and, consequently, can only hold true for objects whose base of support is below the implicit horizon line. Objects above that line must either be floating, in which case there is no necessary relation between their distance and their height in the picture plane, or they must be suspended from, or a part of, a ceiling or cloud cover of some sort. If this is the case, the higher such objects are in the picture plane, the *closer* they are to the station point.

Other Information, Other Invariants

We now have seen how an accurate perspective representation is constructed and how it is that this construction, when it is completed, can make available to an observer information about the spatial layout of surfaces in the scene represented. Let us conclude by briefly considering what the importance is of these techniques and of the information that they represent.

It can be argued that the representation of precise or complicated spatial relations depends upon incorporating into the picture one or more of the forms of information considered in this chapter. Some nongeometrical forms of pictorial information for spatial relations, such as shading and aerial perspective, can contribute significantly to conveying the solidity and relative distances of objects in a scene, but the precision of such information appears to be severely restricted. Limitations on the spatial information that such nongeometrical structures can convey in direct perception are increased in pictorial representations by the lack of precise techniques analogous to the techniques of perspective construction for incorporating such structures into pictures.

Even if the geometrical structures produced by perspective constructions are of considerable importance for the representation of spatial relations, how important is it to be able to depict precise spatial relations in pictures? The obvious answer is that it depends on the particular function each picture or genre of pictures is to serve. It is also true, however, that our theories can bias what we look for in pictures; our ability to analyze the geometrical structures that represent spatial relations may lead us to concentrate on that aspect of a picture, even when it is not appropriate to do so. Gibson's more recent works (1966, 1979) have increasingly pointed to the existence and importance of optic array information for much more than spatial layout. Whether something is edible, is a useful tool, or is friendly toward us can be conveyed by the information in the light reaching our eyes. As our knowledge of the optic array invariants that convey such information increases, our understanding of the ways in which pictures can show us how things look will also grow.

ACKNOWLEDGMENTS

I am grateful to Eve Sedgwick for her thorough critical reading of this manuscript and to Margaret Hagen, Julian Hochberg, and Susan Sawyer for their helpful comments on portions of it. I am also grateful to the Learning Resources Center of the SUNY College of Optometry for the technical production of all of the figures for this chapter.

REFERENCES

Alberti, L. B. [*On painting* and *On sculpture*.] (C. Grayson, Ed. and trans.) London: Phaidon, 1972. (Originally published in Latin in 1436.)

Baltrušaitis, J. *Anamorphoses: ou magie artificielle des effets merveilleux.* France: Olivier Perrin Editeur, 1969.

Barrand, A. G. An ecological approach to binocular perception: The neglected facts of occlusion (Doctoral dissertation, Cornell University, 1979). *Dissertation Abstracts International*, 1979, *39*, 5604B–5605B (University Microfilms No. 7910798).

Bethune, J. D. *Essentials of drafting.* Englewood Cliffs, New Jersey: Prentice-Hall, 1977.

Brunswik, E. *Perception and the representative design of psychological experiments.* Berkeley, California: Univ. California Press, 1956.

Coulin, C. [*Step-by-step perspective drawing for architects, draftsmen, and designers.*] (J. H. Yarbrough, Trans.). New York: Van Nostrand Reinhold, 1966.

Decartes, R. [*Discourse on method, Optics, Geometry,* and *Meterology.*] (P. Olscamp, Trans.). Indianapolis, Indiana: Bobbs-Merrill, 1965. (Originally published in French in 1637.)

Doblin, J. *Perspective: a new system for designers.* New York: Whitney Library of Design, 1956.

Edgerton, S. Y., Jr. *The Renaissance rediscovery of linear perspective.* New York: Harper & Row, 1975.

Farber, J., & Rosinski, R. R. Geometric transformations of pictured space. *Perception*, 1978, *7*, 269–282.

French, T. E., & Vierck, C. J. *Engineering drawing and graphic technology* (12th ed.). New York: McGraw-Hill, 1978.

Gibson, J. J. *The perception of the visual world*. Boston: Houghton-Mifflin, 1950.

Gibson, J. J. Optical motions and transformations as stimuli for visual perception. *Psychological Review*, 1957, *64*, 288–295.

Gibson, J. J. Perception as a function of stimulation. In S. Koch (Ed.), *Psychology: A study of a science* (Vol. 1). New York: McGraw-Hill, 1959. Pp. 456–501.

Gibson, J. J. Ecological optics. *Vision Research*, 1961, *1*, 253–262.

Gibson, J. J. *The senses considered as perceptual systems*. Boston: Houghton-Mifflin, 1966.

Gibson, J. J. The information available in pictures. *Leonardo*, 1971, *4*, 27–35.

Gibson, J. J. *The ecological approach to visual perception*. Boston: Houghton-Mifflin, 1979.

Gibson, J. J., & Cornsweet, J. The perceived slant of visual surfaces—optical and geographical. *Journal of Experimental Psychology*, 1952, *44*, 11–15.

Gibson, J. J., Kaplan, G. A., Reynolds, H. N., & Wheeler, K. The change from visible to invisible: A study of optical transitions. *Perception and Psychophysics*, 1969, *5*, 113–116.

Gibson, J. J., Olum, P., & Rosenblatt, F. Parallax and perspective during aircraft landings. *American Journal of Psychology*, 1955, *68*, 372–385.

Gilman, E. B. *The curious perspective: Literary and pictorial wit in the seventeenth century*. New Haven, Connecticut: Yale Univ. Press, 1978.

Hay, J. C. Optical motions and space perception: An extension of Gibson's analysis. *Psychological Review*, 1966, *73*, 550–565.

Hay, J. C. The ghost image: A tool for the analysis of the visual stimulus. In R. B. MacLeod & H. L. Pick, Jr. (Eds.), *Perception: Essays in honor of James J. Gibson*. Ithaca, New York: Cornell Univ. Press, 1974. Pp. 268–275.

Hochberg, J. E. The psychophysics of pictorial perception. *Audio-Visual Communication Review*, 1962, *10*, 22–54.

Hochberg, J. E. The representation of things and people. In E. H. Gombrich, J. Hochberg, & M. Black (Eds.), *Art, perception, and reality*. Baltimore, Maryland: Johns Hopkins Univ. Press, 1972. Pp. 47–94.

Ittelson, W. H. *Visual space perception*. New York: Springer, 1960.

Janson, H. W. Ground plan and elevation in Masaccio's *Trinity* fresco. In D. Fraser, H. Hibard, & M. J. Lewine (Eds.), *Essays in the history of art presented to Rudolf Wittkower*. London: Phaidon, 1967. Pp. 83–88.

Jones, R. K., & Hagen, M. A. The perceptual constraints on choosing a pictorial station point. *Leonardo*, 1978, *11*, 191–196.

Kaplan, G. A. Kinetic disruption of optical texture: The perception of depth at an edge. *Perception and Psychophysics*, 1969, *6*, 193–198.

Kemp, M. Science, non-science, and nonsense: The interpretation of Brunelleschi's perspective. *Art History*, 1978, *1*, 134–161.

Kennedy, J. M. *A psychology of picture perception*. San Francisco: Jossey-Bass, 1974.

Krautheimer, R. *Lorenzo Ghiberti*. (In collaboration with T. Krautheimer-Hess.) Princeton, New Jersey: Princeton Univ. Press, 1956.

Lawson, P. J. *Practical perspective drawing*. New York: McGraw-Hill, 1943.

Leeman, F. [*Hidden images: Games of perception, anamorphic art illusion: From the Renaissance to the present.*] (E. C. Allison and M. L. Kaplan, Trans.). New York: H. N. Abrams, 1976.

Mastai, M. L. d'O. *Illusion in art*. New York: Abaris, 1975.

Pirenne, M. H. *Optics, painting, and photography*. London: Cambridge Univ. Press, 1970.

Purdy, W. C. The hypothesis of psychophysical correspondence in space perception. *General Electric Technical Information Series*, 1960, No. R60ELC56.

Sedgwick, H. A. *The visible horizon: A potential source of visual information for the perception of size and distance* (Doctoral dissertation, Cornell University, 1973). *Dissertation Abstracts International*, 1973, *34*, 1301B–1302B. (University Microfilms No. 73–22,530).

Walters, N. V., & Bromham, J. *Principles of perspective.* New York: Whitney Library of Design, 1970.

Waltz, D. Understanding line drawings of scenes with shadows. In P. H. Winston (Ed.), *The psychology of computer vision.* New York: McGraw-Hill, 1975. Pp. 19–91.

Ware, W. R. *Modern Perspective* (rev. ed.). New York: Macmillan, 1900.

Warren, R. The perception of ego motion. *Journal of Experimental Psychology, Human Perception and Performance*, 1976, *2*, 448–456.

Wheatstone, C. Contributions to the physiology of vision: On some remarkable and hitherto unobserved phenomena of binocular vision. *Philosophical Transactions of the Royal Society of London*, 1838.

White, G. *Perspective: A guide for artist, architects, and designers.* New York: Watson-Guptill, 1968.

White, J. *The birth and rebirth of pictorial space.* New York: Harper & Row, 1967.

Problems of Magnification and Minification: An Explanation of the Distortions of Distance, Slant, Shape, and Velocity

Introduction 91
Magnification 92
    Earlier Explanations of "Distortions" Attending Magnification 93
    The Approach Taken and Its Underlying Theoretical Assumptions 96
    Analysis 97
Minification 126
    Distortions of Interobject Distance 126
    Distortions of Slant and Shape 126
    Distortions Introduced by Motion 127
Summary 132
References 134

INTRODUCTION

This chapter will attempt to explain the apparent distortions in the distance, slant, and shape of objects in a spatial layout that is viewed under conditions of magnification or minification. Magnification of the optic array reflected from a spatial layout is effected by uniformly enlarging all of the visual angles in the projected optic array. This can be accomplished by certain optical lenses or simply by viewing a normal picture or photograph from a position closer than the center of its geometrical projection. In like manner, minification of the optic array reflected from a spatial layout is effected by uniformly decreasing all of the visual angles in its projection. This, also, can be accomplished by certain optical lenses, or it can result from simply viewing a normal picture or photograph from a position farther than the center of its geometrical projection.

The theory of spatial perception from which these attempts at explication derive is the theory of psychophysical correspondence in spatial perception advanced by Gibson and his colleagues (Gibson, 1950). This theory assumes that under the usual conditions of viewing, the optic stimulus provided by light reflected from textured objects located on a textured surface uniquely specifies the orientation and shape of the objects as well as the relative size and distance. Although absolute distance can be determined if the height of the observation point is given, or if viewing is binocular (Purdy, 1960), we will not be concerned with absolute distance or absolute size. Although the theory of psychophysical correspondence will be utilized in the explications that follow, whatever position the reader may hold regarding the directness of spatial perception, I hope to show that there is nothing about the transformation of magnification or minification per se that makes spatial perception any less direct.

MAGNIFICATION

It is usual for an observer to experience a decrease of apparent depth and distance when viewing a photograph of a three-dimensional scene that was photographed through a telephoto lens, when viewing a televised event that has been magnified with a zoom lens, or when viewing the scene directly through any optical magnifier (e.g., a telescope or binoculars). Careful examination under any of these viewing conditions reveals several alterations in the perception of space which seem to be rather distinct experiences phenomenologically. These are:

1.   Distortions of interobject distance occur when viewing two or more identical objects at increasing distances from the observer causing an apparent decrease in the distance between the objects. Figures 3.1a and b demonstrate this phenomenon, most notably in the projection of the vertical columns spaced at equal intervals along the walls. The photograph in Figure 3.1b was taken under conditions that magnify the optic array by a factor of four. Related to this phenomenon is the fact that under very high magnification at relatively great distance the farther of two closely spaced identical objects may appear larger than the nearer one.

2.   Distortions of slant and shape occur when viewing a slanted surface under magnification, resulting in diminished slant and foreshortened shape. More specifically, any planimetric surface appears to be situated in a more frontal parallel position, and its receding dimension appears

less extensive. Figure 3.1d is a photograph taken under four-power magnification. Note that the apparent slant of the brick wall is more frontal and that the bricks appear shorter than in Figure 3.1c. The effect of such "distortions" upon the perception of a three-dimensional object such as a cube is that the surfaces of the cube appear to intersect at angles more obtuse than right angles and the receding surfaces of the cube appear less extensive (i.e., appear not to be squares).

3. Distortions are introduced by motion. The velocity of objects in radial motion (i.e., moving directly toward or away from the observer) is decreased. An object moving perpendicular to the line of sight appears to change its shape slightly (i.e., to be nonrigid), whereas an object moving along a path oblique to the observer appears to skid both toward and away from the observer. Although the effects of motion have been separately described, on analysis it will be seen that they differ from the effects on perception of discrete objects located at fixed distances only in that the moving objects effect *continuous* projections due to continuous changes in distance.

Earlier Explanations of "Distortions" Attending Magnification

In the late 1950s, investigators studied the relationship between the distance of observation of a mural (large picture) depicting a three-dimensional scene and the perception of three-dimensionality within the scene (Bartley & Adair, 1959; Smith, 1958a,b; Smith & Gruber, 1958). Although varying the distance of observation can produce the same geometric transformation as magnification, investigators have recently dealt with the effects of magnification on the perception of spatiality by directly varying the size of projection while keeping distance of observation constant (Braunstein & Payne, 1969; Pirenne, 1970; Rosinski, 1974). The only attempt at a comprehensive explanation of these phenomena generally available in the psychological literature is by S. H. Bartley, who described and attempted to explain the distortions of magnification on the perceived form of an object and the velocity of radial motion (Bartley, 1951).[1] Whereas Bartley deserves considerable credit for his attempt to explain these two phenomena, certain difficulties with his approach essentially invalidate the utility of his explanation. He seemed to have missed the fact that the only direct transformation of a magnifying lens is the simple

[1] Although it has not been published in the psychological literature, the dissertation of W. C. Purdy (1960) is clearly the most important contribution to the understanding of the problems attending magnification. It is primarily a trigonometric exposition of the psychophysical hypothesis of space perception under normal viewing conditions. However, it also includes the most definitive empirical work on the effects of magnification and extends those trigonometric equations to serve in the prediction of the effects of magnification. Purdy's equations are utilized in this chapter when appropriate, and I am most pleased to introduce his study on magnification into the psychological literature later in the chapter.

(b)

(a)

(c)

(d)

FIGURE 3.1. Comparison of interobject distance as a function of focal length of lenses. (a) Focal length = 50 mm. (b) Focal length = 200 mm. Comparison of magnified slant (θ_m) as a function of focal length of lenses. (c) Focal length = 50 mm; distance = 18 ft; $\theta = \theta_m = 45°$. (d) Focal length = 200 mm; distance = 18ft; $\theta = 45°$; $\theta_m = 76°$.

multiplicative enlargement of all projected angles within the optic array transmitted by that lens. Instead, he utilized the apparently reduced viewing distance perceived under magnification as though it were somehow a direct effect of the magnification. Thus, it would appear that the starting point of Bartley's explanation is actually derived from the relationships of the projected size of the micro- and macrostructure within the magnified optic array. One limitation of this position is clear when addressing the apparent reduction in distance between objects located along a radius from the observer. He simply asserts that magnifying lenses that decrease the apparent distance to an object also decrease the apparent distance between objects. The diagrammatic explanations he utilized to address the phenomenon of distorted form take that assertion as a basic datum. On the topic of the distortion of perception of motion along the line of sight, Bartley's description is somewhat incomplete, and the account is particularly intuitive, providing neither diagrammatic nor trigonometric exposition. Tolansky (1964), a physicist, described the latter phenomenon and independently offered the same limited explanation as did Bartley.

The Approach Taken and
Its Underlying Theoretical Assumptions

It will be argued in this chapter that the distortions experienced under magnification are the consequences of the lessened rate of change of textural density and the lessened slope of linear perspective *per unit area within the projection* of the uniformly enlarged optic array in which all relationships, determined by the real distance, remain unaltered. The impression of three-dimensionality is further reduced because magnifying lenses reduce the field of vision (the sector of the optic array) transmitted. This analysis should facilitate an understanding of the "distortions" of optical magnification as being geometrically equivalent to the distortions that attend viewing a picture or photograph from an observation point closer than the center of its projection. As this analysis is based on trigonometry rather than only diagrammatic exposition, the accuracy of its predictions is not limited by the accuracy with which distance and subtended angles can be transformed to scale values and vice versa. Furthermore, it will provide another opportunity to test the adequacy of our present knowledge of the determinants of spatial perception that have been gained under conditions of normal viewing.

The distortions that will be discussed are experienced when viewing directly through a magnifying system at the physical world, as well as when viewing telephotography or any other picture from an inappropriate station point. Nevertheless, the observational situation that will be assumed in the explanations that follow is that of an observer viewing a hypothetical projection plane of a fixed size, perpendicular to the line of sight, located at an arbitrary but fixed distance in front of the eye. This projection plane also lies within the cross-section of the optic array received by the observer's eye. Utilizing a plane projection surface, rather than dealing with the complexities posed by the concave surface of the retina (which pose no problems unique to magnification), the relationships presented are more obviously pertinent to the viewing of photographs and the viewing of motion projected onto cinema and television screens. However, because the distance of this hypothetical projection plane from the eye is considered as *constant* in all of the ensuing discussions, the term "per unit area of the projection plane" is equivalent to "per unit area of the retina." This is true because, holding distance between the eye and the hypothetical projection plane constant, the relationship will remain constant between a given unit of area of the projection plane and the size of the projection of that unit on the retina.

Analysis

The fundamental relationship underlying the major effects of magnification on the perception of space is the relationship between the projected visual angle and the distance of observation. Figure 3.2 shows this relationship in a rather simplified viewing situation in which the line of sight is the perpendicular bisector of the frontal edge of a rectangular object. Before attempting to apply the projected visual angle function in Figure 3.2 to the apparent distortions listed earlier, it is of some importance to point out that this fundamental relationship must be understood to apply to the visual angle separating any two fixed points lying frontal to the observer or camera lens (e.g., two different points lying on opposite boundaries of the same frontal surface or two horizontally separated elements of the microstructure of a surface). In Figure 3.2 the unit of distance is the physical distance separating two points on the frontal surface, which could correspond to "object size." Because the unit of distance is in terms of the distance separating the two points being considered, this function will always have precisely the same form, regardless of the absolute distance separating the two points (or "object size"). This projected visual angle of a frontal surface is proportional to $1/D$ (where D is the viewing distance). Therefore, with equal increments in the distance from the observer, the visual angle decreases less and less. In other words, the projected visual angle is a decreasing, negatively-accelerated function of viewing distance.[2] However, if the two points in question do

[2] I realize that this statement is not in agreement with that made by Haber and Hershenson (1973): "The frontal dimension of the square elements decrease *linearly* as the distance from the projection plane increases (p. 296)." This statement is in error and might possibly stem from a mis-reading of Gibson's (1950) statement concerning the same relationship: "Geometrically, these frontal dimensions project so as to give a perfectly linear decrease *up the plane of the projection,* and the ends may therefore be joined by a straight line to the vanishing point (italics mine; p.83)." The linear relationship described here by Gibson is that between the *projection* of the frontal dimension and the *projection* of the longitudinal dimension within the plane of projection (i.e., a linear perspective).

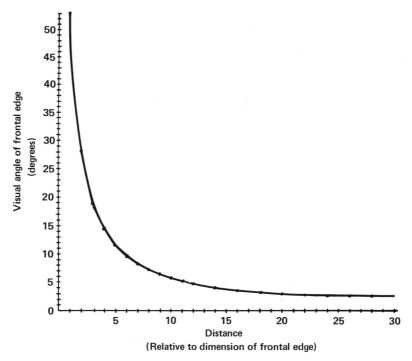

FIGURE 3.2. Projected visual angle as a function of distance of observation.

not lie frontal to the line of sight, a slightly different function is obtained (Figure 3.11 contains such functions). Nevertheless, that function is also a decreasing, negatively accelerated function of viewing distance, and the nature of the argument to be developed using Figure 3.2 applies equally well to the projection of the longitudinal dimension of the object surfaces.

Normally, the portion of the terrain that an observer is viewing under conditions of optical magnification is far enough, relative to object size, so that the visual angle subtended by identical objects in the visual field are very nearly the same size, approaching asymptote. Furthermore, the difference in the projection plane where the objects, spaced at equal intervals from the observer, contact the ground is a decreasing, negatively accelerated function of distance as well (as will be seen in Figures 3.11 and 3.12). The transformation effected by magnification is simply a multiplicative one, thereby leaving the relationship of all these projected angles unmodifed. A projection plane consisting of such large projections of the nearer objects with minimal decrease in projection size of the farther ones, and minimal vertical displacement in the locus of contact with the ground, would normally specify a much closer arrangement of identical objects separated by much lesser distance.

Furthermore, inasmuch as the area of the terrain transmitted by magnifying lenses is considerably reduced, to an extent dependent upon the focal length of the lenses, three-dimensionality will be further reduced. Reducing the field of view in this way excludes reflected rays from nearer surfaces of the foreground, which would normally specify the relative distance from the observer to the object by the inclusion of more expansive perspective and texture gradients. Again, the position taken here is that the apparent distortions effected by magnification when viewing a relatively distant portion of the visual field, where projected visual angles decrease relatively little with increased distance, is due to the fact that (a) these enlarged visual angles retain the same relationship as they do in a nonmagnified array, thereby projecting on the projection plane (and retina) a lesser rate of decrease of texture density and a lesser perspective per unit area and (b) the foreground normally serving to specify the relative distance from the observer to the objects is not retained in the magnified visual field.

Considering what nonmagnified array might be equivalent to a particular magnified array, a decrease in the distance to the nearest object would exclude surfaces previously projected in the foreground (as does magnification) and could be done in such a way as to include only the same physical surfaces in the field as did the magnified array. The reduced distance would also increase the size of all of the projected angles, of course, but the relationship between the size of these projections would not duplicate the relationship effected by magnification from a greater viewing distance. Furthermore, decreasing the distance to the nearest object would also place objects not located along the same line as this object at a slightly different orientation relative to the eye of the observer than would have been the case at the greater distance at which magnification was utilized. Rearranging the placement and orientation of those noncentral objects would still not duplicate the shape projected by them under conditions of magnification, because the receding surface of these forms would not be foreshortened as in magnification. Therefore, among "the complete set of all stationary arrays in an environment comprising all potential stimuli for the eye (Gibson, 1961, p.257)" there is none that corresponds to the transformation effected on any one pattern of optical magnification.

DISTORTIONS OF INTEROBJECT DISTANCE

The distance between two objects that are almost aligned along the line of sight seems diminished when viewed under magnification, particularly when viewed from a relatively great distance (Figure 3.1b). The analysis at this point will be based only on the projected size of familiar objects, as it has been demonstrated that this is sufficient to account for the phenomenon of decreased interobject distance even in the absence of a visible gradient (Gogel, Hartman, & Harker, 1957).

In the context of the projected visual angle as a function of distance, Figure 3.3 graphically depicts a situation in which an individual is observing a vertical rectangular object 2 ft. tall (Object A) at a distance of 45 ft., and a second identical object (Object B) at a distance of 60 ft. With no magnification, the visual angle subtended by the frontal edge of Object A is 2.55° and the visual angle subtended by Object B is 1.91°. These values were computed by Equation (1) introduced in the next section. When these visual angles are multiplicatively transformed by a 7-power lens system, the angles subtended are respectively 17.82° (A′) and 13.37° (B′). Extending a horizontal line from the vertical axis at the value of each of these enlarged projections A′ and B′ to intersect the curve, and dropping a perpendicular from the curve to the horizontal axis, indicates the interobject distance (relative to object size) specified in this magnified

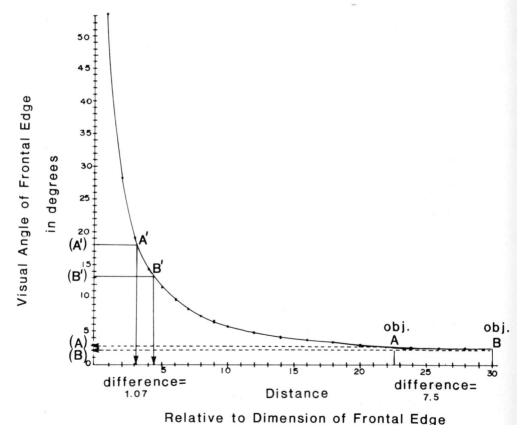

FIGURE 3.3. Projected visual angle as a function of distance of observation with additional details illustrating example in text.

array. The relative distance specified here is equal to the interobject distance at which objects of this size would project this relationship without magnification when the viewing distance is that specified by the enlarged projected size of the nearer object. Remembering that distance units are in terms of the frontal distance between the two points in question, or "object size," and that these objects are 2 ft. tall, the reader can approximate from the scale that the apparent distance between the apparently nearer objects is equal to a little more than the size of the objects (i.e., dimension of the frontal edge). The trigonometry provided later reveals the actual distance specified between the two objects under 7-power magnification to be 2.14 ft. It is no surprise that this interobject distance corresponds to the real interobject distance of 15 ft. divided by the power of magnification (i.e. 15/7).

Outside the context of magnification, Gogel, et al. (1957) have found that distance between familiar objects can be perceived to within a scale factor as a function of the relative size of the projection of familiar objects (without concomitant occurrence of veridical perception of absolute distance). It seems important to mention that they found this to be true although the object utilized was totally planimetric (i.e., a playing card) in a homogeneous field, projecting no gradients of texture. Thus, it seems that apparent distance between the magnified objects can be derived from the difference in projected size.

Consider a special case in which the farther of two magnified identical objects may appear to be larger than the slightly closer object. If the observer were looking through a 7-power magnifying lens system at two identical objects at a distance of about 30 times the frontal edge of the objects with one being farther than the other by a distance equal to only its size (or frontal edge), the projected size of the farther object will be 97% of the size of the projection of the slightly nearer object. Needless to say, although in the magnified array all angles will be increased multiplicatively by a factor of 7, this small 3% difference in projected size is retained. However, especially if the contour of the nearer object overlaps with the farther object, and the farther identical object contacts the ground slightly higher in the visual field than the nearer object (as it must), this unequivocally specifies that the more distant object is farther. Because these enlarged identical objects subtend virtually the same angle, then, as with the Ponzo illusion, the explanation maintains that if one object is specified as farther and yet subtends an equivalent visual angle to the apparently nearer one, this relationship specifies a relatively larger objective size for the farther object.

Without regard to the effects of magnification, a more accurate perception of distance between objects is possible when a texture gradient is present and the density of the texture of the field where the objects contact the ground ("adjacency to more dense texture") is available in the projection of the field (Epstein, 1966). However, texture density is usually fairly uniform within the fairly distant, reduced sector of a magnified array because at that distant portion of the terrain the size of the projected angle between textured elements approaches asymptote. Dunn, Gray, and Thompson (1965) examined the effect of the density of texture elements on perceived distance between objects in an experiment in which they varied the vertical position on a projection plane and the relative size of projection of the objects. They found that less accurate judgments of the distance between objects in the field were made under the condition of uniform texture gradient (similar to the gradients projected under conditions of high magnification at relatively great distance).

Smith and Gruber (1958) found that distance within a magnified projection was perceived within 6% of that predicted from the expectation that the distance perceived would be $1/m$ times the distance specified in a nonmagnified array. By reducing the viewing distance from the picture plane, magnification up to approximately 2 power was effected. In an experiment in which magnification was again produced in the same manner, Smith (1958a) found a somewhat lesser correspondence between the perceived distance and that which was predicted on the basis of the expectation previously specified. In another experiment by Smith (1958b), which is more germane, judgments of distance and relative size were required. The judgment of absolute distance from the observer was consistently underestimated. However, of particular importance was the confirmation of some earlier indications that the perception of relative size (i.e., size constancy) is unaffected by the magnification transformation. The size–distance invariance hypothesis (Ittelson, 1960) asserts that "the retinal projection or visual angle of a given size determines a unique ratio of apparent size to apparent distance (p.58);" that is, a projected visual angle of a certain size can be the consequence of a situation varying all the way from a very large object at a large distance to a very small object at a short distance. However, the values of size and distance are determinant within an inverse proportional relationship. Logically, if somehow size or distance is accurately perceived, then this hypothesis asserts that the other is accurately determined. However, the Smith and Gruber (1958) experiment provides a situation in which the perception of size was not only consistent but also accurate across changes in distance specified within and across all magnification transformations, and yet the perception of the different distances was consistently underestimated. The main point here is that the transformations effected upon the optic array or projection plane by the process of magnification apparently preserve the information necessary to specify objects at different distances as being the same size (i.e., specify relative size). The absolute distance specified, however, is apparently somewhat more equivocal and tends to lead to an underestimate of absolute distance.

DISTORTIONS OF SLANT AND SHAPE

Under a magnification transformation, slant is perceived as more frontal and the receding surfaces of a form are foreshortened. Before addressing the transformation of the projection effected by magnification of a slanted surface, we will address the parameters of the projection of a slanted surface that change as a result of simply increasing the viewing distance. In describing these geometric effects, the equations utilized will be derivatives of Freeman's equations, developed for normal viewing (Freeman, 1956, 1965). Unlike Freeman, however, in this discussion *optical slant* will refer to a deviation from the line of sight. (Of course, the transformations necessitated by our different use of the term have already been made.) This slant will be referred to as θ, and is indicated in Figure 3.4.

The parameters of the projection of the slanted surface that vary with distance and which are depicted also in Figure 3.4 are:

1.　The *projected angle* of the frontal edge (2d in Figure 3.4a) will be referred to as 2β, as indicated in Figure 3.4b. The angle projected by this dimension is a decreasing, negatively accelerated function of distance (as discussed earlier and shown in Figure 3.2), and is portrayed again in

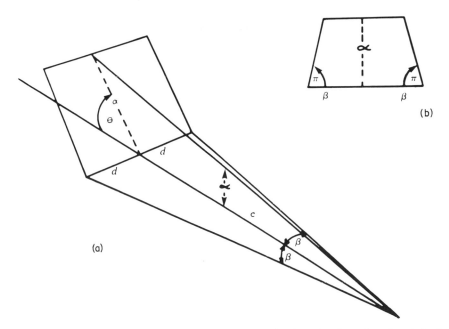

FIGURE 3.4. Specification of the parameters of the projection of a slanted surface (a is the physical layout and b is the projection of the layout).

Figure 3.5 with other projected parameters discussed in this section. The value of 2β can be computed with the following equation, with terms as defined in Figure 3.4:

$$2\beta = \arctan \frac{2cd}{c^2 - d^2} \qquad (1)$$

2.   The *projection* of the vertical dimension, a, in Figure 3.4a will be referred to as α, indicated in Figure 3.4b. The projected angle of this foreshortened dimension is a decreasing, negatively accelerated function of distance as well (an example is contained in Figures 3.11 and 3.12), and is computed by:

$$\alpha = \arctan \frac{a \sin \theta}{c + a \cos \theta} \qquad (2)$$

3.   The projection of the angle of the intersection of the frontal horizontal edge, d, with the receding vertical edge will be called the perspective angle and is indicated by π in Figure 3.4b. This angle is an *increasing*, negatively accelerated function of distance as shown in Figure 3.5. This perspective angle, π, is computed by:

$$\pi = \arctan \frac{c \tan \theta}{d} \qquad (3)$$

4.   The ratio of the projection of the receding, foreshortened longitudinal dimension, α, to the projection of the frontal dimension, 2β, will be referred to as $R_{FS:F}$. The value of this ratio is an *increasing*, negatively accelerated function of distance as shown in Figure 3.5 as well. This ratio can be computed by:

$$R_{FS:F} = \frac{\alpha}{2} \qquad (4)$$

Figure 3.6a portrays the projection of a square slanted at an optical slant of 45° at distance increments equal to the dimension of its frontal edge.[3] As is the case in Figure 3.4, the line of sight is the perpendicular bisector of that horizontal frontal edge. Although, of course, the projected size of all dimensions of this slanted square would decrease with increasing distance, we have deliberately held the projected size of the frontal edge (2β) constant by transforming as necessary the whole projection so that each of the frontal edges is congruent in order to facilitate comparison of perspective angles, π and $R_{FS:F}$. Figure 3.6a provides a direct comparison of the changes in these two parameters of projection with increased distance. These could be the projected forms of a 4-ft. square viewed from 4, 8, 12, 16, 20, 24, 28, and 32 ft., respectively. It will

---

[3] Mark Lumsden programmed the graphics in BASIC language on the Hewlett-Packard HP 2000 Access System, using the Graphic subroutines of ALL, prepared by David Perkins; a hard copy was obtained on the TSP–20 Plotter.

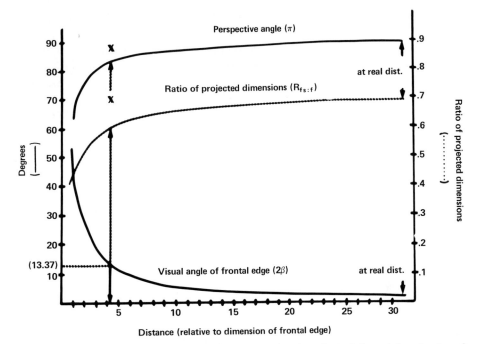

FIGURE 3.5. Projected size of frontal edge (2β), ratio of projected size of foreshortened dimension to frontal edge ($R_{fs:f}$), and perspective angle (π), of a square slanted at 45° as a function of distance.

be seen in the projections corresponding to increased distance both π and $R_{RS:F}$ increase. Figure 3.6b provides the opportunity for the same observation with a more complex surface, a cube. This figure portraying the projections of a cube at increased distances equal to the dimension of its frontal edge was constructed simply by rotating the projections in

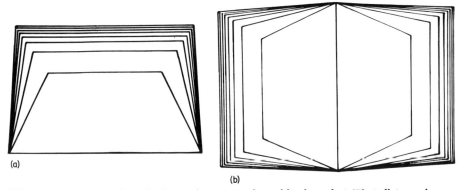

FIGURE 3.6. (a) Equated projections of a square slanted backward at 45° at distance increments equal to the length of the frontal edge. (b) Equated projections of a cube with vertical surfaces at 45° at distance increments equal to the length of the frontal edge.

Figure 3.6a by 90° around the line of sight and then adding their mirror image. The method of composition is related simply to point out the adequacy of our discussion up to this point to account for the changes in the projection of this three-dimensional object with increased distance as a compound instance of the square at a slant. Figure 3.6b graphically portrays the kind of distortion referred to earlier in that the surfaces of the cube do appear to intersect at angles more obtuse than right angles.

Utilizing Equations 1–4 and with knowledge of the distance (c) from which the surface is viewed, the degree of optical slant (θ), and the dimensions of the surface itself (a and 2d), one can determine all of the parameters of this projection. When a surface at a slant is viewed through magnification from any distance, the angles in the optic array are all increased multiplicatively by a factor determined by the focal length of the lens. Thus, the projected angle of the frontal dimension (2β) and the projected angle of the foreshortened dimension (α) are increased by the same factor, leaving relationships among these angles unchanged. That is, the ratio of the projection of the foreshortened dimension to the frontal dimension ($R_{FS:F}$) and the perspective angle (π) are unchanged. *However,* because of the increased area over which the form is projected, there is in this enlarged projection a decrease *per unit area* in the rate with which the projected width of the receding surface decreases as it recedes. One can determine what optical slant, θ_m, is specified by this modified array by replacing the distance specified by the nonmagnified array (c) with the distance specified in the magnified array (c') in an equation derived from Equation 3 so that

$$\text{ctn } \theta_m = \tan \pi \, \frac{d}{c'} \tag{5}$$

The value of c' can be determined by the relationship between projected size and distance (the size–distance invariance hypothesis); specifically, the ratio of c' to c is proportional to the reciprocal of the ratio of the magnified projected angle to the nonmagnified projected angle. That is,

$$\frac{c'}{c} = \frac{2\beta}{2\beta'} = \frac{\alpha}{\alpha'} = \frac{1}{m} \tag{6}$$

where m is the power of magnification. With magnification by a 7-power lens system, c'/c = 1/7, the distance specified by that magnified projection would be 1/7 of the distance specified by the nonmagnified projection. Equation 3 yields a value of π equal to 79.303 for a situation in which d = 1 ft., c = 30 ft., and θ = 10°. Remembering that π will not be changed by a multiplicative transformation of the dimensions of the projection, this value will remain constant at 79.30° under 7-power magnification. The apparent distance (c') is equal to 1/m or 1/7 times the distance (30 ft.), thus $c' = 4.29$ ft. Utilizing Equation 5, we find that the optical slant specified by the magnified array (θ_m) is 39.04°.

Remember also that the ratio of the projected foreshortened dimension to the frontal dimension (which we will now call the *form ratio*) remains invariant under the transformation of magnification. Under the conditions specified above for a slanted square ($a = 2$ ft. and $d = 1$ ft.), Equation 4 for $R_{FS:F}$ yields a value of .1630 and it will have the same value for 7-power magnification. The important question is what is the value of the dimension of the receding surface corresponding to the magnified value of α that is represented in the invariant value of this form ratio at this apparent slant and distance. The magnified projection of this receding surface is equal to 7 times .6224°, or 4.35°. So, substituting this enlarged value of α' (4.35°), and the apparent distance ($c' = 4.29$ ft.), and the slant specified by this magnified array ($\theta_m = 39.014$°) in Equation 2, we find the corresponding value of this receding surface under these conditions (a') is specified as 5.375 in., rather than the 2 ft. specified in the nonmagnified array.

So, the "distortion" of slant related earlier, in which a magnified slanted surface appears more frontal-parallel than it should and the shape is distorted so that it looks like the receding surface is less extensive than it would appear without magnification, is a "veridical perception" because the magnified array does geometrically specify both a more frontal slant and a lesser dimension in the receding direction.

Texture Density and Perspective as Affected by Magnification

The effects of magnification upon texture density and perspective will be discussed utilizing the photos in Figures 3.1c and d, considering the rough microstructure of the bricks as texture and the sequential horizontal contours of the bricks as linear perspective. The photograph in Figure 3.1c depicts a brick wall at an optical slant of 45°. Textural elements are projected with increasing density across the projection plane in a direction corresponding to the increased distance. In like manner, the projection of the parallel lines of the horizontal contours of the bricks converge across the projection plane in a direction corresponding to the increased distance as well. Introducing magnification, as has been done in the photograph in Figure 3.1d, enlarges all visual angles by the factor of m in the projection plane, but our concern now is only for the increase in the visual angles corresponding to the distance between the textural elements and the angles corresponding to the distance between the parallel lines. Because the size of the projection plane remains unchanged, the enlargement of angles results in the reduction of the density of the projection of the textural elements by $1/m$; therefore, the rate of change of the projection of the textural density is reduced by $1/m$ as well. Purdy

(1960) has verified this mathematically and has shown that this relationship holds for the effect of magnification upon any gradient, not only texture density, but perspective and relative size as well. It is worth pointing out, however, that magnification does not alter the "perspective" in the sense of altering the angle of the projection of the receding edges of a projected rectangle (i.e., π). *Magnification does decrease the relative rate per unit area of the projection plane with which the two projected receding edges decrease the relative distance between them.* The situation depicted in Figure 3.7, in which the central projection is magnified, more simply illustrates this point in regard to lessened perpective per unit area of projection plane specifying a more frontal slant.

Purdy (1960) has introduced an equation that geometrically determines the slant specified by magnification of a certain power of a particular optical slant. This equation addresses the question of optical slant during magnification much more directly than do the equations just offered (which also provide other information) and does not require nearly as

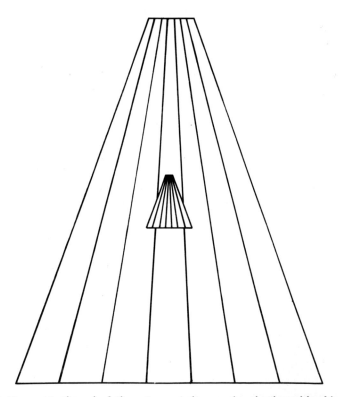

FIGURE 3.7. Demonstration of relative rate per unit area of projection with which projected receding edges decrease the relative distance between them. (The central projection has been magnified by a factor of 7.)

much specific information. This equation was not introduced into the psychological journals until 1974 (Rosinsky, 1974). Certainly, if one is concerned only with determining slant specified by the magnified projection, with no need to know the other parameters of the projected surface, one should take advantage of Purdy's equation:

$$\theta_m = \arctan 1/m \ (\text{ctn } \theta) \tag{7}$$

As indicated earlier, θ corresponds to the deviation of the slanted surface from the line of regard. A trigonometric equivalent of Equation 7 that is easier to utilize is:

$$\theta_m = \arctan \frac{1}{m \tan \theta} \tag{8}$$

Because it is not necessary to know any linear dimensions of the slanted surface in Equations 7 and 8, the slant of the background terrain specified in the magnified array can be determined with the same readiness by Purdy's equation as can a plane of known finite dimensions. Utilizing the equations provided earlier, it would be necessary to arbitrarily assign some dimensions to a hypothetical form lying in the plane of the terrain.

The photograph in Figure 3.1d demonstrated that the slope of the receding surface specified by the magnified array is more frontal, and, considering a single brick as the basic form, the extent of the receding surface of the brick is decreased. The same photo is utilized again as Figure 3.8a for comparison with Figure 3.8b. As indicated earlier, this photograph was taken with a telephoto lens of 200 mm (4 power) with longitudinal axis of the lens at 45° and the camera located at a distance of 18 ft. from the intersection of that axis with the wall. The photograph in Figure 3.8b was taken of the same brick wall with a normal (50 mm) lens at an optical slant that Purdy's Equation (7) indicated was that specified by the magnified surfaces in the photograph in Figure 3.8a (i.e., 76°) and from a distance equal to that specified by the 4-power magnification (4 $\frac{1}{3}$ ft.). It can be seen that both photographs do seem to specify the same optical slant, and that the length of the receding surface of the bricks in the magnified photograph on the left is less than that in the normal photograph.

In Figure 3.6a and b, it is interesting to note that holding the projected length of the frontal edge (2β) constant results in a series of projections that is equivalent to a series of projections of a slanted surface (Figure 3.6a) or a cube (Figure 3.6b) that is viewed at increasing distances equal to the dimension of its frontal edge, *and* magnified in each instance by a power equal to the total number of units of distance. That is to say, that the inside figure represents the projection corresponding to no magnification (1 power) at a distance equal to the dimension of one frontal edge. Going from the inside figure out, the next projection corresponds to viewing from a distance twice as great through 2-power magnification.

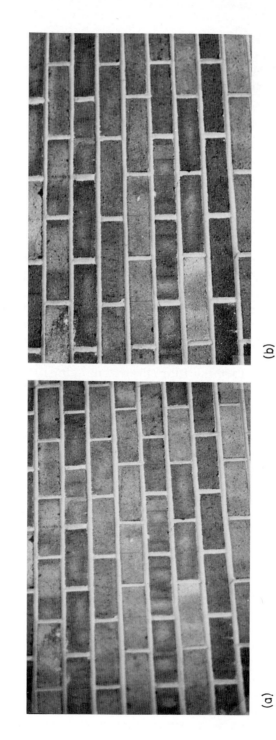

(a)

(b)

FIGURE 3.8. Comparison of slant specified by magnification (θ_m) with its "normal" equivalent slant, demonstrating that the extent of the receding surface in the magnified projection is decreased. (a) Focal length = 200 mm; distance = 18ft; θ = 45°; θ_m = 76°. (b) Focal length = 50 mm; distance = 4.5ft; θ = θ_m = 76°.

The third projection corresponds to the projection from a distance three times as great and viewing through 3-power magnification, and so on. In this manner, Figures 3.6a and b provide rather direct demonstrations of the kinds of distortions taking place under conditions of magnification.

Empirical Study of Effects of Magnification on Perception of
Optical Slant

I am pleased to introduce into the psychological literature the most definitive, empirical study of the effects of magnification upon optical slant of which I am aware. The study was performed by Purdy as part of his doctoral dissertation at Cornell University in J. J. Gibson's laboratory in 1960. Utilizing a point-source projector, Purdy projected texture gradients onto a screen, holding binocular disparity, convergence, and accommodation constant by the planimetric nature and the fixed distance of the projection surface. It is important to note that the visible portion of the projection screen was circular and the projection of the generation surface always filled this circular area. Subject-to-screen distance was held constant across all experimental conditions at such a distance that viewing through a large hole in a reduction screen resulted in a field of view of approximately 25° in diameter. The subject's task was to adjust a rectangular piece of Masonite to a position parallel with the slant perceived on the screen. This adjustable Masonite surface was made visible to the subjects in front of and below their eye level. Magnification was modified by changing the distance of the light point-source to the projection screen while holding constant the distance from the light point-source to the transparent generating surface. The generating surface "was a piece of photographic film, clear except for grid work of fine, clearly opaque lines, spaced 1/8 inch apart. . . . The projection screen was a sheet of lucite, sandblasted on one side to provide a diffusion surface for the image (Purdy, 1960, p.38)." The magnification produced by the apparatus was equal to the ratio of the distance from the light source to the projection screen relative to the fixed distance from the observer to the projection screen. These distances were set so as to produce a magnification of 1.5. The generating surface was set at one of four slants with respect to the horizontal (which was coplanar with the line of sight): 30, 40.9, 52.4, 62.8, and 71.1°, respectively. He selected the values of optical slant of the generating surface to correspond to the predicted, perceived magnified slant of the optical slant one step below in the series of optical slants utilized. This provided the advantage of a built-in control for constant error inasmuch as subjects were also required to respond to nonmagnified projections of these slants as well. Specifically, if the subject responded to a nonmagnified projection of 40.9° in the same was as he responded to a magnified projection of 30° (for which the predicted perceived slant under magnification was 40.9°), then his hypothesis would be confirmed, even though the subject's response on both occasions was incorrect so long as the subject was consistent. That is, constant error can be detected as such and not be permitted to confound the test of his hypothesis concerning the perception of magnified arrays.

Although Purdy's data revealed an average constant error of 2.12° in setting the adjustable board at the perceived slant of the magnified array, the same constant error attended the settings for the corresponding non-magnified array as well. More to the point of the experiment, the pre-dicted matches were obtained with only an average "error" of about 1°. Specifically, the judged slant for the 30° magnified projection was per-ceived as equivalent to the 40.9° nonmagnified projection within .65° on the average; the judged slant for the 40.9° magnified slant was perceived as equivalent to the 52.4° nonmagnified slant within 1.81°; and the judged slant of the 52.4° magnified projection was perceived as equivalent to the 62.8° nonmagnified projection within .69°. This test of the effects of mag-nifying an optic array was designed conceptually to test the adequacy of an analysis of the optic stimulus in terms of the hypothesis of psycho-physical correspondence. It was predicted that the transformation ef-fected by magnification would change the perceived slant toward the frontal orientation according to the function provided. The data agreed with the predictions within very acceptable limits.

Braunstein and Payne (1969) also utilized displays equivalent to various magnification transformations. Although the primary aim of their exper-iment was different from that of Purdy, they found, as did Purdy, that when a perspective gradient is magnified, responses are given confirming the perception of a more frontal slant.

Slant Specified by Lenses of Various Focal Lengths

The focal length of a lens is the optical parameter that determines the extent to which the transmitted image is magnified. Given the lens–film distance and the diagonal of the negative produced by a 35 mm single lens reflex camera, a lens system with a focal length of approximately 50 mm is considered to project a "normal" image (i.e., actually effects no magnification of the optic array). In Figure 3.9, the relationship between slant specified by the projection of this 50-mm normal lens (θ_m) and the actual slant between the line of regard and the plane surface (θ) is de-picted by the straight diagonal originating at the origin of the graph. That is, the slant specified by this "normal" lens corresponds to the actual optical slant for all degrees of optical slant. It will be seen in this figure that lenses of longer focal length specify a slant greater than the optical slant for each value of optical slant. Furthermore, lenses of shorter-than-normal focal length specify a slant less than the optical slant.

It is interesting to note that the maximum discrepancy between the slant specified by magnification and actual optical slant lies on each of these curves at the point at which these curves would intersect a diagonal drawn from the value of magnified slant of 90° to the value of optical slant of 90°. The amount by which any curve deviates from the curve of the normal 50-mm lens for a particular value of optical slant is the extent of slant "distortion" for that lens and for that particular value of optical slant. The lenses included in this figure correspond to those that are commercially available.

Slant Specified by Varying the Station Point from Which a Picture is Viewed

Gibson formulated rules for observing a picture surface: (a) It should be seen with one eye, (b) it should be seen upright and perpendicular

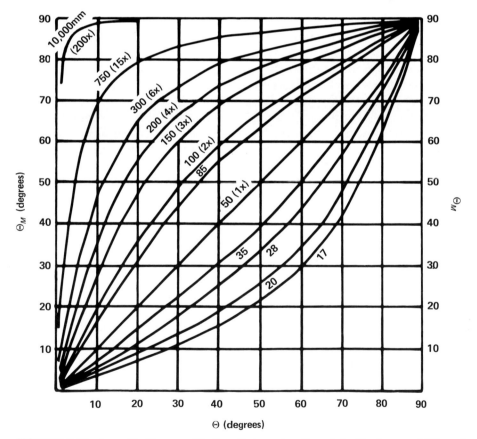

FIGURE 3.9. Slant specified by magnification (θ_m) as a function of slant for lenses of different focal lengths.

to the line of sight, and (c) there should be an aperture in front of the eye hiding everything but the picture itself (Gibson, 1971). The conditions specified in (a) and (c) also correspond to the basic conditions for viewing through the view finder of a camera and other optical devices, but let us consider the applicability to viewing through a telescope. Viewing through a telescope is monocular and the visual field is truncated in such a way that only a portion of the optic array potentially available to the naked eye is projected to the eye. However, there is also a very crucial difference in that when viewing through a telescope one is receiving an optic array transmitted through magnifying lenses. As mentioned earlier, this means not only that the effective visual field is reduced, but also that a multiplicative transformation has been made on all the visual angles in the reduced section of the optic array transmitted by the lens. The projected visual angles are increased by a factor of m, decreasing all gradients by a factor of $1/m$. This condition is geometrically equivalent to a person viewing a picture from a station point closer than the center of the projection, precisely only $1/m$ as far as would be required to receive the normal geometric projection. For example, the transformation upon the optic array effected by a magnifying lens of a focal length of 200 mm (200/50 = 4-power) is the same as that occurring when viewing a photograph taken from the same distance with a normal lens of 50-mm focal length but viewing that photograph from a station point only one-fourth of the appropriate viewing distance along a perpendicular to the center of the photograph. However, in the latter case, the visual field would include more of the nearer terrain than would the photograph produced by optical magnification.

It has just been stated that by reducing viewing distance to less than that required to receive the normal geometric projection, one can effect magnification of the surfaces represented in a normal photograph or picture. Additionally, by appropriately increasing the distance of the station point, one can manage to receive the normal geometric projection from a photograph of a scene that was magnified with a telephoto lens. Furthermore, appropriately decreasing the distance of the station point, one can manage to receive the normal geometric projection from a photograph of a scene that was minified by a "wide-angle" lens. The appropriate viewing distance is determined by multiplying the focal length of the lens by the enlargement factor. The enlargement factor is the factor by which the diagonal of the printed photograph exceeds the diagonal of the negative from which it was made. Consequently, the proper viewing distance for photographs taken with lenses having longer-than-normal focal lengths will be greater than that for photographs taken with normal lenses by the distance equal to the difference in focal length of these two lenses multiplied by the enlargement factor. For example, consider a negative that had been made with a 50-mm lens utilizing a single-lens reflex 35-mm camera. The negative size for such a camera is 24-mm × 35-mm, with a diagonal of 42.44 mm. If this is utilized in printing an 8 in. × 10 in. photograph that has a diagonal of 12.8 in. (or 325.12 mm), the enlargement factor is equal to 7.7 (i.e., 325.12/42.44 = 7.7). Consequently, the appropriate station point for viewing this enlarged print taken with a normal lens is equal to 50-mm × 7.7, giving a distance of 385 mm (or 15.16 in.). On the other hand, if the camera had remained in the same position but utilized a lens having a focal length of 200 mm, then the proper station point for viewing the enlarged 8 in. × 10 in. photograph would be 200 mm × 7.7, giving a distance of 1540 mm (or 60.6 in.). The *difference* in the distance from the enlargement at which these two photographs should be viewed is equal to 1155 mm (or 45.5 in.). This is more readily calculated as (200 mm − 50 mm)7.7 = (150 mm)7.7 = 1155 mm (or 45.5 in.). Normally, we view all photographs from the same distance determined by convenience. Clearly, the viewing distance necessary for receiving the center of projection of this 8-in. × 10-in. photograph taken with a 200-mm telephoto lens (approximately 5 ft.) is much greater than that normally utilized in viewing photographs. Even when viewing from the proper viewing distance, it may well be that some flattening is still experienced due to the additional effect of the truncated field. It follows from these considerations, of course, that photographs taken with shorter-than-normal focal lengths must be viewed from correspondingly lesser distances in order to receive the center of projection, remembering that the equation for determining the proper station point is focal length times the enlargement factor.

Utilizing the trigonometric equations and the graphic portrayal of relationships provided in this chapter, one can predict the slant specified by surfaces contained within normal photographs and pictures viewed at various distances (i.e., effecting various degrees of magnification). Specifically, one would determine what value of m is effected by a particular viewing distance by first determining what the distance is from the center of the photograph along its perpendicular bisector to the center of the projection (i.e., the distance to the appropriate station point). With a photograph, this is computed by the method just indicated. Pirenne (1970) tells how this can be determined with some pictures as well. Then one should determine the ratio between that appropriate distance and the viewing distance to be utilized in a particular situation. That ratio is the power of magnification or minification (m).

Now, if one knows the optical slant of a particular object in a photograph when it is viewed from the proper station point (θ) then the slant specified when viewing at a particular inappropriate distance (θ_m) can be determined by using Equation 7. If the value of m closely approximates the power of one of the lenses characterized in Figure 3.9 (the power is indicated in parentheses beside the value of the focal length in that figure), then that individual curve will provide the slant specified from that distance for all the slants indicated along the horizontal axis of the figure.

Effects of Reduction of the Visual Field

In studies quite unrelated to the concern of this chapter, it is frequently reported that when viewing a slanted surface through an aperture in a reduction screen, the plane of that surface seems be more parallel to the plane of the reduction screen. This is particularly true if the aperture is very small and texture is minimal (Katz, as cited in Gruber & Clark, 1956). Gruber and Clark (1956) experienced the same difficulty in trying to determine the optimal size of an aperture used when having subjects make judgments of the slant of a surface viewed through an aperture. Their pilot work revealed an average constant error of 25° toward greater frontality, the discrepancy increasing with increased distance. Enlarging the aperture beyond 7° of visual arc did not appreciably increase the accuracy of judgments of the slant. Gibson (1950), as well as others utilizing this reduction screen technique of slant presentation, consistently obtained a large constant error and, as was the case with Gruber and Clark (1956), the error seems to always be in the direction of a more frontal plane. In an experimental attempt to determine the effects of such truncation of the visual field upon jugement of slant, Hagen, Jones, and Reed (1978) have demonstrated that reduction of the visual field by picture frames, boundaries of projection screens, etc., result in a "frontal shift in the localization in the visual field." As already discussed, viewing through magnifying lenses reduces the sector of the optic array in the same fashion as viewing through a reduction screen. The relevance of all these various means of reducing the sector of the optic array is to occlude the nearer portion of the visual field extending from the foot of the observer to objects retained in the central sector of the transmitted array that would otherwise specify relative distance to these objects and, perhaps, specify the slant of the terrain more definitively.

Figure 3.10 diagrammatically shows the relative reduction in the visual field accompanying viewing through lenses of the focal length indicated. When one plots the size of the visual field as a function of focal length, it is clear that the angle of viewing is a decreasing, negatively accelerated function of the focal length of the lens. It may be that the slant actually specified by the magnified optic array per se is somewhat less frontal than that experienced and reported by subjects due to the fact that the magnified optic array is also truncated (e.g., by lenses, by the boundaries

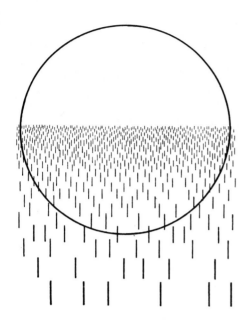

**NORMAL LENS (55 mm) PERMITS
43° ANGLE OF VIEW**

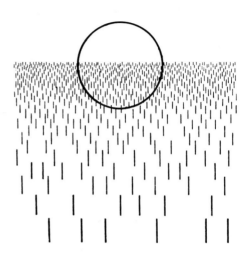

**135-mm LENS (2.5x) PERMITS
18° ANGLE OF VIEW**

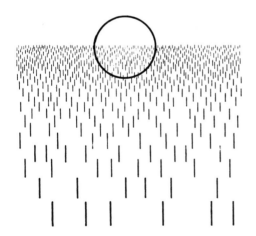

**200-mm LENS (3.7x) PERMITS
12.5° ANGLE OF VIEW**

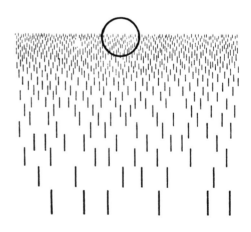

**300-mm LENS (5.5x) PERMITS
8° ANGLE OF VIEW**

FIGURE 3.10. Demonstration of the reduction of visual field effected by lenses of greater focal lengths (i.e., greater magnification).

of the photograph, TV screen). This is quite feasible, as Hagen, *et al.* (1978) did demonstrate that truncation alone is sufficient to produce a statistically significant greater frontal slant. Even in Purdy's experiment (1960), he obtained an identifiable constant error of about 2°, which may have been due to the truncating effect of his reduction screen which allowed only 25° of visual field). It would seem that this possible source of influence upon slant perception could be experimentally separated from the effects of magnification per se, in the same magnified projection.

DISTORTIONS INTRODUCED BY MOTION

The following discussion pertains to changes specified by magnification of objects in motion that are projected through optical lenses (direct observation) or projected on a motion picture or television screen. Apart from the truncated visual field, the same changes should be produced by viewing normal projections on these screens from a station point nearer than that appropriate to receive the center of projection.

Velocity of an Object Moving Along the Line of Sight Is Decreased
During Magnification

Figure 3.3, which shows that projected size is a decreasing, negatively accelerated function of distance, is again useful here. Consider that an object moves from point B to point A. If this object is 10 ft. in its major frontal dimension, it will have moved from a position of 300 ft. to a position 225 ft. from the observer, having traveled a distance of 75 ft. toward the observer. The function indicates that the projected size of the approaching object will have increased very little concomitant with the 75-ft. decrease in observing distance. Furthermore, the function indicates that moving this same distance toward the observer from successively less distance positions would result in successively greater change in the size of projections. In short, this familiar function in Figure 3.3, relating projected size to distance, is also a "zoom–loom" function, depicting the projected size of the same object as it moves toward or away from the observer. If a 10-ft. object moves from 300 ft. (a distance 30 times as far as the object size) toward the observer to a point 225 ft. from the observer while being viewed with 7-power magnification, that magnification will specify that it moved from a position at point B' to point A'. The reason it will appear to begin movement from B' rather than B is that, under the conditions of relative size and distance, and the power of magnification indicated here, it will project a visual angle equal to that projected if it were located at B' (i.e., the distance that is specified by the magnified angle of projection). (However, the terrain would have a more frontal

slope due to the magnified gradient of the terrain.) During the time interval in which the object actually travels from point B to point A, the
magnified angle will increase from the visual angle corresponding to the
distance at B′ to the visual angle corresponding to the distance at A′.
Therefore, during the time that the object was actually moving from a
distance of 300 ft. to a distance of 225 ft. (a distance equal to $7\frac{1}{2}$ times the
object size), the magnified projection specifies much less relative movement. In Figure 3.3, we have extended a horizontal line from the vertical
axis at the value of the enlarged projection at the beginning of movement
(B′) and another from the value at the end of the movement (A′) to intersect the curve, and dropped a perpendicular from the curve to the
horizontal axis. The difference between these points of intersection with
the horizontal scale of relative distance indicates the distance that was
specified by magnification in units of object size. It can be seen that the
distance traveled, specified by the enlarged projection, is a distance equal
to little more than the size of the object. Utilizing an equation provided
earlier reveals the distance specified to be 10.72 ft., instead of the actual
distance of 75 ft. Given that the time of observation was, of course, unchanged by the process of magnification, and the specified distance traveled was decreased to one-seventh, or $1/m$ of the real distance traveled,
then the specified velocity is decreased to only one-seventh, or $1/m$, of
the actual velocity.

The lesser distance specified by the enlarged, expanding visual angle
is also accompanied by a disproportional rate of descent in the projection
plane. The rate of descent is actually less than would occur if the object
were really moving across the lesser distance specified by magnification
from this closer distance specified by the enlarged image. For purposes
of this analysis, let us take a simple case in which the line of regard or
the longitudinal axis of the magnifying instrument is parallel with the
geographical terrain and the object being viewed is positioned perpendicular to the line of regard and the terrain. At relatively great distances,
movement of a certain fixed extent toward the observer will result in less
angular displacement down the projection plane than would be the case
for the same amount of movement toward the observer from a much
closer distance. This situation is diagrammed in Figure 3.11. In discussing
this situation, the crucial unit of distance on the terrain is the height of
the observation point. It can be seen that the farther the distance from
the observation point, the smaller the visual angle subtended by equal
increments or decrements in observation distance. Figure 3.12 demonstrates this relationship better as it shows the continuous change in projected visual angle corresponding to the *difference* in the vertical projection in the visual field effected by changes in the distance from the
observer for lenses of three different focal lengths: one wide angle, one

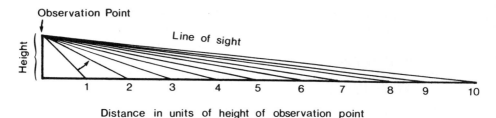

Observation Point

Height

Line of sight

Distance in units of height of observation point

FIGURE 3.11. Diagram illustrating the viewing situation assumed in Figure 3.12.

normal, and one telephoto lens. The solid portion of each of the curves portrays the rate of change in projection of 5-ft. increments from the point on the terrain included in the sector of the optic array that is transmitted by the lens with its longitudinal axis parallel with the terrain from a height of 5 ft. The point of all this for the effects of magnification is that while the magnified expanding visual projection of the object specified movement of that object from a distance corresponding to 42.86 ft., to a point 32.14 ft. from the observer, the amount of movement down the projection plane (actually caused by moving 75 ft. over a much more distant expanse) is not as much as would occur if, in fact, such an object were moving over this short distance of 10.72 ft. at this much shorter distance from the observer. Given that time is constant, the *rate* of movement down the projection plane is considerably less. In addition to this "distorted" rate of movement down the projection plane is the appearance that the surfaces of the moving object seem more frontal to the observer than would be the case if the object were, in fact, moving across the nearer and lesser distance interval specified by the magnified optic array.

I have been struck with the drama of these combined effects in some motion pictures, particularly in "The Graduate," when Dustin Hoffman was running to intervene in the wedding of Katherine Ross. The obviously great muscular effort expended and the anguish on his face consistent with his real velocity seemed inconsistent with his slowly expanding optic projection and tortuously little movement down the projection plane. The effect was to convey a sense of great frustration, much like the "treadmill" running in nightmares. There is a perceptual paradox here that I would like to relate, utilizing an equation apparently first introduced by Purdy in one of his unpublished manuscripts referenced in his dissertation (Rosinski, 1974). This equation, which permits the computation of "time to collision" (TC) of an approaching object with a stationary observer, is:

$$TC = \frac{a_1}{(a_2 - a_1 / (t_2 - t_1)} \qquad (9)$$

Considering a_1 to be the projected size of the moving object at its greatest distance of 300 ft., $a_1 = 1.91°$, and a_2 to be the projected size of this moving object at 225 ft., $a_2 = 2.55°$, and $t_1 = 0$ and $t_2 = 1$ sec., then the "time to collision" with the observer from the end of the observed movement is 3.0 sec. Now, if we substitute the magnified projected angles into this equation while holding time of travel constant $(t_2 - t_1)$, the "time to collision" from the end of the observed movement is unchanged (i.e., it is still 3.0 sec). So, although the object appears to start from a closer point and travels an apparently lesser distance toward the observer, the apparent velocity is proportionately less, so that the object would not collide with the observer any sooner. Mathematically, this is the case because the change in the numerator (a_1) effected by magnification is the same as that effected upon the difference between a_1 and a_2 (the only one of the two factors in the denominator that can vary, inasmuch as the time interval is unchanged by magnification). Therefore, TC must remain invariant across changes in magnification.

Of course, an object does not have to be moving exactly along a path leading directly toward or away from the observer (radial motion) in order for the effects in this section to apply. To the extent that the path of movement changes the observer's distance at all, the velocity of displace-

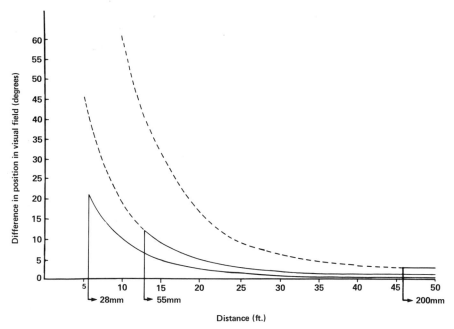

FIGURE 3.12. Difference in projected position in visual field as a function of distance for a wide-angle lens (28 mm), a normal lens (55 mm), and a telephoto lens (200 mm). Note: Height of observation point is 5 ft. above ground level.

ment in that radial directional component will be decreased by 1/*m* under magnification. It may be of methodological interest to note that if one wished to study the effect of different specified approach velocities (zoom rates) while holding "time-to-collision" constant, this could be done by simply using different powers of magnification upon the same approach array.

Changing Shape (Nonrigidity) of Objects Moving Perpendicular to the Line of Sight

As a rectangular object, such as an automobile, moves by an observer on a path perpendicular to the line of sight, its visible surfaces will present a continuous change in optical slant. However, as Figure 3.9 indicates, for any given level of magnification the slant specified by a magnified projection differs from the real optical slant and discrepancy is not uniform across all values of the magnified optical slant. Therefore, and particularly if the moving object has two or more visible planimetric sides, magnification will continuously specify differing slants and shapes (as discussed earlier) of the surfaces and a nonrigid object in motion will be perceived.

Although I am unaware of empirical research directly specific to the situation just described, the unpublished dissertation of Farber (1973) performed in Gibson's laboratory at Cornell University is, at least, consistent with that expectation. Farber utilized a point-source shadow caster consisting of a rigid wire grid rotating about a vertical axis. The shadow of this rotating grid was rear-projected onto a translucent screen. Magnification was changed by varying the position of the lamp relative to the projection screen, while holding constant the distance from the observer to the projection screen. Twenty-four magnification ratios between .6 and 2.2 were utilized. Subjects were simply asked to describe the changes, if any, in the vertical and horizontal dimension of the object projected on the screen and to attempt to describe the path of movement involved. The major results were that magnification produced phenomenal nonrigidity for most observers under those conditions. Although Farber utilized motion around a vertical axis, this experiment would seem to be relevant to the extent that some of the projections generated by an automobile moving perpendicular to the line of sight across the visual field are quite similar to those projected by an automobile simply rotating about a stationary vertical axis.

"Paradoxical Skid" of an Object Moving Along an Oblique Path to the Observer

The "paradoxical skid" is due to the fact that a magnified array specified surfaces more frontal to the observer than are specified under conditions of no magnification. This has been discussed earlier in the account of the distortion of slant and shape specifically addressed to the observation that the surfaces of a cube appear to intersect more obliquely under magnification. This paradoxical skid is the manifestion of the effects of motion on such a distorted "cube." When observing an automobile moving on a straight racetrack or on a freeway under high magnification, the path of movement is specified by the car's deletion and accretion of background textural elements in the terrain and by the projected visual angle relationships. However, this movement is not quite perpendicular to the front surface of the vehicle. This is due to the high magnification, which specifies a much more frontal slant than is actually the case. Thus, the front surface of the vehicle appears to be oriented obliquely to the path of movement. Another way of describing this is that the front surface is less oblique to the observer than is the path of motion. Considering only the front surface, this is a condition which would obtain if a rigid, orthogonal automobile were to be skidding away from its path and deviating *toward* the observer. On the other hand, the other side of the vehicle visible to the observer is also more frontal in its projection than would be the case without magnification. Considering only this other side, this is a condition which would obtain if a rigid automobile were skidding away from its path and deviating *away* from the observer (i.e., the rear end of the automobile would appear closer to the observer than would be consistent with its path of motion). In summary, the distortion of "paradoxical skid" is due to the increased frontality specified by magnification for each of the surfaces of a multisurfaced object that is in motion along a path oblique to the O.

MICROSCOPY

Distortions attending the magnification of both the macrostructure and the microstructure have been discussed. Again, the macrostructure consists of objects and planar discontinuities of sufficient magnitude so as to be easily perceived as separate entities by the unaided eye, and the microstructure consists of texture elements, varying in degree of coarseness, comprising the surface of objects, terrain, etc. At this point, we will extend the same principles used in accounting for the effects of the extreme magnification of even smaller "objects" than those elements comprising the microstructure (i.e., microscopic organisms). Preparatory to this discussion, it is important to remember that in the relationship between the projected visual angle and the observer's distance (Figure 3.2) the unit of distance is object size (more specifically, the physical distance separating the two points in space such as two points lying on the opposite boundaries of the frontal edge of an object).

Distortions of Interobject Distance

The distance from the objective lens of an optical microscope to the organism is relatively quite large in units of the organism's size. Furthermore, the third dimensional expanse (depth) over which microscopic preparations are extended is relatively shallow, even when measured in units of the organism's size. Consequently, organisms located within this shallow depth can differ relatively little in their distance from the object lens. Thus organisms of the same objective size would project visual angles of almost identical size and, therefore, would seem to be lying in the same plane (although the depth of field of microscopic lenses is so shallow that organisms at varying distances from the objective lens cannot all be in focus and must be observed sequentially by refocusing the lenses).

Distortions of Slant and Shape

In Figure 3.9, the top curve reveals that a 200-power microscope projects an image specifying about 88° slant for an object slanted only 10° from the line of sight! Given that most optical microscopes utilize lens systems effecting 100 power and above, it will be clear that organisms, regardless of their objective slant relative to the line of sight (optical slant), will be projected in a magnified array as specifying a position virtually perpendicular to the line of sight. This could lead to some fairly erroneous conclusions regarding the shape of a microorganism inasmuch as the organism will appear relatively shorter than is in fact the case, considering our earlier determination that a 2-ft. surface deviating from the line of sight by 10° would appear to be only a little over 5 in. when viewed from a distance of 30 ft. through a 7-power telescope. Furthermore, when the same organism is under continued observation, while moving about in such a manner as to change its slant in regard to the line of sight, it will appear under this extreme magnification to remain in the frontal plane. Therefore, it would seem that this could result in the perception of a frontal-parallel organism, changing shape. On first blush, one wonders how much is the ascribed ability of an amoeba to change *shape* actually due to the projective transformations effected by change in orientation onto a frontal plane. How much of the variability in *size* among different members of the same species of microorganisms is due to the circumstance of observing a number of different individuals at varying slants relative to the line of sight, but each appearing to lie in the frontal plane due to high magnification? Of course, these distortions of distance, shape, and slant would all be contained in microphotographs as well.

Distortions Introduced by Motion

Tolansky (1964) relates his experience upon being shown some pond life through a fairly high-powered microscope and being struck quite forcibly with the rapid flashing movements of the organisms: "Some whipped and thrashed their flagellae; small spherical objects rolled past rapidly, worm-like creatures twisted and turned violently. Everything was furiously active; even hairs on some objects whipped frantically (p. 152)." He, like many of us, had carried the impression that microorganisms are violently active and lively. When we learn, however, that the average velocity of a paramecium is only 3 mm/sec or approximately 12 yards per hour, it leads me to feel that somehow something in the equation relating the relevant parameter for perceived velocity is not fully appreciated. To the extent that the distortion experienced by the observer corresponds to that specified by the magnified optic array, lateral motion is not ex-pected to change. However, I suspect that the perceived distance does not correspond to the correct distance due to the lack of information usually available to assess distances to objects in the field (e.g., gradients of texture, perspective) and lack of familiarity with the real microscopic size of the organisms, etc.

In many ways, observing a microorganism move across the field under great magnification is like the situation described by Gibson (1950) in which an unfamiliar airborne object moves across the textureless space between the observer and the clouds, (i.e., size and distance are inde-terminant). In the absence of distance and size information, the perceived velocity may be primarily a function of the relationship between the size of the angle projected by the organism and the angular velocity of that organism. On this assumption, one can set up an equivalent viewing situation involving objects and space of more comprehensible dimen-sions. For example, viewing a paramecium of 225 mμ in length move across a field of view of 1.86 mm (the linear extent corresponding to the visual field transmitted by a 100-power microscope), moving at 3 mm/sec, produces a situation comparable to viewing a typical automobile (of 17.7 ft. in length) moving across a visual field 146 ft from a distance of 126 ft. at a velocity of 166 mph when viewed with the unaided eye. Observing the same paramecium move with the same objective velocity (3 mm/sec) under 400-power magnification across a visual field of only .46 mm (field of view under the 400-power magnification condition) is comparable to observing the same automobile move across a distance of 36 ft. from a distance of 31.3 ft. at a velocity of 166 mph.

So, in general, the effects of the extraordinary level of magnification required in microscopy are such that under these viewing conditions a change in slant of the same identical organism can be perceived as a change in shape, and different identical organisms at different slants can be perceived as being of very different shapes. Furthermore, due to the indeterminant relative viewing distance, the velocity of the tiny, slow creatures is vastly exaggerated.

MINIFICATION

Distortions introduced by minification occur when viewing a photograph taken with lenses of shorter-than-normal focal length from the distance usually used when viewing normal photographs, or by viewing any picture from a station point farther from the picture plane than is appropriate to receive the normal projective geometry. Of course, these same distortions are experienced when viewing directly through lenses of shorter-than-normal focal length. The effects of minification are of the same nature as those experienced when viewing under conditions of magnification, but are opposite in direction.

Distortions of Interobject Distance

When viewing two identical objects at increasing distance from the observer, it seems that the radial distance between the objects appears to be very much exaggerated. Figures 3.13a and b demonstrate this phenomenon in the projection of the vertical columns spaced at equal intervals along the walls. Figure 3.13b is a photograph taken through a 35-mm lens which minified the optic array by a factor of .70. (35 mm/50 mm = .70).

Distortions of Slant and Shape

When viewing a slanted surface under minification, the slant relative to the line of sight is less frontal and form is distorted in that its receding dimension appears to be more extensive. In Figure 3.13d, note the effect of .70 minification on the apparent slant of the brick wall, and the apparent length of the bricks. The net effect of these distortions upon the perception of a three-dimensional object such as a cube is that the surfaces of the cube appear to intersect at angles more acute than right angles, and its receding surfaces appear more extensive.

Distortions Introduced by Motion

When one is viewing movement through a lens system having a focal length shorter than normal or when viewing a TV or motion picture screen from a distance greater than that appropriate to receive the center of projection, one experiences an increase in the velocity of objects moving toward or away from the observer along the line of sight. An object moving perpendicular to the line of sight appears to change its shape slightly (i.e., to be nonrigid). An object moving along a path oblique to the observer, paradoxically, appears to skid away and toward the observer. Both of the latter effects introduced by the minification of movement are in the opposite direction also from those introduced by the magnification of movement.

Of course, the same logic applies to the explanation of these distortions as it does to the distortion of magnification. All of the equations provided earlier pertain to this situation as well: c' (i.e., distance to the picture plane) will simply be greater than that appropriate rather than less, and the values of m in Purdy's equation will be less than 1.0 rather than larger. Nevertheless, it may be worthwhile to apply the arguments made there to the distortions of minification at least to the extent necessary to convince the reader of the validity of that approach to the "minification problem."

Utilizing Figure 3.3 (which was generated initially to explicate distortions of interobject distance due to magnification), we can similarly explain the apparently greater distance between the objects under minification. In this section this figure is used in the reverse order from the manner in which it was used with magnification, although using this familiar figure will necessitate the use of somewhat cumbersome values for distance, and lenses of unusual focal length. Suppose that one were viewing an object that is 10 ft. along its frontal edge from a distance of approximately 32 ft. (at A'), at which distance it would subtend a visual angle of approximately 19°. Simultaneously, one is viewing a second identical object along the same line of sight at a distance of approximately 43 ft. (at B'), at which distance it would subtend a visual angle of 13.4°. Note that the relative distance between the objects is a little greater than the size of the object. If viewing were through a lens system having a focal length of only 7.14 mm (that is, one-seventh of the focal length of normal lenses of 50 mm), then the nearer object would subtend a visual angle of only one-seventh of what it would subtend without minification. That is, it would subtend a visual angle of only 2.55°. This corresponds to the size that such an object projects from a distance of 225 ft. (point A in the graph). The farther object would subtend a visual angle of approximately 2.0°, which corresponds to the size such an object would project from a distance of 300 ft. (point B on the graph). The interobject distance specified by relative projected size in this minified array is 7.5 times the object size (75 ft., rather than 10.7 ft.). This increase in apparent distance is the basis for the apparent increase in velocity, of course, inasmuch as the time interval is not affected by minification.

Turning now to determine how it is that a less frontal surface slant is

(b)

(a)

(c)

(d)

FIGURE 3.13. Comparison of interobject distance as a function of focal length of lenses. (a) Focal length = 50 mm. (b) focal length = 35 mm. Comparison of minified slant as a function of focal length of lenses. (c) Focal length = 50 mm; distance = 18 ft; $\theta = \theta_m = 45°$. (d) Focal length = 35 mm; distance = 18 ft; $\theta = 45°$; $\theta_m = 35°$.

specified by minification, let us first review that m equals the focal length of the lens in question divided by the normal focal length. Therefore, the m value for a lens of 35-mm focal length is equal to 35 mm/50 mm, or .70. Therefore, $1/m = 1/.70 = 1.43$. Generalizing then, when m is less than 1 (i.e., minification), $1/m$ will exceed the value of 1. Again, noting that in the normal photograph in Figure 3.13c of a brick wall at an optical slant of 45°, there are a certain number of texture elements projected with increasing density across the photograph in a direction corresponding to the increased distance. Introducing minification in the photograph in Figure 3.13d decreases the projected distance between the textural elements as well as the parallel lines. However, because the size of the projection plane (photograph) remains unchanged, there will be more textural elements included in it. Consequently, the rate of the change of the density (i.e., the texture density gradient) *per unit area* of the projection is correspondingly greater. In like manner, the distance separating the converging projections of the horizontal contours of the bricks is lessened; therefore, the slope of linear perspective per unit area of the projection is increased. Specifically, the space between all the elements and lines is decreased by the factor m which equals .70. Or conversely, the density of the projection of the texture elements and the slope of the linear perspective is increased by the reciprocal of the power of magnification ($1/m = 1/.70 = 1.43$).

Due to the increased density of the gradients and the greater perspective specified by minification, the slant departs less from the line of sight, or is less frontal. As Figure 3.9 indicates, the shorter the focal length of the lens relative to normal lens, the more the slant specified by the minified array deviates from the real optical slant in a direction away from the observer. Interobject distance is exaggerated in the photograph taken with a lens of shorter-than-normal focal length, not only because of the minification of the objects maintained in the same relationships, but also because the texture gradient of the terrain, increased by $1/m$, specifies a greater distance between them, as well as to them.

It was demonstrated in Figure 3.10 that the visual field is smaller as focal length increases; conversely, as focal length decreases, visual field is larger. In that figure it can be seen that more terrain nearer to the observer is included in the visual field subtended by the 55-mm lens than is included with the 200-mm lens. This is shown in a different fashion in Figure 3.13, which also includes photos taken by lens of shorter-than-normal focal length, Figures 3.13b and 3.13d. In Figure 3.14, the arrows intersect the horizontal axis at the relative distance from the objective lens at which the boundary of the projection plane (photograph) excludes the nearer terrain. Note that the wider-angle lens (28 mm) includes more of the nearer terrain and recall that the *rate* of change of projected ele-

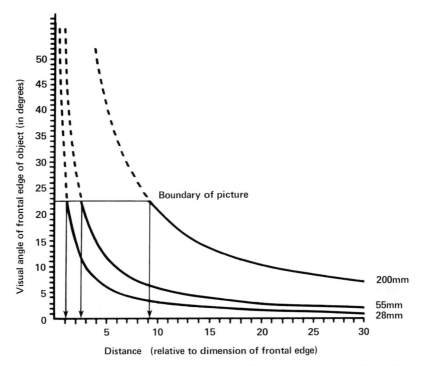

FIGURE 3.14. Projected visual angle as a function of distance of observation for a wide angle lens (28 mm), a normal lens (55 mm), and a telephoto lens (200 mm).

ments and perspective is greater with the minification lenses than normal or magnifying lenses.

With very wide-angle lenses, objects located at the extreme lateral periphery are also included in the visual field. The projective geometry of objects so located departs considerably from normal due to the acute angle to the nodal point of the lens. However, if photographs taken with such lenses were viewed from a distance determined by dividing this shorter focal length by the enlargement factor (defined earlier), and the eye remained fixated upon the center of the projection plane, the projection upon the retina would be "normal" (i.e., the same as that received if the eye were located at the nodal point of the lens where the photograph was taken). Such distortions as can be effected by extremely wide-angle lenses approximate the kinds of distortions that attend viewing a picture plane along a fairly oblique line of sight. The deliberations that have been addressed to that particular kind of distortion (Olson, Pearl, Mayfield, & Millar, 1976; Perkins, 1972, 1973; Vogel & Teghtsoonian, 1972; and Ward, 1976) may have some relevance for distortion obtained in the lateral periphery with shorter-than-normal lenses.

SUMMARY

Normal geometric projection results from observing a real three-dimensional scene through a normal lens or viewing a picture of a real scene from the appropriate station point. Under such "normal" viewing circumstances, one does not experience systematic distortion of distance, slant, shape, or velocity. However, to the extent that the focal length of the lens is longer than normal, or to the extent that one observes a picture from a station point closer than appropriate, the geometric projection is magnified. The apparent distance to the objects and the radial distance between objects are lessened by a factor equal to the reciprocal of the power of magnification ($1/m$). Slant specified by the magnified projection is more frontal and is readily determined by Equation 7. A somewhat foreshortened shape is specified, the dimension being determinable by the use of Equation 2. Inasmuch as the perception of motion is based on the continuous changes in the size of projection effected by continuous changes in distance, velocity along the line of sight that is specified by magnification is also decreased. Just as the decreased velocity of radial motion is related to the apparent decrease in distance to and radial distance between static objects, there are two other phenomena introduced by movement that are similarly related to the distortion of slant and shape evident in viewing static surfaces:

1. When an object moves perpendicular to the line of sight, its surfaces change orientation in regard to the observer. The continuous apparent changes in specified slant and the extent of the receding surfaces specified by magnification are such as to specify a nonrigid object in motion.
2. When an object moves along a path oblique to the observer, the apparent orientation of the surfaces of the moving object is not consistent with the perceived direction of motion. The perceptual result is a "paradoxical skidding" of the object. The object seems both to skid toward the observer (indicated by the more frontal orientation of the farther visible side) and skid away from the observer (indicated by the more frontal orientation of the nearer visible side).

The effects of the extraordinary magnification introduced by microscopy (preserved in microphotographs as well) are such that a change in the slant of the same identical organism can be perceived as a change in shape, and different identical organisms at different slants can be perceived as being of very different shapes. Furthermore, when viewing through a microscope, the perceived velocity of tiny, slow-moving organisms is vastly exaggerated due to the indeterminant relative viewing distance.

To the extent that the focal length of the lens is shorter than normal, or to the extent that one observes a picture from a point farther than that appropriate to receive the center of projection, the projected optic array is minified. Under these viewing circumstances, all of the effects are opposite in direction from those specified by magnification (i.e., apparent distance to the objects and the radial distance between objects are increased, specified slant is less frontal, and the extent of the receding surfaces is increased). Correspondingly, the velocity of radial motion is increased, and the nonrigidity specified in an object moving perpendicular to the line of sight is opposite to that specified by magnification, as is the "paradoxical skid" indicated for objects moving oblique to the observer.

The principles applied to the explanation of magnification are also applied to distortions of minification, regardless of the means by which magnification or minification is effected. In brief, the explanations developed in this chapter are based primarily on the fact that the projected visual angle (of the distance between any two points) is a decreasing, negatively accelerated function of distance. The *relationship* between all projected visual angles in the projection plane is, of course, determined by the real distance, and this relationship remains unchanged in the projection regardless of degree of magnification or minification. By uniformly enlarging the optic array, magnification lessens the density and rate of change of density of textural elements as well as the slope of the linear perspective *per unit area* within the projection. A lessened density and lessened density gradient or linear perspective gradient specifies a nearer surface and a more frontal slope, both determinable by the use of equations provided in this chapter. Furthermore, magnifying lenses truncate the visual field, excluding the nearer terrain that normally specifies the relative distance to objects in the visual field. All of these factors converge in the explanation of the manifestations of reduced spatiality described.

In a like manner, under conditions of viewing leading to minification, there is an increase in the density and the rate of change of the density of textural elements, as well as an increase in the slope of linear perspective *per unit area* within the projection of the minified array. An increased density, increased density gradient, or a linear perspective gradient specify a greater viewing distance to a less frontal receding surface of greater length, all determinable, of course, by the use of the same equations as just referred to in discussing the effects of magnification (Equations 2 and 7). Furthermore, lenses of shorter-than-normal focal length transmit a wider than normal expanse of the nearer terrain which encompasses more expansive gradients. These gradients also will be transformed by minification to more dense ones specifying greater distance to the objects in the field beyond them. All of these factors converge in the explanation of the manifestations of increased spatiality described in our discussion of minification.

REFERENCES

Bartley, S. H. A study of the flattening effect produced by optical magnification. *American Journal of Optometry*, 1951 Monograph, 119.

Bartley, S. H., & Adair, H. J. Comparisons of phenomenal distance in photographs of various sizes. *Journal of Psychology*, 1959, *47*, 289–295.

Braunstein, M. L., & Payne, J. W. Perspective and form ratio as determinants of relative slant judgments. *Journal of Experimental Psychology*, 1969, *81*, 584–590.

Dunn, B. E., Gray, G. C., & Thompson, D. Relative height on the picture plane and depth perception. *Perceptual and Motor Skills*, 1965, *21*, 227–236.

Epstein, W. Perceived depth as a function of relative height under three background conditions. *Journal of Experimental Psychology*, 1966, *72*, 335–338.

Farber, J. M. The effects of angular magnification on the perception of rigid motion. *Dissertation Abstracts International* 1973, *33B*, 4540-B.

Freeman, R. B. Effect of size on visual slant. *Journal of Experimental Psychology*, 1956, *71*, 96–103.

Freeman, R. B. Ecological optics and visual slant. *Psychological Review*, 1965, *72*, 501–504.

Gibson, J. J. *The perception of the visual world.* 00: Boston: Houghton-Mifflin, 1950.

Gibson, J. J. Ecological optics. *Vision Research*, 1961, *1*, 253–262.

Gibson, J. J. The information available in pictures. *Leonardo*, 1971, *4*, 27–35.

Gogel, W. C., Hartman, B. O., & Harker, G. S. The retinal size of a familar object as a determinant of apparent distance. *Psychological Monographs*, 1957, *442*, 1–16.

Gruber, H., & Clark, W. C. Perception of slanted surfaces. *Perceptual and Motor Skills*, 1956, *6*, 97–106.

Haber, R. H., & Hershenson, M. *The psychology of visual perception.* New York: Holt, Rinehart, and Winston, 1973.

Hagen, M. A., Jones, R. K., & Reed, E. S. On a neglected variable in theories of picture perception: Truncation of the visual field. *Perception and Psychophysics*, 1978, *23*, 326–330.

Ittleson, W. H. *Visual Space Perception.* New York: Springer, 1960.

Olson, R. K., Pearl, M., Mayfield, N., & Millar, D. Sensitivity to pictorial shape perspective in five-year-old children and adults. *Perception and Psychophysics*, 1976, *20*, 173–178.

Perkins, D. N. Visual discrimination between rectangular and nonrectangular parallelopipeds. *Perception and Psychophysics*, 1972, *12*, 396–399.

Perkins, D. N. Compensating for distortion in viewing pictures obliquely. *Perception and Psychophysics*, 1973, *14*, 13–18.

Pirenne, M. *Optics, painting and photography.* Cambridge, England: Cambridge Univ. Press, 1970.

Purdy, W. C. The Hypothesis of psychophysical correspondence in space perception. *General Electric Technical Information Series*, 1960, No. R60ELC56.

Rosinski, R. R. On the ambiguity of visual stimulation: A reply to Ericksson. *Perception and Psychophysics*, 1974, *16*, 259–263.

Smith, O. W. Comparison of apparent depth in a photograph viewed from two distances. *Perception and Motor Skills*, 1958, *8*, 79–81. (a)

Smith, O. W. Judgments of size and distance in photographs. *American Journal of Psychology*, 1958, *71*, 529–538. (b)

Smith, O. W., & Gruber, H. Perception of depth in photographs. *Perceptual and Motor Skills*, 1958, *8*, 307–313.

Tolansky, S. *Optical illusions*, Elmsford, New York: Pergamon, 1964.

Vogel, J. M., & Teghtsoonian, M. The effects of perspective alterations on apparent size and distance scales. *Perception and Psychophysics*, 1972, *11*, 294–498.

Ward, J. L. The perception of pictorial space in perspective pictures. *Leonardo*, 1976, *9*, 279–288.

RICHARD R. ROSINSKI
JAMES FARBER

CHAPTER **4**

Compensation for Viewing Point in the Perception of Pictured Space

Introduction 137
Decoding Spatial Layout through Linear Perspective 140
Effects of Viewing-Point Dislocation 143
    Magnification 143
    Shear 144
Pictorial Space Perception 148
    Effects of Magnification 151
    Effects of Shear 155
Perceptual Compensation for Geometric Distortion 156
References 175

INTRODUCTION

A fundamental problem in the study of picture perception simply involves explaining how two-dimensional pictures and photographs are capable of producing accurate impressions of three-dimensional spatial layouts. In part, this representational quality is based on similarities between the optic array projected from the picture and that from the real scene. Under "ideal" conditions a picture can present to the eye a near simulation of the scene it represents. Given a near identity of the two arrays, any theory can explain picture preception.

137

But this ideal case is rarely achieved or even closely approximated. As Evans (1960), Pirenne (1970), and others have noted, the pictorial array may differ from the environmental array in many respects: the presence of texture from the picture surface, a narrowing of the range of colors and luminances, the presence of borders, and so forth. Furthermore a picture is rarely viewed from the correct point of observation. Consequently, there may be striking geometrical distortions in the array that is projected to the observer's eye.

To the extent that perception of spatial relationships in pictures depends on detailed geometric isomorphism, we should expect that viewing a picture from an incorrect location would affect the perception of layout. Yet ordinary experience suggests that such effects are weak or nonexistent under some conditions. As we walk past a painting or photograph, we perceive, apparently accurately, what is depicted in the picture. The existence of such a constancy phenomenon has suggested to some (e.g., Pirenne, 1970) that the perception of pictures must involve a compensation process that enables viewers to discount the effects of projective transformations on the depicted space. If such constancy processes exist, they must work only within certain circumscribed limits. A simple demonstration that such limits exist can be seen in anamorphic art. Even the simplest projective transformation used in anamorphic art can not be discounted or compensated for when the picture is viewed from the frontal parallel. Perception of the object or scene depicted in the anamorphic painting occurs only when the painting is viewed so that the projection to the eye is similar to the projection from the real object (i.e., when geometric similarities exist between the object and its representation).

Because the precise relationships between viewing point dislocations, geometric transformations, and perceptual accuracy is unknown, determination of the correct viewing point for a display and of the effects of displacement is crucial for a further understanding of picture perception. Clearly any discussion of the way in which the visual system treats pictures, as well as any investigation of "pictorial compensation," must be based on a knowledge of the transformations induced by viewing-point displacement. In spite of this, there have been relatively few attempts to specify or control such transformations.

In the present chapter, we discuss the geometric effects of changing the viewing point of a picture, and consider the theoretical and empirical status of the concept of "pictorial constancy." For the purposes of this discussion we adopt the convention of speaking in terms of photography and photographic images; of course, identical considerations hold for any geometrically representative display that has a single center of projection (e.g., TV or radar images, line drawings, computer graphics). We distinguish between the optic arrays produced by the picture and by the environment by referring to the pictorial and environmental arrays. For a picture viewed from a given point, the spatial layout that could have generated an array equivalent to that pictorial array will be called the *virtual space*. Thus for each viewing point, there exists a corresponding virtual space. By definition, then, the "correct" viewing point for a picture is one in which the virtual space is identical with the geographic space that originally generated the picture (i.e., when the pictorial and environmental arrays are isomorphic).

To obtain this identity in viewing a photograph, the relationship between the eye and the photograph must preserve the relationships that exist between the lens node and the film plane. With a rigid (box) camera, the lens axis is centered on a line perpendicular to the center of the film plane, so the correct viewing point must be along a line perpendicular to the center of the photograph. The distance of the correct viewing point along this line is equal to the actual focal length of the lens multiplied by the degree of enlargement of the photograph. Thus, if the focal length of the lens when the picture was taken was 70 mm, and the negative is enlarged 8 times, then the correct viewing distance is 560 mm. Note that the correct distance is jointly a function of the focal length and the degree of enlargement. Viewing distance for a particular photograph is too close or too far away only with reference to lens and enlargement. An implication of this fact is that geometrically, transformations are not solely due to the use of particular lenses, but to the combination of lenses and viewing point. For example, the so-called "telephoto effect" is not the result of using a telephoto lens, but rather of viewing a photograph from an incorrect (too near) point given a particular lens.

Similar considerations hold for determining the correct viewing point of a picture taken with a flexible (view) camera. All spatial relationships between the lens axis and the film plane must be identical to the relationship between the line of sight and the photograph. Thus, a 3 cm rise of the film plane puts the correct viewing point 3 cm (times the degree of enlargement) above the center of the photograph. The pictorial and environmental arrays are identical if the distance and orientation of the photograph relative to a line from the eye to the center of the photo are identical to the distance and orientation of the film plane relative to the line from the lens node to the center of the negative. If these conditions are not maintained, then the pictorial and environmental arrays will differ, and the virtual space projected from the picture will differ from the environmental space.

One way to define the geometric distortions resulting from changing the viewing point is to describe the virtual space that is produced. To demonstrate this point, let us consider the object in Figure 4.1. If this drawing is viewed from the correct point along a line perpendicular to the center of the photo, then the virtual object for the pictorial array is a cube. If the photo is viewed from another point, the virtual object for

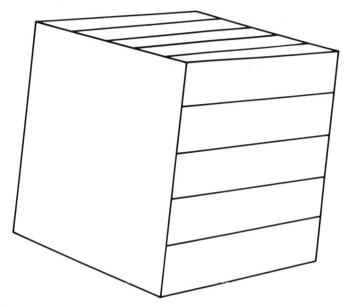

FIGURE 4.1. This drawing of a cube corresponds to a projection of an infinite number of virtual objects to an infinite number of viewing points. The object is a cube only when seen from one viewing point.

that projection will not correspond to a cube, but to some other object. If we can describe this other object, then we will have described the effects of the geometric transformation.

This section will examine the geometrical basis of pictorial space perception via linear perspective representations. We will consider photographs, drawings, paintings, or other representations that can be analyzed by the principles of linear perspective, describe the rules by which the virtual space specified by such a picture can be determined, and show how the geometry of the virtual space is affected by the location of the point of observation. In particular, the way that ''incorrect'' points of observation produce specific transformations of the geometry of the virtual space will be explained. Although our analyses will be developed for linear perspective, the same general principles, and the same conclusions, apply to pictorial representations of spatial layout in general, as we have shown elsewhere (Farber & Rosinski, 1978).

DECODING SPATIAL LAYOUT
THROUGH LINEAR PERSPECTIVE

The rules of linear perspective can be used to represent a desired spatial layout. A picture can be constructed using these rules, so that it projects the same array to some point as a real scene. This is a case of using linear perspective for the *synthesis* of a spatial representation. The same principles can be used to *analyze* a given representation (i.e., to determine the corresponding spatial layout), given the picture and point of observation. It is possible to determine the three-dimensional shape, the relative sizes, and the orientations of objects in a picture if the scene lends itself to linear perspective analysis. We will first review some rules for decoding layout from linear perspective, and then consider their implications for virtual space projected to "incorrect" points of observation.

In a linear perspective representation, parallel lines converge to a common vanishing point. There exists a point in the picture plane (corresponding to the "point at infinity" in space) that is common to all parallel lines. The direction of the vanishing point relative to the point of observation is the common direction of all lines in the sheaf. Consequently, the direction of the vanishing point specifies the direction or orientation of the set of parallel lines. Furthermore, lines that are *coplanar* converge to vanishing points that are collinear. The lines on a plane all have vanishing points that are on a line in the picture plane. Thus, there is a horizon line corresponding to each plane.

These facts are sufficient to deal with most cases of general interest. Figure 4.2 is the projection of a simple ground plane, consisting of a regular, rectangular texture. There is a central vanishing point at V, the intersection of one family of parallel sides. The orthogonal sides also project into lines that intersect in a vanishing point V_2, but the vanishing point for these lines cannot be represented in the figure, as it is at infinity in the plane of the illustration. There are two other implicit vanishing points which are of particular importance for our discussion: V_3 and V_4 are the vanishing points for the diagonals of the ground lattice. Although the diagonals are not directly represented in the illustration, they do intersect at V_3 and V_4 because, for a regular ground texture, the diagonals form two sets of parallel lines.

In order to determine the geometry of the space of Figure 4.2, we need a scale for depth. That is, we need to know the depth shape of the ground elements; the ratio of depth to width (d/w ratios). This requires that we specify a point of observation. We assume the viewing point for Figure 4.2 is at O. Note that although we have represented O in the illustration, it does not exist in the actual picture plane.

We can now determine the shape of the ground elements. This is not trivial, since trapezoidal figures, even if we assume them to correspond to rectangles, might correspond to rectangles of a wide range of shapes (d/w ratios). In fact, only for a specific center of projection does the figure represent a square ground lattice. This point is located where the angle between the observation point and the primary vanishing points V_1 and V_2 (the angle $\angle V_1, O, V_2$) is 90°; therefore the sides of the ground texture

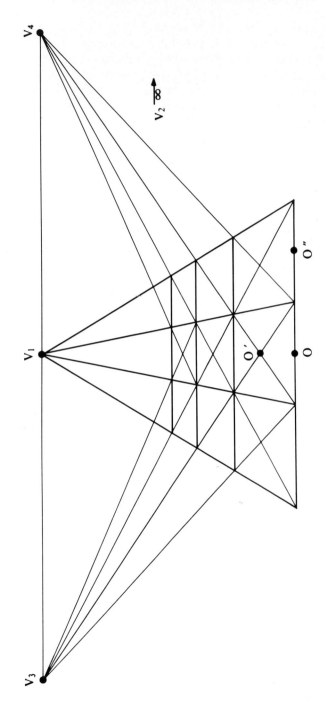

FIGURE 4.2. Schematic representation of the geometric relations important in an illustration of a ground plane of regular elements. Vanishing points of the surface are V_1, V_2, V_3, and V_4. The observation points, O, O', and O'' do not lie in the picture plane, but are represented in this illustration to depict angular relations.

elements are orthogonal, and their shape is rectangular. If the angles between the diagonals and the main vanishing points ($\angle V_3$, O, V_1 or $\angle V_4$, O, V_1) are 45°, each element corresponds to a square, rather than any other rectangle. Of course, the absolute size of the ground elements is not specified, unless we make some assumption about the height of the original center of projection above the ground plane, but the relative sizes and distances are fully determined by the angular relationships among the vanishing points and the viewing point.

In a similar fashion, the orientation of planar surfaces can be analyzed in terms of vanishing-point relationships in the pictorial array. In the environment, a line from the vanishing point of a plane surface to the eye must run parallel in space to the surface. Thus, the orientation of the lines from the eye to the various vanishing points relative to the gravitational coordinate system is identical with the orientation of the surface in space. If a picture is viewed from the correct viewing point, lines from the eye to the pictorial vanishing points have the same orientation as the represented surfaces.

EFFECTS OF VIEWING-POINT DISLOCATION

As the preceding analysis shows, if a picture is viewed from the correct point of observation, the angular relationships between the viewing point and the various vanishing points specify the internal depth, relative size, shape, and orientation of depicted layouts. Clearly, then, if one changes the position of the viewing point relative to the photo, these angular relationships are altered, and the pictured space is geometrically transformed.

Magnification

If the same picture is viewed from a different point, a different virtual space is specified. For example, if the center of projection were at O' rather than O (on the same perpendicular line, but closer to the picture plane), the diagonal vanishing point angles would be shifted. In particular, if the distance from V_1 to $O = z$, and if the distance V_1 to $O' = z'$, then the angle $\angle V_3$, O, V_1 is increased relative to $\angle V_3$, O, V_1, by a factor depending on the ratio z/z'. If we call these angles θ and θ', then

$$\tan \theta' = k \tan \theta, \tag{1}$$

where $k = z/z'$.

In the present case, this amounts to an increase in the diagonal angle, and implies a decrease in the depth to width ratio. Hence, a decrease in the distance of the center of projection corresponds to a decrease in the depth scale of the pictorial space. Such a change in virtual shape is illustrated in Figure 4.3 (Purdy, 1960).

So far, we have been considering the analysis of a picture, given a known center of projection. But if we analyze pictorial representations in terms of the corresponding virtual space, the same conclusions should follow for the effects of viewing a picture from a point of observation displaced along the perpendicular. Viewing a picture from a point of observation closer than the theoretical center of projection produces, at the eye, an array corresponding to a space of compressed internal depth; viewing from too far produces an array corresponding to a space with an expanded internal depth scale.

Although we have been concerned with a single ground plane, the same arguments and analyses generalize to scenes containing planes in different orientations, or containing objects of different shapes, as long as linear perspective still applies. For example, consider Figure 4.4 (a slanted lattice against a textured ground). The ground plane is defined as in Figure 4.2, but there is now another vanishing line, corresponding to the horizon of the slanted checkerboard. The slant of the plane is specified by the direction of its horizon. For the case illustrated in Figure 4.4, and for the point of observation indicated by O, the slant is about 45°. But for a nearer center of projection (point of observation), the elevation of the horizon is increased—hence, the specified slant approaches the frontal-parallel. In addition to compressing depth in the ground plane, moving the point of observation closer to the picture also changes the specified slants of other planes. In fact, all of the effects of changing the distance of the point of observation can be summarized by the statement that the internal depth of the corresponding virtual space is compressed by a factor $k = z/z'$. This implies the changes of slant, shape, and internal depth.

Shear

The effects discussed are produced by varying the distance of the center of the projection or point of observation. We will now consider the effects

SQUARE   RECTANGLE

FIGURE 4.3. The angular length–width ratio and the diagonal angles of a ground element define its shape. Because magnification compresses internal depth it alters element shape.

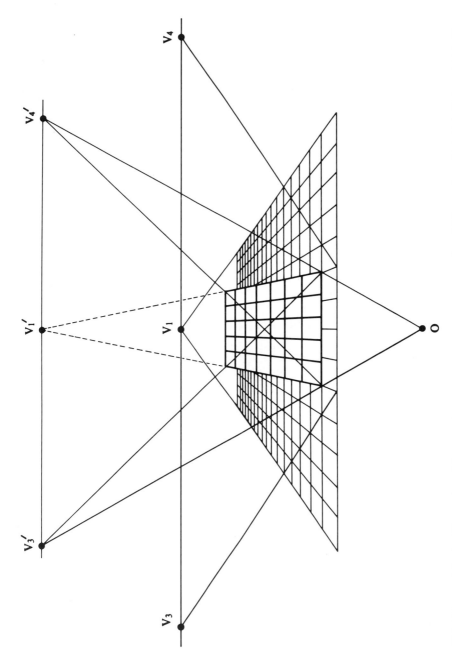

FIGURE 4.4. A lattice-like surface lying on the ground plane creates a set of vanishing points, V_1', V_2', V_3', and V_4'. These vanishing points help specify the surface's characteristics and its spatial relationship with the ground. The observation point, O, does not lie in the picture plane, but is represented in the illustration to depict angular relations.

on the virtual space of lateral displacements of the point of observation (parallel to the picture plane), as illustrated by point O'' in Figure 4.2. Once again, we need consider only the effects on the angular relationships among the vanishing points and the point of observation. Obviously, moving O to O'' (e.g., where O'' is to the right of O) shifts the direction of V_1, and consequently the direction of the lines intersecting at V_1. It also alters the angle between V_1, O'', and V_2. The angular direction of V_2 is unaffected by the lateral shift, but V_1 is shifted leftward; so the angle $\angle V_1$, O'', V_2 is now greater than 90°. This means that the sides of the ground elements are no longer orthogonal. The "element" of ground texture is no longer a rectangle, but a parallelogram. The effect of the lateral displacement of the point of observation is to produce a shear in the virtual space. Of course, not only ground elements, but all angular relationships among nonparallel lines (as long as they are not in the same frontal plane) are sheared. In particular, although frontal-parallel lines and planes remain unchanged by a lateral shift (because their vanishing points are unaffected), the orientation of nonfrontal planes is angularly shifted opposite to the direction of displacement.

Usually, both perpendicular and lateral shifts of the point of observation may occur. It is intuitively clear that the effects described should be additive: Viewing from too near and too far to the right, for example, should produce both a depth compression (due to the approach along the perpendicular), and a lateral shear. We have described the quantitative relationship in Farber and Rosinski (1978).

The preceding analysis outline provides a simple way of decoding all spatial transformations of pictured space resulting from viewing-point dislocation. As we have shown previously (Farber & Rosinski, 1978), all such distortions can be analyzed into a linear combination of magnification and shear factors. Vanishing-point relationships combined with some simple trigonometry can be used to determine precisely the nature of transformed virtual space.

As an example of how such determinations can be made, consider the situation schematically depicted in the side view in Figure 4.5a. An observer at O views a picture, Π, of a slanted surface. The vanishing line of this surface, in the picture plane is located at V. Because a line from a point of observation to a surface's vanishing line is parallel to the surface (i.e., it has the same slant), the orientation, θ, of line $O\ V$ relative to the horizon (V) is identical to the surface slant.

If the relationship between the center of the projection and the viewing point is changed by rotating the picture plane about the axis (A) a new virtual space results. The nature of this transformation is depicted in Figure 4.5b. Since V is displaced to V', the virtual surface orientation is transformed to θ'. The relationship between the original and transformed

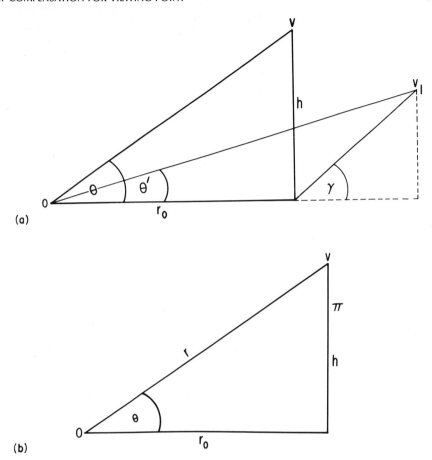

FIGURE 4.5. (a) A schematic side view depicting geometric relationships between a point of observation (O) and the picture plane Π. The vanishing point for a surface depicted in the picture is V. A line drawn from the point of observation to the vanishing point makes the same angle θ, with the perpendicular as the surface does. (b) If the picture is slanted back by δ, the vanishing point is moved to V_1, and the virtual orientation of the surface is changed to θ'.

orientation is as follows. The original surface slant (θ) is given by

$$\sin \theta = \frac{h}{r'} \tag{2}$$

and by

$$\cot \theta = \frac{r_0}{h} \tag{3}$$

The picture plane has been rotated so that it makes an angle, δ, with the horizontal. The transformed surface slant (θ') can be expressed as

$$\cot \theta' = \left(\frac{r_0 + h \cos \delta}{h \sin \delta} \right) = \left(\frac{\cot \theta}{\sin \delta} + \cot \delta \right) \tag{4}$$

and as

$$\sin \theta' = \frac{h \sin \delta}{r'} = \left(\frac{r}{r'} \sin \delta \right) \sin \theta. \tag{5}$$

But,

$$\frac{r}{r'} = \frac{1}{\sqrt{(1 + \cos \delta \sin 2\theta)}}, \tag{6}$$

and therefore,

$$\sin \theta' = \sin \theta \left[\frac{\sin \delta}{\sqrt{(1 + \cos \delta \sin 2\theta)}} \right] \tag{7}$$

Rotating the picture plane affects the relationship among vanishing points of surface element diagonals. In a directly analogous fashion, such change can be analyzed as an index of shape distortion.

It is important to note once again that the effects we are discussing are "geometrical," in the sense that the transformations of virtual space are determined on the basis of considerations concerning the geometry of projection, and not on the basis of a theory about the operation of the visual system. We do not claim that the transformations of pictorial space that are geometrically specified necessarily occur in perception. That is a separate, empirical matter.

PICTORIAL SPACE PERCEPTION

The experimental literature on the effects of spatial transformations on pictorial space perception is small. There is, however, convincing evidence that, under some conditions, perceived and virtual space are in correspondence. As Gibson (1971) has argued, pictures can be representational whenever monocular arrays from a picture and from the world coincide (i.e., when perceived and virtual space are isomorphic). This, of course, corresponds to our definition for viewing a picture from the correct station point.

Such isomorphism of perceived and virtual space exists, at least for viewing under specialized conditions. Schlosberg (1941) suggested that photographs can lead to compelling and highly realistic impressions of spatial layout under conditions that restrict the monocular field of view to the photograph. Gibson (1951) had subjects view a corridor and a photomural of that same corridor. The observer's view in both conditions was through a small aperture that restricted the field of view and kept the eye at the correct point of observation. Subjects were asked to decide which corridor was real and which was a picture. Gibson reported that only 60% of the subjects were correct. The results were surprising in view of the fact that the two stimulus situations differed in overall brightness, contrast, and color. Because the virtual space projected by the picture was identical to the environmental space only in terms of their geometry, difficulty in discriminating between the two indicates that geometric factors played a large role in the perceptual discrimination of the two conditions.

A similar experiment by Smith and Smith (1961) illustrated this point more dramatically. In their experiment, people looked through an eye piece positioned at the correct viewing points and viewed a photograph of a room containing a target on the floor. The observers were asked to toss a ball into the target under conditions that restricted their view of the picture after the ball had been tossed. There were two important aspects of the results of this study. First, the ball-tossing responses of the observers were all quite accurate—the ball would have landed on or near the target in all cases. The virtual location of the target in the pictorial space, then, determined the perceived location of the target. More strikingly, Smith and Smith report that, although no attempt was made to achieve versimilitude (beyond assuring that the geometrical structure of the pictorial array matched that of the environmental array), none of the subjects reported knowing that they were looking at a photograph rather than the actual room. Thus, both in terms of qualitative impressions as well as quantitative accuracy, the structure of the geometric array is an important determiner of a pictorial space perception.

This fact, however, raises a difficult problem for an information-based theory of picture perception. If there is an isomorphism between perceived space and virtual space, pictures should be accurately representational only when they are viewed from the correct center of projection. Each projection to other viewing points specifies a unique virtual space, therefore, each viewing point should give rise to its own unique perceived space.

It has been pointed out numerous times that, intuitively at least, such alterations in virtual space are not reflected in perception (Haber, 1978; Pirenne, 1970). It seems that we perceive a pictorial representation of space veridically, even when the geometric projection to the eye is greatly distorted. Moreover, pictures apparently look the same regardless of the viewing point.

Some individuals (e.g., Hagen, 1974; Pirenne, 1970) have speculated that picture perception involves a special perceptual process by which viewers are able to discount the distortion of virtual space caused by dislocations of viewing point. For viewing from the correct geometrical station point, perception is determined by the projected information. When a picture is viewed from the wrong viewing point, a special pictorial perceptual process is "triggered," engaging different mechanisms for compensation. Hagen, like Pirenne, believes this triggering of a new process is related to picture plane cues, but she gives no indication of the mechanism involved. Hagen's position has been criticized elsewhere (Rosinski, 1974).

The various notions of compensation suggested by other theorists are vague regarding the nature of these processes. The basic problem each of them addresses is the lack of correspondence between virtual and perceived space. Because perceived space apparently corresponds more closely to environmental space than to the distorted virtual space, a mechanism is proposed to account for this perceptual anomaly. It has been difficult to determine the nature of this mechanism because an analysis of the distortions of virtual space has been only recently available.

An inability to compare perceived with virtual space makes it impossible to specify precisely the extent and nature of perceptual compensation. Assertions regarding the existence of compensation may be in error if crucial relationships among perceived, virtual, and environmental spaces are not determined. Yet, virtually every writer on pictorial distortion (the present ones included) has appealed to the reader's intuitions. For example, Haber (1978, p. 41) in discussing expected perceptions of a distorted pictorial space argues that "most picture lookers know that this does not happen." It is worth pointing out that neither such casual phenomenology nor the more experimental phenomenology of Pirenne is relevant here. The fact that observers are not consciously aware of distortions in virtual space does not imply that the nature of virtual space is unregistered by the visual system. Furthermore, one's introspections about the nature of perceptual distortions are irrelevant. To comment on whether a picture seems distorted is to assess the correspondence between virtual and environmental space. A judgment of a distortion of space implies that virtual space is registered and somehow compared to environmental space. But, observers cannot judge that a scene is distorted unless they know what it is supposed to look like. This information is not available at the incorrect viewing point. Logically, one's estimate of the distortion present in virtual space can not be accurate unless an impossible object results.

A second kind of logical problem has arisen due to difficulty in specifying the virtual and environmental spaces, and assessing their effects on perception. For example, viewing-point dislocation does not affect the relative sizes of surfaces lying in planes parallel to the picture plane. Relative sizes in any virtual space always coincide with relative sizes in the environmental space. Consequently, the perceived relative size of objects in photographs is logically irrelevant to the problem of determining the nature of perceptaul compensation. The concept of compensation only need be invoked when the virtual and environmental space differ. This makes it especially important to determine whether alterations of virtual space are reflected in the perception of space.

Effects of Magnification

One of the clearest demonstrations of the effects of magnifying the pictorial array was provided by Purdy (1960). Purdy had his subjects make reproduction judgments of the slant of a textured surface under experimental conditions in which there was either no magnification or a 1.5 magnification. In addition to determining whether the conditions differed, or whether the data deviated from the predictions, Purdy used an ingenious procedure to eliminate the effects of constant errors. Because a slant of 40.9° (0.713 rad) under a 1.5 magnification geometrically specifies a surface at 52.4° (0.914 rad), Purdy had his subjects judge both the 40.9° (0.713 rad) surface under 1.5 magnification as well as 52.4° (0.914 rad) surface without magnification. Thus, a direct intrasubject comparison of the perceived slant could be obtained. The two magnifications were created by maintaining a constant distance from the subject to the display, but changing the location of the center of projection. Thus, available information specified the virtual orientation of the surface.

Purdy found a significant difference between judgments with and without magnification. Furthermore, the average deviation between the judged surface slant under magnification and the geometrically predicted judgment without magnification was only 1.05°. Thus, there was a remarkably close correspondence between the perceived slant of the surface and the virtual slant specified by the structure of the magnified pictorial array.

A similar correspondence has been found in other studies. Smith and Gruber (1958) used a direct scaling technique to determine the effect of viewing distance on the perception of distance in photographs. On each trial, subjects viewed a corridor and a photomural of the corridor through an aperture. The experimenter designated a point in the photo, and the subject expressed the distance of that point as a fraction or multiple of the perceived distance to the corresponding point in the real corridor. The correct geometric viewing point for the photomural was at a distance of 2.1 m. The actual viewing distances used, however, were 1.0, 1.3, 1.6, 2.0, 2.4, and 2.8 m. Viewing from these observation points should result in compression or expansion of the virtual space depicted in the photograph. Smith and Gruber found that the judgments did differ significantly from one another across viewing distance. In addition, by reanalyzing their data, we can see that the ratio judgments actually made in the various conditions closely matched those predicted by the distortion of the virtual space. As $k = 2.1$ at the nearest viewing distance, and $k = .75$ at the farthest distance, the consequent compressions and expansions of virtual space differ by a factor of 2.8. In fact, the conditions differed by a factor of 2.86. Smith and Gruber point out that within any of the viewing conditions, the obtained judgment did not differ by more than 6% from those predicted.

The magnifications in the Smith and Gruber study were induced by varying the distance between the observer and the display. However, viewing was through a reduction aperture, which reduced display plane information. In terms of both optical information and results, the Purdy study and the Smith and Gruber study agree.

In a further experiment, Smith (1958a) had subjects view a similar photomural from two distances and estimate the number of paces needed to go from their position to a set of pipes at the end of the hall. As one might expect from the expansion of virtual space, subjects' judgments of these distances varied directly with the viewing distance of the photograph. However, the match between geometric predictions and the actual judgments was not as close in this study as in previous ones. Given the two viewing distances used, the judgments from the far viewing point should have been about 4.5 times greater than those from the near point. Although the judgments differed in the predicted direction, the difference between all conditions was only a factor of about 2.5. These results suggest that the geometry of virtual space affected the perception of distance, but that other factors may have been operating to reduce the effect relative to that theoretically expected.

A similar conclusion can be drawn from another study performed by Smith (1958b). In this experiment, subjects viewed photographs of a plowed field with 15 white stakes of varying heights positioned in the foreground and a single white stake positioned in the background. Subjects viewed these photographs at either 75% ($k = 1.33$) or 250% ($k = 0.40$) of the geometrically correct viewing distance (resulting in a magnification or minification respectively), and made judgments of the height and distance of the stake in the background. The geometrical analysis previously presented indicates that under these two conditions, the virtual space of the photograph should be compressed and expanded. Qualitatively, the results followed this pattern. Judgments of distance in the two viewing conditions differed by a factor of 2.7, with the mean judgments at the 75% viewing distance to be underestimations and those from the 250% distance to be overestimations of the actual distance to the target object. Thus, these results generally follow expectations based on the geometric distortion of the virtual pictorial space.

However, a precise reanalysis of the Smith data indicates that the match between the geometrically expected results and the data is not very close (see Figure 4.6). For example, the average distance of the standard was 203 yards (186 m). Under the viewing conditions used in the study, the geometric compression of virtual space predicts mean judgments of 152 yards (139 m) in the 75% condition because (1/1.33) × 203 = 152, and 507 yards (464 m) in the 250% condition because (1/0.4) × 203 = 507. In fact, the actual means for these two conditions were 110 yards (100.5 m) and 297 yards (271.5 m), respectively. Thus, it is clear that there was considerable underestimation relative to the geometrically predicted distances. Secondly, there are reasons to suppose that the effects of the 250% minification condition were even less than the stated comparisons suggest.

Smith did not use a control condition in which subjects viewed the same photographs from the correct station point. However, Gibson and

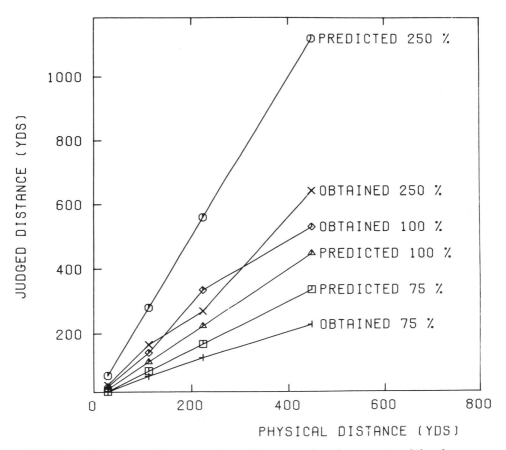

FIGURE 4.6. Mean judged distance, and predictions based on the geometry of virtual space for the physical distances used in Smith's experiment.

Smith (unpublished) did perform such a study using the same photographs later used by Smith (1958b). Smith used this other set of data as a comparison for magnification or minification. For an average distance of the standard of 203 yards (136 m), the mean distance judgment when viewing the photograph from the correct station point was 261 yards (289 m). Thus, when viewing from the correct point, subjects overestimated the distance of the standard. The virtual space projected to the correct viewing point, or with 250% minification, differed by 304 yards (278 m). Yet as shown in Figure 4.6 the actual difference between these two conditions was only 36 yards (33 m), scarcely 12% of the predicted difference. The distance judgment phase of the Smith (1958b) study demonstrates that magnification of the pictorial array does exert an influence on the perception of distance, when magnification is induced by moving the viewing point relative to the picture. However, the correspondence between the obtained and predicted judgments is so slight as to suggest that other factors are influencing the judgment. Unfortunately, the stimulus conditions are not specified in sufficient detail to determine exactly what other factors might have been operating.

The Smith (1958b) study was also constructed to determine the effects of magnification and minification on the perception of size. According to the analysis of the virtual space previously presented, the relative frontal size of the object in the virtual space is not affected by the viewing distance to the photograph. Subjects made size judgments by matching the object in the distance with one of 15 objects in the foreground. Smith found an extremely close correspondence between the judged and actual size of the stimulus object so that object size appears unaffected by the viewing distance. The actual size of the target object in Smith's study was 69-in. (175.26 cm) high. Subjects in the magnification and minification conditions made matching (relative size) judgments, and selected objects with mean sizes of 68.8 and 68.4 in. (174.25 cm and 173.74 cm) respectively. Thus, regardless of the magnification, there was no effect on the perceived size of the target object. It should be noted, however, that although the data and predictions regarding size perception match exactly, the Smith (1958b) data must be regarded as only weak support of the proposition that virtual space affects the judgment of size. As Smith points out, the judgments of size and distance appear to be independent. Although perceived and virtual size correspond, perceived and virtual distance do not. The exact reason for this lack of correspondence cannot be directly determined, but it seems clear that some source of relational information for size may have played a role in the subjects' judgments (Sedgwick, 1973). The combination of the virtual size in the pictorial space with relational information could have resulted in near perfect judgments as relational size is not affected by magnification.

Effects of Shear

There are few experiments on the effects of the shear transformation on pictorial space perception, perhaps because of the relative complexity of these geometrically predicted transformations of virtual space. To our knowledge, there are no studies of the effects of shear on the perception of distance or orientation. The existing studies address themselves to questions of relative size and shape perception.

Perkins (1972, 1973) conducted two studies providing information about the effects of shear transformation on the perception of shape. In the first, Perkins (1972) had individuals judge whether drawn parallelopipeds were rectangular or nonrectangular—their judgments were highly accurate. Line drawings of boxes were constructed so that half of them could not have been geometric projections of rectangular parallelopipeds. In general, a line drawing of a box could be a representation of a rectangular solid only when the drawing could have been the geometric projection of a rectangular object. Perkins suggested that in the perception of shape, the visual system imposes geometric regularities (such as symmetry and rectangularity) on the object, but only to the extent that such regularities are consistent with the geometric projection. Thus, the structure of the pictorial array sets a limit on the perception of stimulus regularities.

In a second experiment, Perkins (1973) used the identical stimulus materials, but had his observers view the pictures obliquely from angles 41° (.72 rad) or 26° (.45 rad) relative to the picture plane. As in the previous experiment, the observers' task was to judge whether the represented box was rectangular. These specific, oblique-viewing angles were chosen to determine the effect of the pictorial array on the judgment. Under these viewing conditions, boxes that were orthogonally rectangular (i.e., satisfied a geometric criterion of rectangularity when viewed normally) could be either rectangular or nonrectangular in the virtual space. Similarly, some of the orthogonally nonrectangular boxes (i.e., not meeting the rectangularity criterion under normal viewing) could be rectangular or not in the virtual space. Thus, Perkins was able to create a conflict situation between the virtual object specified by the pictorial array and the object represented in the drawing.

There are several noteworthy aspects of the Perkins data. First, the accuracy of judgment (defined as judgments in accordance with the orthogonal classification, or in accordance with the depiction) was less accurate during oblique viewing. Generally, the transformation of the virtual shape of the object did affect perceptual judgments. However, this conclusion must be qualified. When the picture was viewed at 41° (.72 rad) from the picture plane, there was no effect of the virtual space on judgment. Whether the virtual object projected to the eye was rectangular or not, did not affect judgments. It is clear then, as Perkins points out, that in this case subjects were unaffected by or able to discount the effects of the projective transformation of the virtual space induced by the dislocation of the viewing point. In the 26° (.45 rad) viewing condition, however, the conflict between the orthogonal and virtual object resulted in substantially inferior performance. There was clear evidence that in the 26° condition the perception of shape was affected by the structure of the virtual space. Thus, the perception of shape is partly determined by nonoptical factors and is not in simple correspondence with the virtual space, but geometric transformation does exert some influence on judgment.

PERCEPTUAL COMPENSATION FOR GEOMETRIC DISTORTION

It is unfortunate that there is some inconsistency among studies performed in the past. Under some conditions, space perception of transformed pictures seems to be directly influenced by the geometry of the virtual space represented by the pictorial array. Other research indicates that factors in addition to the simple geometry of the virtual space affect perception. Of course, the differences among studies must be directly related to display content and viewing conditions. Unfortunately, many of the early experiments are not sufficiently descriptive to allow us to unequivocally explain discrepancies among studies. Some provide virtually no information regarding viewing conditions, and others provide insufficient descriptions to allow a determination of exactly what information was available to the observer.

There are, however, certain common threads throughout the literature suggestive of certain constraints on the operation of a compensation process. First, it appears that perception of familiar objects or objects within a familiar spatial context is relatively unaffected by distortion of virtual space. Familiarity apparently overrides distortions in the array. Second, perception seems to be in greater correspondence with the virtual space when picture plane cues are eliminated or minimized, or when the optic distortion is not induced by changes in viewing point (as in Purdy's experiment).

We can see why familiarity and/or availability of display plane information moderates the effect of distortion by analyzing the nature of pictorial perception. Operations and states involved are represented in Figure 4.7. In the simplest case, there exists an environment represented in the display. If the display is viewed from the station point, the transformation is an isomorphic one and virtual space and environmental

FIGURE 4.7. A minimal set of operations and states involved in perceptual compensation for distortion in virtual space.

space are identical. Perceived space corresponds to environmental space within the limits of the pick-up process, and there is no need for any compensation. This is, of course, the simplest circumstance, and one that corresponds to one aspect of the Gibsonian position.

The intriguing problem occurs when we introduce a transformation. How is it possible for perceived space to correspond to the environmental rather than the virtual space? One trivial possibility is that familiarity overrides any distortion of virtual space. For example, we know somehow that this is a picture of our friend and see her despite the distortion. This is scarcely perception, of course, but more like social cognition.

As a second method of accounting for "compensation phenomena," this chapter hypothesizes a passive perceptual mechanism that renders the visual system relatively insensitive to distortions of virtual space. There are at least two related ways that this could be passively accomplished, either through perceptual persistence or categorization. This chapter proposes a situation analogous to that reported by Julesz (1971) for binocular vision. In stereopsis, if two stereogram halves are fused, disparity may be increased well beyond Panum's area before diplopia results. In similar fashion, once an object, scene, or spatial relationship is identified or categorized, distortions of virtual space must be extreme before they affect judgments.

Although he is not explicit on this point, this would appear to be a type of mechanism consistent with the findings of Perkins (1973). Perkins suggested that there is a minimal geometric criterion for rectangularity. Consider a two-dimensional line drawing in which three lines meet at a point. For this configuration to be a geometrically possible projection of a rectangular corner, the three angles must all be greater than 90°; or in a special case, two of the angles must be exactly 90°.

If an object satisfied this minimal criterion, it would be seen as rectangular. Subjects viewed pictures of boxes from viewing angles of 41° (.72 rad) or 26° (.45 rad) from the picture plane. When the picture was viewed from the 26° (.45 rad) location, judgments were strongly affected by the virtual space. Such results suggest that, for certain familiar objects such as parallelopipeds, categorical perception may occur. As Pirenne (1970) has suggested, shifting perceived shape away from the familiar category may take a substantial distortion of virtual space.

It seems also that such a view would be consistent with a recent portion of Gibson's theorizing. He holds that under certain conditions (correct viewing?) the pictorial array can act as a surrogate source of information. Under other circumstances (those in which projective equivalence is lacking) pictures may simply function as mediators or symbols for objects or spatial environments. We also acknowledge that one aspect of the perception of pictorial distortion may simply be a case of pattern matching or categorical judgment.

However, a more interesting aspect of compensation is how an unfamiliar scene might be treated. It could be recognized as a scene via pattern matching, but details of layout are not given in the categorization of unfamiliar landscapes. The observer has available only the virtual scene projected to the eye. Accurate perceptual judgments corresponding to the environmental space require knowledge of the transformation operating on the scene. However, such knowledge is not available in the optic array. There is an infinity of distortions or transformations and none of them can be determined for an unfamiliar scene solely on the basis of the virtual space. If judgments do not conform to the virtual space but show a correspondence to the environmental space, the transformation must be estimated by the visual system even though there may be no mathematically sufficient basis for the estimate. The importance of display plane information suggests that the ability to determine viewing point relative to the display affects this estimate.

We propose, as an explanation of pictorial compensation, an active perceptual process that undoes or discounts the effects of distortions of virtual space. There are several necessary characteristics of such a process. Ideally, such an active compensation mechanism would operate when virtual space distortions were present, but not when virtual and environmental space were isomorphic. Yet, as we have pointed out, there is no way that one can tell that virtual space is distorted without having knowledge of the correct environmental space. The operation of an active compensation process must depend, then, on certain assumptions and inferences about viewing pictures.

Such an active process would operate when the actual viewing point (given by stereopsis, parallax, accommodation, etc.) did not correspond to the assumed correct viewing point. Assumptions regarding the correct viewing location could be based on a variety of experiential or optical considerations. For example, paintings, drawings, and photographs are often prepared for viewing from a point along a perpendicular to the center of the display. Consequently, the center of projection may correctly be assumed to be along a line normal to the display plane.

Distance along this line may be given by experience or optical clarity. For example, standard print formats have evolved so as to insure that they subtend approximately the same angle at the standard viewing distances. Approximately the same distance relationships are given in considering the fidelity of televised pictures. For standard television displays, signal to noise ratios are highest at viewing distances of approximately twice the height of the display. Thus, for both photographic and electronic displays, presentation conditions may lead to an assumed correct viewing point along a line perpendicular to the center of the display and at a distance of twice the display height.

Such a set of assumptions provides a specification of the correct viewing point in terms of the relationship to the picture plane. It is important to point out certain important consequences of the assumptive approach. First, it is obvious that such assumptions are learned on the basis of exposure to specific displays. Children or others with restricted experience may not have developed such abilities. In much the same fashion, technological and cultural differences may affect specific learning. For example, use of a different video standard (e.g., the European standard) gives slightly different signal-to-noise ratios as a function of distance, which may cause assumptions regarding video displays to be somewhat altered. Individuals deprived of pictorial experience may have no learned assumptions about pictorial viewing; their picture perception may be based totally on the virtual space or on pattern matching. For them, space perception in pictures may simply be a case of pattern matching of virtual space.

Additionally, it is necessary to acknowledge that the various compensation mechanisms proposed here are interrelated. For example, both familiarity with, and assumptions about the environmental space could contribute to the estimation of the correct viewing point. If certain assumptions are made about what is depicted, the range of potentially correct viewing points is greatly reduced. Consider a display containing two surfaces meeting in a dihedral angle. The lines from the viewer's eye to the two implied vanishing points must meet at the same angle as the two planes. Therefore, if it were assumed that the corner were rectangular, the possible correct distance of the viewing point would be constrained to one value. Similarly, if it is assumed that a plane is perpendicular to the frontal plane, then the correct viewing point must lie along a line perpendicular to the implied horizon. In this way, perceptual assumptions about the nature of surfaces and orientations could indicate positions for the correct viewing point. Deviations from such an assumed correct point could be the basis for compensation.

If compensation is based on an assumed, correct viewing point relative to the picture plane, the availability of picture plane information should affect the degree of compensation. Recently, we have completed several experiments in our laboratories which bear on these various mechanisms for pictorial compensation. In the first, observers were required to make modulus-free magnitude estimates of the sizes of objects depicted in photographs. The objects were gray, square parallelopipeds, 6 cm in height and varying in width. The photos were prepared using a 4 × 5 view camera so that three facets of the object were visible, and the center of projection was 25 cm away from the center of the photograph. The photographs were viewed at distances of 25 cm, 50 cm, or 75 cm by observers whose heads were held motionless in a chin rest (photos were held motionless on an optic bench). All viewing was binocular, with the matted photograph held in a rectangular frame.

The three viewing conditions employed in this study correspond to magnifications of 1.0, 0.5, and 0.33. The effects of such viewing conditions on virtual spaces are easily determined. Using the rationale presented earlier, minification results in an expansion of virtual space so that the width of the object is affected. The precise amounts of geometric expansion under these three conditions are presented in Table 4.1.

Although the estimates of the subjects were in abstract, nonmetric units, we can easily determine the relationship between environmental, virtual, and perceived space. It is well known that the relationship between the magnitude estimate of size and physical extent is linear (i.e., a power function with an exponent of 1.0 [Marks, 1974]). If perceptual compensation for viewing point occurred, all functions should be linear

TABLE 4.1
Actual Size and Virtual Size of Object under Two Minifications

Actual size $(m = 1.0)$	Virtual size $(m = 0.5)$	Virtual size $(m = 0.33)$
1.0	1.56	2.21
1.5	2.34	3.31
2.0	3.14	4.41
2.5	3.90	5.52
3.0	4.68	6.62
3.5	5.46	7.73
4.0	6.24	8.83
4.5	7.02	9.94
5.0	7.80	11.04
5.5	8.59	12.14
6.0	9.37	13.25
6.5	10.15	14.35
7.0	10.93	15.46
7.5	11.71	16.56
8.0	12.49	17.67
8.5	13.27	18.77
9.0	14.06	19.89
9.5	14.86	21.00
10.00	15.61	22.10

with a slope of 1.0. If the perceived space matches the virtual space, we should expect slopes equivalent to the relationships in Table 4.1. That is, with $k = 1.0$, the slope should be 1.0; with $k = 0.5$, the slope would be 1.40; and with $k = 0.3$, the slope should be 1.99.

The results of this experiment are presented in Figure 4.8. It is immediately clear from the figure that almost complete compensation occurred. There was essentially no effect of the virtual space relationship on judgment. Almost identical results were obtained using line drawings that were projectively equivalent to the edges of the objects in the photograph. Figure 4.9 depicts those data. Although different subjects were used, and consequently a different modulus is evident, almost identical relationships are obtained. It is clear that almost complete compensation takes place for expansion of virtual space due to minification.

One difficulty with these results is that although we are assured that compensation occurred, we have no means of determining its basis. Given the experimental conditions, any or all of the mechanisms discussed above could have been operating. For example, the objects may have been categorized as rectangular regardless of the virtual space, and subjects' estimates based on shape relationships. Or an assumption about the correct viewing point could have been made based on picture plane location or on vanishing point relationships. In order to avoid such difficulties, and to determine more precisely the extent and nature of pictorial compensation, we have undertaken several other experiments examining other indicators of perceptual accuracy.

One consequence of the expansion compensation of space resulting from changes in the viewing point involves changes in virtual orientation. Magnification makes the virtual orientation of surfaces more frontal, minification makes it less frontal. Therefore, to evaluate the nature of compensation for distortion, we have used observer's direct-scale estimates of orientation of lattices. In our studies of magnifications, slanted lattices were computer-generated and displayed on a television screen (CRT). Observers viewed the display binocularly and made direct estimates of orientation in degrees, expressing their responses on a computer keyboard. The convention was adopted with 90° being the frontal, and orientations with the top edge further away were denoted as less than 90°. In the first experiment, observers always viewed the display from 112 cm; however, the correct center of proportion across conditions was 28, 56, 84, 112, 225, 337, and 450 cm. Thus, 7° of magnification ($k = 4.0$ to $k = 0.25$) were induced. The virtual orientation of surfaces under these magnification ratios is depicted in Figures 4.10 and 4.11. No independent information for the slant of the lattice was available, and the distance between viewer and display was constant. Consequently, the exact nature of the transformation and its degree is not specified optically. Under such conditions, one expects that judgments would be determined

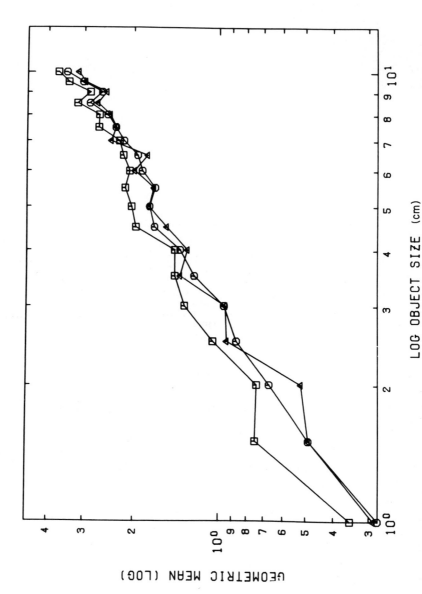

FIGURE 4.8. Mean magnitude estimates (log scale) as a function of object size. Viewing distance is a parameter. Data collected for photographs. (○, 75 cm; △, 50 cm; □, 25 cm.)

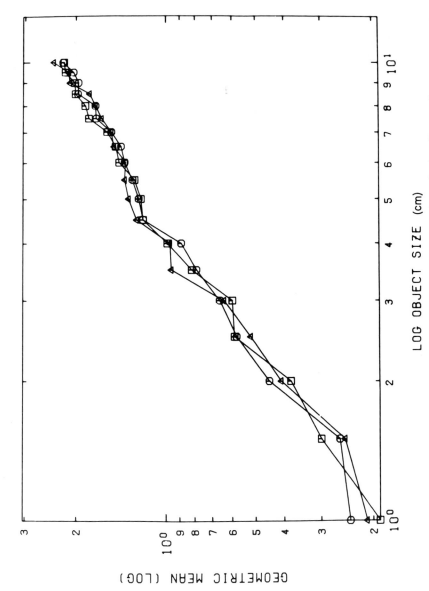

FIGURE 4.9. Mean magnitude estimates (log scale) as a function of object size. Viewing distance is a parameter. Data collected for line drawings. (△, 75 cm; ○, 50 cm; □, 25 cm.)

163

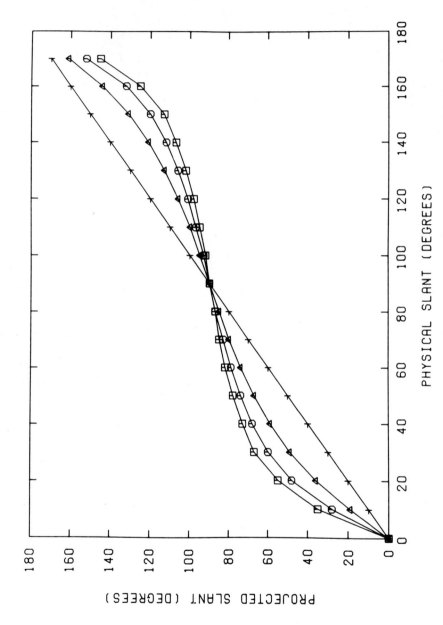

FIGURE 4.10. Virtual surface orientation as a function of physical orientation and degree of magnification. (□, M = 4.0; ○, M = 3.0; △, M = 2.0; +, M = 1.0.)

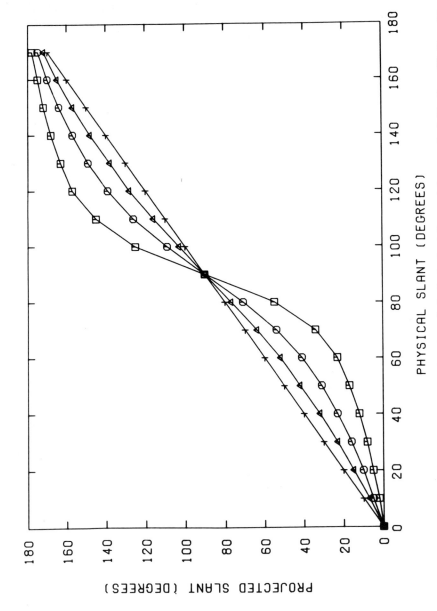

FIGURE 4.11. Virtual surface orientation as a function of physical orientation and degree of minification. (□, M = .25; ○, M = .50; △, M = .75; +, M = 1.0.)

by and in correspondence with virtual space, at least within limits imposed by familiar size and shape.

The data for this experiment are depicted in Figure 4.12 for magnifications, and in Figure 4.13 for minifications. It is evident from comparison of these figures that the range of judgment is restricted. As has been verified in numerous experiments, slant judgments in a variety of experimental circumstances tend to be more frontal than is specified by the virtual space. Such a tendency is evidenced in the figures, as none of the mean judgments occur below the slope (1.0) line. The reduced range of judgment in the present case is probably the result of the conflict between monocular perception and binocular information for the display plane. However, there is no doubt that, within the general accuracy constraints for slant perception, virtual space exerts a significant influence on perception. For the most extreme minification of .25, the relationship between judgments and geographic slant is primarily linear with a slope of approximately .8. For the most extreme magnification, the relationship is cubic. It is worth pointing out that based solely on the geometry of the virtual space, virtual slants are shifted toward the frontal with magnification. The existence of such a shift in judged orientation suggests that perception was heavily influenced by the virtual space. Because of the degree of correspondence between virtual and perceived space, we conclude that no active compensation is evident under conditions that provide neither an assumptive nor informational basis for the geometric distortion.

A second experiment provided similar optical magnifications, but by varying the viewing-point location in this experiment, lattices were computer generated with the correct viewing point 112 cm from the screen. Magnification or minification was induced by having the participants view the display from distances of 28, 56, 112, 225, 337, and 450 cm. Again, 7 degrees of magnification were induced ranging from $k = 4.0$ to $k = 0.25$. Optically, the virtual spaces were equivalent to those used in the previous experiment. However, the amount of magnification was perfectly related to the viewer distance specified by binocular vision, convergence, and accommodation. Again, observers made direct-scale estimates of orientation. The results are depicted in Figures 4.14 and 4.15. Although there is a small condition effect in the higher slants, it can easily be seen that all conditions virtually overlap. Although the virtual orientation differs by as much as 70° over conditions, perceived orientation scarcely differs at all.

We take these results as the first demonstration of total compensation for magnification. Note the description as *total* rather than perfect. Compensation is obviously not perfect, because the perceived space does not match the environmental space. But the psychophysical functions are isomorphic, and they are apparently uninfluenced by virtual orientation,

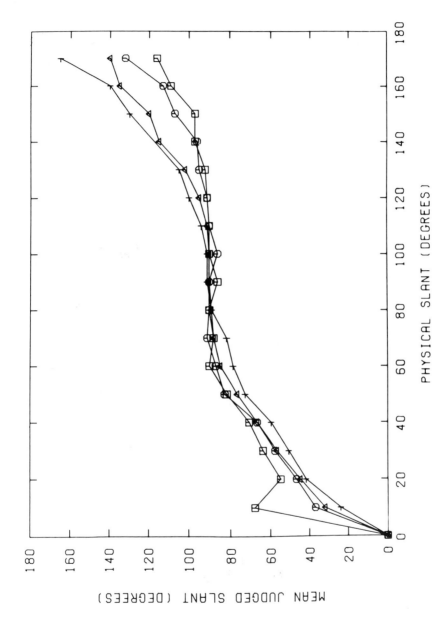

FIGURE 4.12. Perceived orientation of physical slants under magnification. (□, M = 4.0; ○, M = 3.0; △, M = 2.0; +, M = 1.0.)

PHYSICAL SLANT (DEGREES)

MEAN JUDGED SLANT (DEGREES)

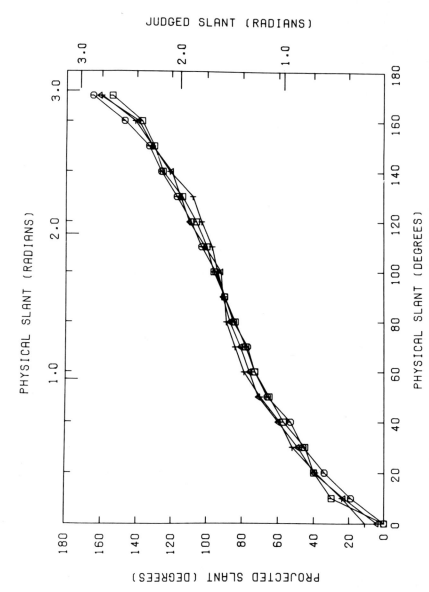

FIGURE 4.13. Perceived orientation of physical slants under minification. (□, M = .25; ○, M = .50; △, M = .75; +, M = 1.0.)

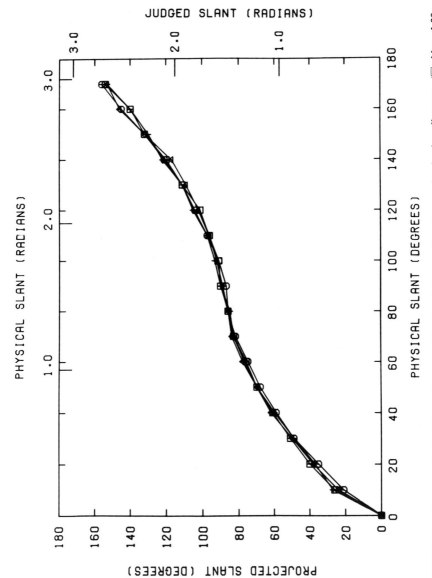

FIGURE 4.14. Perceived orientation when magnification is induced by changes in viewing distance. (□, M = 4.00; ○, M = 2.00; △, M = 1.33; +, M = 1.00.)

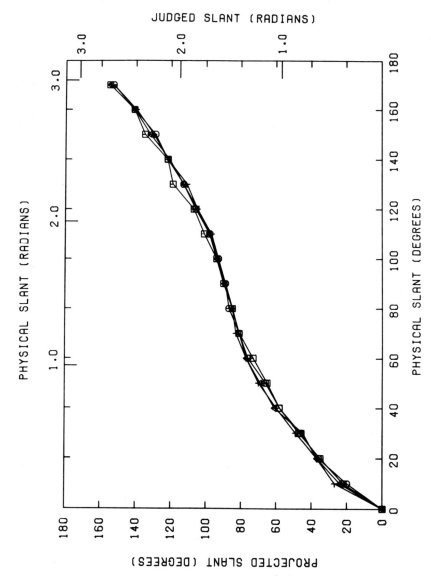

FIGURE 4.15. Perceived orientation when minification is induced by changes in viewing distance. (□, M = .25; ○, M = .33; △, M = .50; +, M = 1.00.)

therefore, although compensation is not perfectly accurate, it is complete.

The particular form of this function is not linear as would be expected if judgments did perfectly match the environmental slant. Rather, a specific cubic form is shared by all 7 magnification conditions. This clearly indicates that different amounts of compensation occur depending on magnification, or viewing distance. Seven viewing distances were used, and all functions overlapped. This implies that distortion was estimated relative to a single, assumed, correct viewing point and each actual viewing distance is compared to this value in computing the amount of distortion to be compensated for. Any active compensation process would only be effective if it were modulated by the amount of distortion.

An interesting question involves the location for the assumed, correct viewing point for these televised displays. A comparison of the data with the virtual orientations depicted in Figures 4.10 and 4.11 reveals that all conditions correspond to a virtual space for a magnification of 2.0. As in all conditions the center of projection was located at 112 cm, the judgments correspond to the virtual orientation projected to 56 cm. We can provide a speculation as to why 56 cm appears to be the assumed correct point for the CRT display. Because the display screen was approximately 27-cm high, the assumed correct point is at a distance of twice the height of the display. As we pointed out earlier, this distance is also optimal in terms of providing a maximal signal-to-noise ratio for conventional TV displays. It may be that with video displays, an observer learns an assumed correct viewing point on the basis of optical picture clarity. One implication of this inference is that assumed correct points may vary depending on the nature of the display and one's experience with it. The extent of such idiosyncracies, or even their existence, has yet to be determined. However, a basic conclusion regarding magnification can be drawn from this particular set of studies. If the nature of the distortion can not be estimated, virtual orientation influences perceived orientation. If viewing distance is perceptually specified, the location of the viewing point combined with an assumed correct point for that display modulates an active compensation process.

We have, in addition, found evidence of almost total compensation for the effects of shear on surface orientation. As we showed in the derivation presented, the virtual slant (θ') of a surface with physical slant θ, is affected by rotation of the picture plane, δ, as in Equation 7.

To determine whether virtual orientation affected perception, we required college students to view a photograph of a slanted, striped surface, and make judgments of surface orientation under two conditions. In the first condition, viewing was monocular, through an aperture, and the photographic display was placed in a viewing box with no rectangular frame present. In this situation, subjects viewed the photographic displays along a horizontal line of sight that was either perpendicular to the center, or was at an angle of 135° (2.36 rad). Judgments corresponded to virtual orientation (see Figure 4.16). In the second condition, subjects viewed the identical stimulus displays binocularly, while the displays were held in a rectangular frame in a lighted room. Viewing was along a horizontal line of sight either 135° (2.36 rad) or 45° (.79 rad) from the display plane. Although the virtual surface orientations differed by as much as 90° from the two viewing points, judgments of orientation did not differ at all (see Figure 4.17). Furthermore, judgments from both the 135° and 45° viewing position were primarily linear with no higher order components, and the relationship between judged slant and physical slant was essentially equivalent to that obtained with normal viewing. Thus, a shear transformation affects perception greatly when display plane information is minimized, but compensation for shear is total if adequate display-plane information is available.

These results suggest that compensation for display plane orientation occurs when the viewing angle from the eye to the display varies from some system reference value. Such a set of picture-viewing assumptions would account for the operation of a compensation process. This chapter

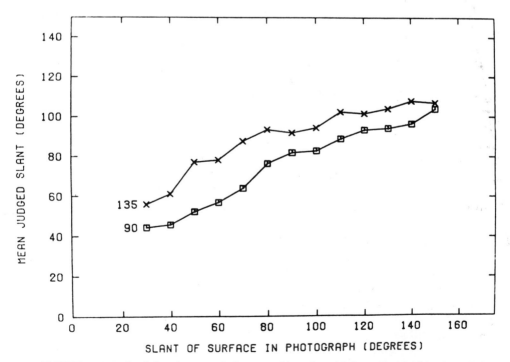

FIGURE 4.16. Judged slant in rotated pictures with reduced information for location of picture plane.

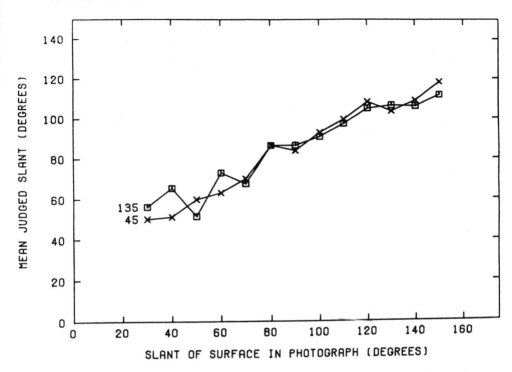

FIGURE 4.17. Judged slant in rotated pictures with complete information for picture plane location.

proposes that this process is relatively simple and discounts the effects of viewing-point dislocations. Consider a situation in which an individual makes judgments of the orientation of a surface while viewing a display that is slanted relative to the line of sight. As θ' is specified by surface gradients, and δ by binocular vision or frame perspective, exact correspondences for θ could be determined using the relationship defined in equation 7.

Although such a process may appear rather complex, a function of the sort described above is necessary. In our experiment, virtual orientation was a curvilinear function of environmental orientation when the display plane is viewed at a slant. Yet for both the 45° (.79 rad) and 135° (2.36 rad) viewing angles, judgments of orientation were collinear without higher order components. This indicates that the compensation process is a nonlinear one, and also indicates that simple differences between θ and δ can not be the basis of compensaion.

The present hypothesis can also account for the paradox of picture-in-a-picture perception (Pirenne, 1970). Consider a slanted surface viewed directly with a horizontal line of regard, then surface slant (θ) equals projected slant (θ'). If a photograph of the surface is viewed from the wrong station point, the projected slant θ' is a function of surface slant (θ) and angle δ as given by Equation 7. If this photograph is itself photographed and the second photo is viewed from the wrong station point, a second transformation occurs, and projected slant, θ'', is a function of θ', θ, δ, and δ'. The paradox results from the fact that it is apparently difficult to compensate for the transformation while viewing the second photo. If the second photograph is viewed from its correct station point, a situation geometrically equivalent to that in the previous experiment is obtained, and compensation could only occur if δ (the inclination of the first photograph relative to the optical axis of the camera taking the second picture) is known (see Pirenne's Figures 8.1 and 8.2 in this regard). Two transformations occur when the second photograph is viewed from the wrong station point and compensation (i.e., accurate perception of θ) requires accurate estimates of θ'', θ', and δ', and δ. Consequently, errors in estimating any of these parameters will result in errors of compensation. Additionally, as the two transformations involve nested calculations, such errors will be exaggerated. Furthermore, because binocular or ocular cues do not specify the orientation of the first picture relative to the second picture or relative to the observer, an estimate of δ may be unavailable to the observer.

A similar process can be proposed based on the assumed content of the display rather than the assumed viewing relationships. For a familiar object, the discrepancy between θ' (registered) and θ (assumed) is an indicator of δ. This value of δ can then be used in applying compensation processes to other objects and surfaces depicted in the display. There is evidence that such assumptions regarding context can affect compensation. Cooper (unpublished) required adults to judge rectangularity of parallelopipeds that were distorted in virtual space by a shear. When the object was included in the display so that its edges and sides were parallel to the corners and walls of the room (also in the display), judgments were essentially perfect. When the position of the target was altered so that edges and sides were not parallel to the room's corners and walls, judgmental accuracy decreased. The relationship between the distorted objects and the reference axes provided by the assumed rectangularity of the room provided a way to discount distortions of virtual space.

In summary, the lack of a strict correspondence between perceived and virtual space, coupled with the existence of correspondences between environmental and perceived space suggest that pictorial perception involves a unique visual compensation process. We propose two possible mechanisms involved in such compensation. First, a simple, passive pattern matching may be involved. Once an object or pattern meets certain minimal criteria, categorization occurs. Extreme distortions are necessary before such categorization can be overcome.

Second, we propose the existence of an active perceptual compensation process that discounts optical distortions caused by changes in the viewing point. Because there is no optical information for the correctness of viewing point, such compensation must be based on assumptions regarding appropriate viewing conditions for representational displays. Our research indicates that observers can compensate for both the effects of shear and magnification on spatial layout. Our data suggest that compensation is a nonlinear process, modulated by the difference between actual and assumed correct-viewing points. The actual location of these assumed correct points, and the way such assumptions develop, are clearly two important issues for future work in pictorial space perception.

ACKNOWLEDGMENTS

Preparation of this chapter was partially supported by The Office of Naval Research, Engineering Psychology Programs, under Contract No. N00014-77-1-0679 to Richard R. Rosinski.

REFERENCES

Evans, R. M. *Eye, film, and camera in color photography.* New York: Wiley, 1960.

Farber, J. & Rosinski, R. R. Geometric transformations of pictured space. *Perception*, 1978, *7*, 269–282.

Gibson, J. J. A theory of pictorial perception. *Audio-Visual Communications Review 1*, 1951, 1–23.

Gibson, J. J. The information available in pictures. *Leonardo*, 1971, *4*, 27–35.

Haber, R. N. Visual perception. In M. R. Rosinzweig & L. W. Porter (Eds.), *Annual Review of Psychology*, 1978, *29*, 31–59.

Hagen, M. A. Picture perception: Toward a theoretical model. *Psychological Bulletin*, 1974, *81*, 471–497.

Julesz, B. *Foundations of cyclopean perception.* Chicago: Univ. Chicago Press, 1971.

Marks, L. E. *Sensory processes.* New York: Academic Press, 1974.

Perkins, D. N. Visual discrimination between rectangular and nonrectangular parallelopipeds. *Perception & Psychophysics*, 1972, *12*, 396–400.

Perkins, D. N. Compensating for distortion in viewing pictures obliquely. *Perception & Psychophysics*, 1973, *14*, 13–18.

Pirenne, M. H. *Optics, painting, & photography.* Cambridge: Cambridge Univ. Press, 1970.

Purdy, W. C. *The hypothesis of psychophysical correspondence in space perception.* Ithaca, New York: General Electric Advanced Electronics Center, September, 1960. (NTIS No. R60ELC56).

Rosinski, R. R. Picture perception and monocular vision: A reply to Hagen. *Psychological Bulletin*, 1974, *83*, 1172–1175.

Schlosberg, H. Stereoscopic depth from single pictures. *American Journal of Psychology*, 1941, *54*, 601–605.

Sedgwick, H. A. *The visible horizon: Potential source of visual information for the perception of size and distance.* Unpublished doctoral dissertation, Cornell University, 1973. (University Microfilms No. 73–22, 530)

Smith, O. W. Comparison of apparent depth in a photograph viewed from two distances. *Perceptual and Motor Skills,* 1958, *8,* 79–81. (a)

Smith, O. W. Judgments of size and distance in photographs. *The American Journal of Psychology,* 1958, *71,* 529–538. (b)

Smith, O. W., & Gruber, H. Perception of depth in photographs. *Perceptual and Motor Skills,* 1958, *8,* 307–313.

Smith, P. C., & Smith, O. W. Ball throwing responses to photographically portrayed targets. *Journal of Experimental Psychology,* 1961, *62,* 223–233.

PART II

APPLICATIONS AND LIMITATIONS OF THE PROJECTIVE MODEL OF PICTORIAL INFORMATION

CHAPTER **5**   SAMUEL Y. EDGERTON, JR.

The Renaissance Artist as Quantifier

Introduction 179
Renaissance Art Influences Scientific Development 180
The Unique Characteristics of Renaissance Art 181
Renaissance Art verus Eastern Art 185
Renaissance Art and the Advent of the Printing Press 189
   The Exploded View 192
   The Transparent View 195
   Applications of Illustrative Techniques 197
Conclusion 211

INTRODUCTION

More than 20 years ago, in a memorable symposium at the Metropolitan Museum of Art in New York, the late, great art historian Erwin Panofsky delivered one of his dazzling lectures, grandly entitled, "Artist, scientist, humanist; Notes on the Renaissance Dämmerung."[1] In this performance,

---

[1] Panofsky's lecture was delivered in 1952 and published by the Metropolitan Museum of Art in *The Renaissance, a symposium, February 8–10, 1952,* New York, 1953. A revised and expanded version was published again in Wallace K. Ferguson *et al, Six Essays . . . The Renaissance,* New York, 1962, pp. 121–182.

179

Panofsky laid down a thesis that Renaissance art and Renaissance artists were a necessary ingredient to the oncoming scientific revolution of the seventeenth century. If the fifteenth and sixteenth centuries in Western Europe were not in themselves the *loci* of modern science, the artists of that period, with their abilities to render *chiaroscuro* (the illusion of the third dimension through shading) and linear perspective, at least achieved a "decompartmentalization" (Panofsky's word) of the old medieval categories of things, and then recompartmented the natural and physical world into forms preparatory for the true scientific study that followed.

Seven years later, Harcourt Brown responded to Panofsky in another memorable lecture, more modestly entitled, "The Renaissance and historians of science."[2] Brown advised that Panofsky was wrong, even "silly" as he put it, to suggest that scientists ever depended on pictures for their inspiration. Art, even Renaissance art, Brown stated, is essentially "intuitional." Any intuitional experience, he emphasized, is *ipso facto* unscientific. Professor Brown went on:

> For the scientist, if a statement is not mathematical, exact, impersonal, objective, capable of producing identical meaning in all hearers, referring to cumulative and repeatable effects, it is not scientific. For him, interesting, disconnected statements about the world in general, inexact, subjective, asking the use of intuition, special insights, do not count as science even if they are impressive and present exciting interpretations of phenomena.[3]

And Brown continued further:

> [The scientist is] not interested in the diagram, the visual statement. . .however accurate or in perspective. . .but in what can be done with it, how it [can be] used, improved on, not artistically, but as a tool in the quite special enterprize that is science [because] the scientist is not interested in the. . .object. . .except as it leads him to knowledge of the class or classes of objects of which the individual is a member. He does not, *qua* scientist, stand still to admire the object without reference to larger issues which the characteristics of the object reveal.[4]

RENAISSANCE ART INFLUENCES SCIENTIFIC DEVELOPMENT

Now, I would say that Harcourt Brown missed Panofsky's point, which was that Renaissance art was different from all other art *because* it conformed almost exactly to Brown's own definition of a scientific statement.

[2] Brown's paper was first delivered at the New England Renaissance Conference, Brown University, on October 16, 1959, and was first published in *Studies in the Renaissance*, 1960, 7, pp. 27–42.

[3] Brown, *Studies in the Renaissance*, p. 30.

[4] Brown, *Studies in the Renaissance*, p. 33.

Nevertheless, many historians of science, modern scientists, and even psychologists still think brown's argument is correct. "What proof has ever been presented," they ask, "that Galileo [even though he lived in Renaissance Florence, expressed a firmly favorable opinion of Renaissance art, and was something of a Renaissance drarfsman himself] ever depended on a Renaissance picture as he developed his theories of motion and the heliocentric universe?" "What proof has ever been given that William Harvey [even though he studied medicine in Padua not long after Vesalius had produced his great illustrated treatise on anatomy there] ever needed a Vesalian diagram to formulate his theory about the circulation of the blood?" Unfortunately, these questions must be answered even by me in the negative. If revolutionary scientists such as Galileo and Harvey were inspired by Renaissance pictures, they left us no *written* record.

What must we do then—we who are convinced that Renaissance art did influence science on the eve of the scientific revolution? We have not been successful so far in convincing our scientist colleagues that the *visual* document (i.e., the contemporaneous picture) should carry the same weight as a written affidavit. How may we build a convincing case, on the basis of pictorial evidence alone, that the scientific revolution begining in Florence, Italy with Galileo's experiments was no mere accident of place and time? How may we demonstrate that the Renaissance of art in Western Europe and the explosion of modern science had a direct and working relationship?

I would like to propose that instead of trying to discover elusive, one-on-one connections between individual geniuses of Renaissance art and seventeenth-century science, we concentrate our investigations on the shared uniqueness of the Western European scientific *and* artistic revolutions. If everyone recognizes that the scientific revolution of the seventeenth century was a uniquely Western European experience, that nothing like it had ever occurred in other civilizations of the world, then we should re-examine Panofsky's point, that Western Renaissance art was quite as revolutionary, that nothing like *it* had ever occurred in the world before, not even in China or Islam which had equally distinguished traditions in the sciences and the arts. I am not speaking of mere changes in style, a matter which confused Professor Brown, but am considering the possibility that Renaissance art was different in *kind* than any other artistic expression in human history.

THE UNIQUE CHARACTERISTICS OF RENAISSANCE ART

Although Renaissance art certainly had its aesthetic and intuitively subjective side, it also had an application impossible to any other art form no matter how sophisticated or aesthetically beautiful. This was its ability to translate physical objects and their surrounding spaces into geometrical quantities that could be imagined as three-dimensional forms even though figured on a two-dimensional surface. In other words, Renaissance art was capable, as no other art form in human history ever was, in Professor Brown's own words, "of mathematical, exact, impersonal, objective. . .statements. . .producing identical meanings in all [viewers], referring to accumulative and repeatable effects (p. 30)."

Figures 5.1 and 5.2 may make this clearer. They are prints from two sixteenth-century German treatises on drawing in perspective; Hieronymus Rodler and and Johann II of Bavaria, *Ein schön büchlein und unterweisung der Kunst des Messens*, 1531, and Erhard Schön, *Unnderweissung der proporzion*, 1540. In these prints one notes how artists of the time were being taught to think of their pictures as *maps,* with nature represented as fitting to the fixed coordinates of a cartographic grid.[5] Quite obviously, the Renaissance artist, even *"qua* artist," was not just "standing still to admire his object." He was surely concerned with the "larger issues," and even forced the "characteristics of his (depicted) objects to reveal the (mathematical) class or classes of objects to which the individual is a member (p. 33)."

In this sense, Renaissance art was different not only from the preceding arts of the Middle Ages but also the highly sophisticated forms of the East. I did not say *better than,* only qualitatively *different.* The mathematical aspect of Renaissance art also allowed it to be used as a special visual language, more communicative than oral or written language, particularly when describing tangible objects. Although Chinese artists could express ineffable feelings and poetic contemplation in their prictures, they could not represent the purely physical appearance of things as well as Western artists. Once again, I am not making a value judgment about Chinese art vis-à-vis the West. I would only argue that the unique quantifying quality of Western Renaissance art conferred advantage if the artist and his viewer wished only to study the strictly physical appearance of objects in nature.

Art historians can demonstrate that Western European artists were pursuing this quantifying quality as early as the thirteenth century, as is evident in the frescoes of the upper church of St. Francis at Assisi. Figure 5.3 shows a set of three scenes from the *Life of St. Francis* painted about

[5] On the relationship between cartography and art in the fifteenth century, see Samuel Y. Edgerton, Jr., "Florentine interest in Ptolemaic geography as background for Renaissance painting, architecture, and the discovery of America," *Journal for the Society of Architectural Historians,* 1974, *33,* pp. 275–292.

FIGURE 5.1. *Woodcut Print of Artist Drawing a Scene through a Gridded Window.* [*From Hieronymus Rodler and Johann II of Bavaria, Ein schön büchlein und unterweisung der Kunst des Messens, 1531. Photo author.*]

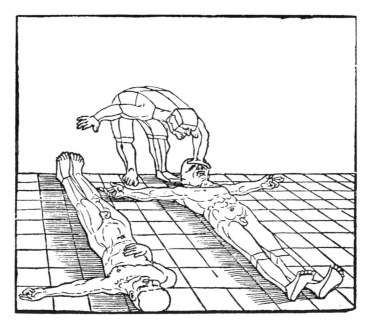

FIGURE 5.2. *Woodcut Print of Human Figures Foreshortened on a Gridded Floor in Perspective.* [*From Erhard Schön, Unnderweisung der proporzion, 1540. Photo author.*]

**FIGURE 5.3. Giotto (?), *Three Frescoed Scenes from the Life of St. Francis of Assisi.* [*From the Upper Church of San Francesco, Assisi, c. 1300. Photo author.*]

1300, perhaps by the Florentine, Giotto. Whoever the artist in these frescoes, he has surely tried to create the illusion that one is looking at real-life scenes as if through a *window*. This window notion had always been a uniquely Western tradition, first applied to picture making by the ancient Greeks and Romans. However, with the influx of Christianity (and new artistic traditions rooted in the East), this concept was forgotten as European artists abandoned their pursuit of illusion in favor of more spiritual expressions. A better explanation is that European artists allowed the picture-as-window idea to slip into a state of suspended animation, revivable, as Panofsky mused, only by Renaissance "warmth and moisture." In any case, the intense religiosity of late-medieval Europeans, especially those inspired by the cult of St. Francis, forced artists to resucitate the old Western tradition as a means of giving, literally, a "you are there" experience to people who wanted to have their holy stories brought back to life. In Figure 5.3, one observes, for instance, that all three scenes share a common painted frame. The frame is an illusionary architectural opening that the artist painted in the form of a surmounting cornice on modillions and supported by columns between each story. Although these stories individually show only a naive use of perspective (as was characteristic of medieval art generally), the painted frame clearly indicates that the artist intended the viewer to look at all three pictures together from a single viewpoint in the center. Furthermore, even though the three stories in this set from the *Life of St. Francis* happened at different times and places, the painter showed them as all lighted from the same source (i.e., each figure and object illuminated on its right side and shaded on its left). The frescoes of St. Francis of Assisi were first planned, incidentally, at about the same period that science historians identify as containing the fetal heartbeat of the scientific revolution evidenced in the writings of precocious thinkers associated with the new Franciscan order like Robert Grosseteste and Roger Bacon.

RENAISSANCE ART VERSUS EASTERN ART

I would emphasize again that this notion defined in the paintings at Assisi (i.e., that the picture be thought of as a window) was another uniquely Western idea unshared in the arts of the East. Its effect upon artists and viewers of the time was to force them not only to depict the details in their pictures with optical consistency, but to more closely examine the natural world which served as their model. In other words, they were motivated by the picture-as-window concept to look for, admire, and understand the more physical characteristics of the natural

FIGURE 5.4. Ambrogio Lorenzetti, Fresco Painting of Good Government in the Country. *[From Palazzo Pubblico, Siena, c. 1335. Courtesy of Fratelli Alinari S.P.A., Florence and Editorial Photocolor Archives, Inc., New York, New York.]*

world. We can follow this inexorable logic right on through the fourteenth century. Figure 5.4 is another Italian fresco, this time from the Palazzo Pubblico in Siena, painted by Ambrogio Lorenzetti about 1335. It shows a scene entitled *Good Government in the Country* in which the city walls appear on the left and rolling farmlands on the right of the painting. Overhead (on the left) is a flying female figure holding an inscription, the didactic message of the picture. This inscription is written on a curving scroll. The artist, as he included these words, took care that they were represented according to the same perspective principles as all the other solid objects in his illusionary pictorial space "behind" the fictional window.

The inclusion of such curving scrolls for titles and inscriptions became commonplace in Western art, but there is no such convention in Eastern pictures. For example, see Figure 5.5 a Chinese painting dating from about 1530, by Chou Ch'en, entitled *Dreaming of Immortality in a Thatched Cottage*. It shows a scholar in his hut at the lower right. In his dreamy contemplation he projects himself into the infinite landscape where we see him again, mystically levitated, as he ponders the transcience of nature. Whether the artist intended this lovely mountainscape to be an illusion of extending space or not, he still added the inscription (at the upper left) as if it were perfectly flat, right on the picture surface with no apparent conflict in his mind that the flatness of the inscription contradicted the illusion of pictorial depth. Chinese painters like Chou Ch'en never considered that they should portray nature as if it were seen through a window, and they never felt bound to the consistency the fixed viewpoint demanded of their Western counterparts.

FIGURE 5.5. Shou Ch'en (?), *Scroll Painting of a Scholar Dreaming of Immortality in a Thatched Cottage,* **c. 1530.** [*Courtesy of the Smithsonian Institution, Freer Gallery of Art, Washington, D.C.*]

By the fifteenth century, the Western artistic urge to replicate nature through a window finally forced painters to work out a completely mathematical solution for defining how objects appear behind this window. This was the science of linear perspective, the earliest demonstration of which we can attribute to Filippo Brunelleschi of Florence in about 1425.[6] Figure 5.6 is a developed example of this purely Western European achievement, a painting of *St. Jerome in His Study* by Antonello da Messina from about 1450–1455. It is interesting to compare this masterpiece of the flowering Western Renaissance to Chou Ch'en's masterpiece of Chinese painting, especially as the Scientific Revolution was still years away, and Chinese science and technology at the time was hardly inferior to that of the West.

What these two pictures together show is not just a difference in artistic style, but a monumental difference in attitudes toward nature itself. In the Chinese painting, the philosopher floats mystically in the vapor of infinity. His thoughts, like the rationale for his levitation, transcend the fixed limits of Euclidian geometry—a science that the Chinese did not know until it was introduced to them by the Jesuits in the early seventeenth century. In Antonello's painting, *St. Jerome*, the quintessential Western philosopher sits rationally in a perfectly tangible space, constructed through the use of illusion but according to the same geometrical principles as any real carpentered room. This illusionistic room is filled with light and shadow, according to the exact laws of geometric optics— the same science from which the principles of linear perspective derive. St. Jerome ponders immortality just as his Chinese counterpart; however, in Western Christian thought, the ineffable is fixed and static, conforming to mathematical law. Christian artists, especially after the thirteenth century, were always encouraged to represent it, however mysterious, in terms as palpable and physical as possible. Indeed, the very laws of optics, so beautifully applied in Antonello's painting, were also believed, by the Christian fathers, to explain how God spreads His Divine Grace throughout the universe.

Antonello's *St. Jerome* is the perfect paradigm of a new consciousness of the physical world attained by Western European intellectuals by the late fifteenth century. This consciousness was shared especially by artists such as Leonardo da Vinci, Francesco di Giorgio Martini, Albrecht Dürer, Hans Holbein, and more, all of whom, as we shall see shortly, had even developed a sophisticated "grammar and syntax" for quantifying natural

[6] For an analysis of the cultural milieu and a reconstruction of Brunelleschi's perspective demonstrations, see Edgerton, *The Renaissance Rediscovery of Linear Perspective*, New York, 1975.

FIGURE 5.6. Antonello da Messina, *Oil Painting of St. Jerome in His Study,* c. 1450–1455. [*Courtesy of the Trustees, National Gallery, London.*]

phenomena in pictures. In their hands, picture making was becoming a pictorial language that, with practice, could communicate more information, more quickly, and by a potentially wider audience than any verbal language in human history.

RENAISSANCE ART AND THE ADVENT OF THE PRINTING PRESS

What a fecund coincidence then that the technology of printing arrived in Europe just at the time that Renaissance art, with its *chiaroscuro* and linear perspective, was the prevailing means of pictorial expression. It is a cliché that the advent of movable type revolutionized European education in the sixteenth century and was, therefore, an essential ingredient to the coming Scientific Revolution. In fact, it has been stated boldly, and with many believers, that the printing press changed Europe from an "image culture to a culture of words."[7] Nothing, I argue, could be further from the truth.

Rather, the printing press remade Europe into a wholly new kind of "image culture"—a broad audience receptive to the new geometric pictorial language of the Renaissance. In spite of the great masterpieces of painting and sculpture in the fifteenth century, most Europeans probably were not responsive to these changes in representation until they became popular in printed woodcuts and engravings after 1500. One of the most astounding technical achievements in history was the quick adaptation of Renaissance art to the printmaker's black and white media. I believe that the printed *illustration*, not the printed word, is the reason why the press in the West proved to be an instrument of dramatic change, whereas in China, where printing had been practiced since the ninth century, it had been a force for preserving orthodoxy. In the West, even if the subject of the printed text were unscientific, the printed picture always presented a rational image based on the universal laws of geometry. In this sense, the Scientific Revolution probably owes more to Albrecht Dürer than to Leonardo da Vinci. Figure 5.7 is a characteristic example of Dürer's extraordinary technical mastery of the woodblock medium. It is a print from his *Apocalypse* series published in 1498, showing the scene from Rev. 10: 1–11, where the Apostle John describes a "mighty angel come down from heaven, clothed with a cloud, and a rainbow was upon his head, and his face was as if it were the sun, and his feet as pillars of fire." Dürer has represented this arcane image from the most mystical book of the Bible in a remarkably literal and believable way. He even has the Apostle "eat the book" exactly as the angel commanded.

Leonardo's own ingenious contributions to Renaissance scientific illustration remained, unfortunately, in manuscript form and were seen by only a few *cognoscenti* during the sixteenth century.[8] Had the great Florentine never lived at all, it is probably true that the Scientific Revolution would have carried on exactly as it did. In fact, there were many artists before and during Leonardo's lifetime who, even without his brilliance, were developing the same pictorial conventions. One of these

---

[7] For examples, see Lawrence Stone, "Literacy and education in England, 1640–1900," *Past and Present*, 1969, *42*, p. 78; also Elizabeth L. Eisenstein, "In the wake of the printing press," *The Quarterly Journal of the Library of Congress*, 1978, *35*, p. 184.

[8] For an excellent analysis of Leonardo's ability to think out mechanical problems by drawing pictures, see Bert S. Hall and Ian Bates, "Leonardo, the Chiaravalle clock and a reply to Antonio Simoni," *Antiquarian Horology*, 1976, *9*, pp. 910–917.

FIGURE 5.7. Albrecht Dürer, *Woodcut Print of St. John Devouring the Book,* **c. 1498.** [*Courtesy of the Museum of Fine Arts, Boston.*]

was a relatively obscure Sienese named Mariano di Jacopo called Taccola, who lived and worked from the 1420s through the 1440s and died when Leonardo was but 1 year old.

Taccola also wanted to be a an engineer and visited the great Brunelleschi who cautioned him against plagiarists who would steal his ideas.[9]

---

[9] Some of Taccola's manuscripts have been edited and published by James H. Beck (Ed), *Liber tertius ingeneis ac edifitiis non usitatis di Mariano di Jacopo detto il taccola,* Milan, 1969; Gustina Scaglia (Ed.), *Mariano Taccola de machinis; the Engineering Treatise of 1449; Introduction, Latin Texts, Description of Engines and Technical Commentaries,* Wiesbaden, 1971; Frank D. Prager, "A manuscript of Taccola, quoting Brunelleschi, on problems of inventors and builders," *Proceedings of the American Philosophical Society,* 1968, *92,* pp. 131–150; and Scaglia and Prager, *Mariano Taccola and His Book De Ingeneis,* Cambridge, Mass., 1972.

He was a modest artist who seems not to have been interested in Brunelleschi's epocal perspective demonstrations as such. Nonetheless, he was the first Renaissance draftsman to apply certain concepts inherent in the perspective system to the drawing of complex machinery. Taccola passed his ideas on to his fellow Sienese, Francesco di Giorgio Martini, who in turn gave them to Leonardo da Vinci. At any rate, these sophisticated drawing techniques were already conventionalized and shared among many Renaissance artists before the spread of printing.

The Exploded View

Figures 5.8, 5.9, and 5.10 are of pages from two of Taccola's surviving manuscripts and show sketches of military and various other mechanical

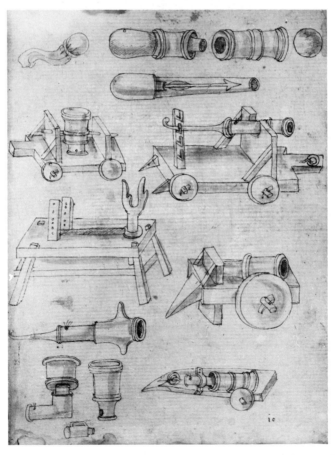

FIGURE 5.8. *Drawings of Military Machines.* [*From Taccola, De ingeneis, ms. Cod. Pal. 766, Biblioteca Nazionale, Florence, c. 1433. Courtesy of Biblioteca Nazionale, Florence.*]

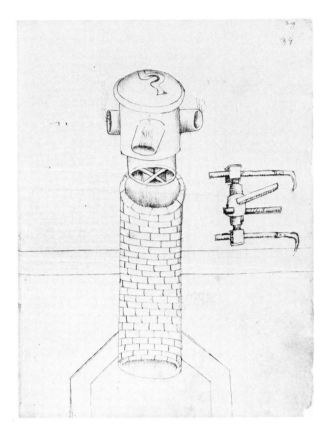

FIGURE 5.9. *Drawing of a Chimney Pot.* [*From Taccola, De ingeneis, ms. Cod. Lat. 197, Bayerische Staatsbibliothek, Munich, c. 1427. Courtesy of the Bayerische Staatsbibliothek, Munich.*]

devices. At the top of the page in Figure 5.8, one sees a drawing of a cannon. In order to make the picture clearer, Taccola tried to depict the cannon as if it were split apart, with the powder chamber pulled away from the barrel and the cannon ball (on the right) suspended in front. Here is, perhaps, one of the first "exploded views"—as modern engineers now term this convention. Oddly enough , linear perspective and *chiaroscuro*, which supply geometric stability to pictures, also allow the viewer a momentary suspension of his dependence on the law of gravity. With a little practice, the viewer can imagine solid volumes floating freely in space as detached components of a device. The viewer need only have some reference to scale and the proper size proportion of the parts of each other, and then he can understand how they fit and function, individually and together.

Figure 5.9 is one of a series of drawings Taccola made showing chimney

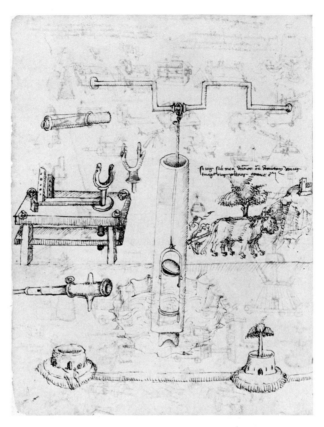

FIGURE 5.10. *Drawing Showing a Suction Pump.* [*From Taccola, De ingeneis, ms. Cod. Lat. 197, Bayerische Staatsbibliothek, Munich, c. 1427. Courtesy of the Bayerische Staatsbibliothek, Munich.*]

pots and fireplaces. In order to prevent downdrafts which cause fireplaces to smoke, Taccola designed devices that diverted the smoke away from the prevailing winds. These were to fit and rotate in the top of chimneys. To show the internal structure of the pot, the artist drew it not only "exploded" above the chimney top, but as if both ends were seen at once, as if each end were rotated away from its true perspective position and turned toward the viewer so that he might inspect both above and below. This "rotated view" can not be dismissed as a symptom of Taccola's poor ability as a draftsman. He employed it purposefully throughout his notebooks. The same convention was later picked up by Francesco di Giorgio Martini, who also used it consistently even though he was a much better artist than Taccola.

The Transparent View

This "Sienese Archimedes," as Taccola liked to be called, developed yet another convention of perhaps even wider applicability than the exploded view. Figure 5.10 shows his design for a suction pump. He has drawn it as a "transparent view" so that the viewer may observe the complexities of the pump-piston inside the encasing cylinder. The artist indicated the cylinder exterior with shading in order to emphasize its three-dimensional shape, but he also allowed the viewer to see through its surface to understand how the flap-valve on the piston head operated (forced open by the water as the piston descends, and be closed as the piston is raised). Taccola's rather crude little drawing was copied again and again by later artisan–engineers who found his transparent view the most convenient way to explain this complex mechanism. In a working model of the suction pump, the essential parts are never seen. Only a transparent view allows one to know what is happening inside the cylinder and what physical principles are affecting the pump's operation.

It is important to consider that Taccola probably designed this suction pump on paper without first building a working model. Indeed, what the new Renaissance pictorial language allowed (and what Taccola may have been the first to exploit) was the ability to design machines solely by means of drawings without asking the patron to finance expensive constructions.[10] One should note that Taccola's suction pump, although theoretically workable, was still not very efficient. He designed the connecting rod or rope to be raised and lowered by a crank. Whether Taccola thought of it or not, the crank makes a rotary motion which would force the piston tight up against the cylinder side-walls on every up and down stroke. Some years later, Francesco di Giorgio Martini added a modification to Taccola's design, and, once again, he may have conceived of this invention entirely on paper. Figure 5.11 is of a page from Francesco di Giorgio's own notebook (circa 1480).[11] In the lower-right corner it shows a complex of suction pumps operated by one reciprocating crank. Francesco, however, carefully compensated for the rotary motion of the crank by designing a loop in the connecting rod for every pump. A hollow

[10] On the basis of this unique drawing, Sheldon Shapiro, in "The origin of the suction pump," *Technology and Culture*, 1965, 5, pp. 571–580, has assumed that Taccola was the first to invent the device. Two other historians of technology have made seminal comments on the importance of pictures to the inventive imagination: Eugene S. Ferguson in "The mind's eye: Nonverbal thought in technology," *Science*, 1977, 26, pp. 827–836; and Bert S. Hall in *Technical treatises 1400–1600: Implications of early non-verbal thought in technology*, Unpublished address read before the Meeting of the Society for the History of Technology, Washington, D.C., October 22, 1977.

[11] Francesco di Giorgio Martini's major manuscripts have been published in facsimile and transcribed by Corrado Maltese and Livia Maltese Degrassi (Eds.), *Francesco di Giorgio Martini, Trattati di architettura ingegneria e arte militare*, Milan, 1967.

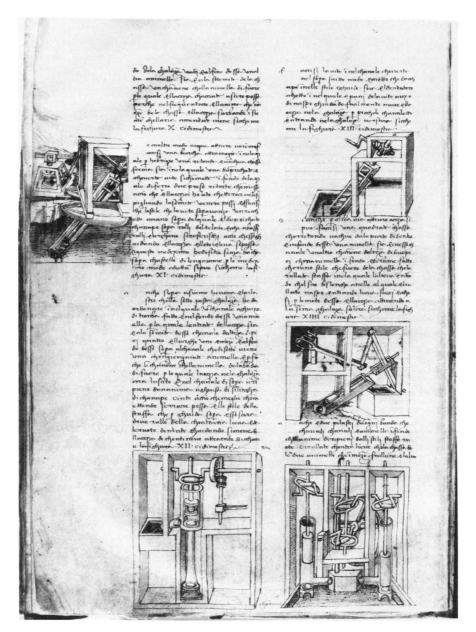

FIGURE 5.11. *Drawings of Water Pumps.* [*From Francesco di Giorgio Martini, Trattato, ms. Cod. Ashb. 361, Biblioteca Laurenziana, Florence, c. 1480. Courtesy of Biblioteca Laurenziana, Florence.*]

roller was also designed around the arm of each crank, which slipped inside the connecting rod loop, thus allowing the connecting rod to move up and down and remain vertical with each crank rotation.

Applications of Illustrative Techniques

The exploded and transparent views (and a more convincing form of the rotated view), first adapted to the new rules of *chiaroscuro* and perspective by Taccola and Francesco di Giorgio Martini, passed into the international, printed pictorial language of the Renaissance during the sixteenth and seventeenth centuries, serving every possible application. Figure 5.12 is of a page from a German-language surgical text published in 1518.[12] The artist, probably Hans Wechtlin of Strasbourg, depicted an open cadaver obviously from "life." Although not exactly a transparent view, the technique produces the same result. Moreover, the artist added exploded views of the head. Wechtlin showed the brain in various stages of removal from the skull, in separate figures suspended about the central drawing.

Figure 5.13 shows yet another application of the transparent and exploded views to a more mechanical situation. This is of a page from Georg Bauer Agricola's *De re metallica*, the classic Latin-language tome on mining and metallurgy first published in 1556.[13] The unknown artist here has modified the transparent view by imagining the earth cut away to expose the mine shaft, similar to Wechtlin's cadaver which was split open to expose the viscera. In this mine shaft is a double suction pump, and the artist has also depicted its parts exploded and disassembled on the surrounding ground, including also a transparent view of the box holding the crank and connecting rods.

Figure 5.14 is an example from Agostino Ramelli's beautifully engraved treatise on machines published in French and Italian in 1588.[14] The plate is of a windlass for raising water from a well. The operator turns a vertical crank which then turns a latern gear beneath the ground but is exposed in a cutaway, transparent view. This gear, lettered "B," rotates another, lettered "C," which is attached to a reel around which is wound a rope.

[12] Published in Laurentius Phryesen (Fries), *Spiegel der Artzney*, Johannes Grüninger Press, Strasbourg, 1518.

[13] Agricola's *De re metallica* has been republished in facsimile with English translation and notes by Herbert Clark Hoover and Lou Henry Hoover, London, 1912 (reissued in New York, 1950).

[14] Ramelli's book has been reprinted in facsimile without translation in Oxford, England, 1975, and in English translation with extensive notes by Eugene S. Fergusen and Martha Teach Gnudi (Eds.), *The various and ingenious machines of Captain Agostino Ramelli*, Baltimore, 1976.

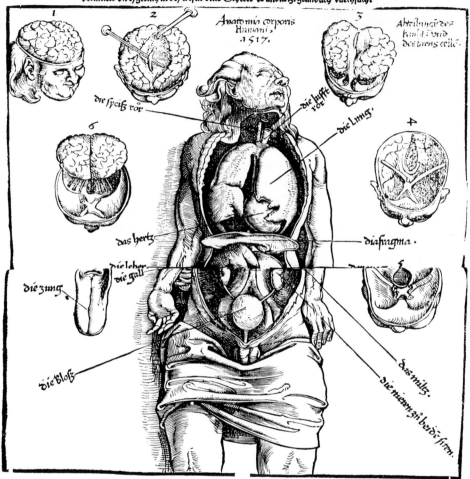

Ein contrafact Anatomy der inneren glyderen des menschen durch
den hoch gelerten physicam vnd medicine docrom Wendelinü Bock von Brackenau/zü Straßburg
declariert vn eygentlich in bey wesen viler Scherer Wundartzt gründlich durchsucht

FIGURE 5.12. Hans Wechtlin, *Woodcut Print of Cadaver Showing Situs of Visceral Organs.*
[*From Laurentius Phryesen, Spiegel der Artzney, 1518. Courtesy of the Francis A. Countway Library of Medicine, Boston.*]

This rope can be followed, or rather imagined, as running under the ground to where it reappears again in an adjacent, cutaway opening. Here we see it around a pulley where it is directed above the ground and on to the windlass "E." At the lower left of the engraving is another view of the same gear and reel "C," suspended so we may examine it in more detail.

LIBER SEXTVS.   139

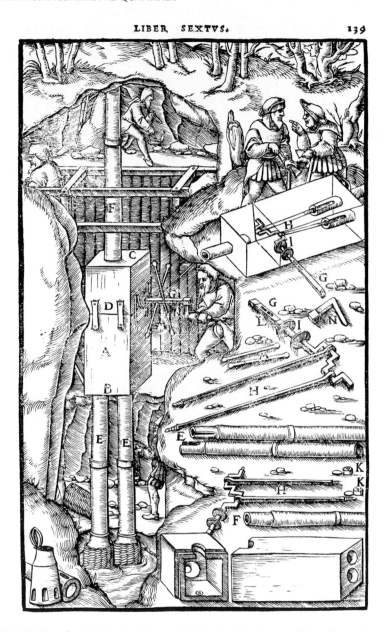

FIGURE 5.13. *Woodcut Print of a Mine with Twin Suction Pumps.* [*From Georg Bauer* [*Agricola*], De re metallica, 1556. *Courtesy of the Francis A. Countway Library of Medicine, Boston.*]

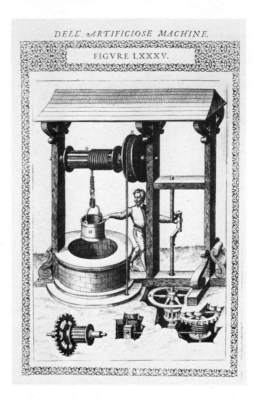

FIGURE 5.14. *Engraving of a Windlass Pump.* [*From Agostino Ramelli, Le diverse et artificiose machine, 1588. Courtesy of the Houghton Library, Harvard University, Cambridge.*]

Figure 5.15 is of an especially interesting application of the new Renaissance, didactic, pictorial vocabulary. It is noteworthy because the scene here has nothing to do with science but with teaching the Roman Catholic religion. This engraving is one of more than 150 published in 1593 by a Spanish Jesuit, Hieronymus Nadal. He collected these into a book to be used by Jesuit missionaries serving in China and Japan. The purpose of this *Annunciation* scene, and all the others, was to furnish the missionaries with field propaganda.[15] The engravings were to be used

---

[15] Nadal's book, published 13 years after his death, was one of the most ambitious undertakings of the famed Christophe Plantin press of Antwerp. Plantin himself spent years of time and trouble on it, seeking out artists to do the engravings and sponsors to put up the capital. He too died for the book's completion, and it finally went to press under his successor Martinus Nutius. The engravings in Nadal's book and their influence on contemporaneous Chinese Christian art have been discussed by Pasquale D'Elia, S. J., in *Le origini dell'arte cristiana cinese, 1583–1640*, Rome, 1939. See also Josef Jennes, *Invloed der Vlaamsche Prentkunst in Indiä, China, en Japan, tijdens de XVIe en XVIIe eeuw*, Lauvain, 1943.

FIGURE 5.15. *Engraving of the Annunciation.* [*From Hieronymus Nadal, Evangelicae historiae imagines, 1593. Courtesy of the Institutum Historicum S.I., Rome.*]

as tools of the faith, just as the machine and anatomical illustrations we have been examining were tools of science.

In the Christian religion, all gospel stories are related and divinely ordained. The Annunciation, for example, was predetermined when God created Adam. It then foretold the death of Jesus on the Cross. Since early Christian times it was commonplace in art to have one main gospel scene represented in the picture center surrounded by miniature scenes of other typologically related stories. This tradition continued even after the advent of linear perspective. Renaissance viewers became accustomed to suspending their sense of time unity in these religious representations, just as they could suspend their sense of space unity in scientific illustrations. Religious art, like scientific art, shared a common didactic enterprise, and both relied on similar pictorial conventions when projecting their messages. In the Nadal *Annunciation* (engraved by the Wierix brothers of Antwerp), we see, behind the main figures, a small *Crucifixion* as if in the distance (G); a miniature of *God Appointing Gabriel* ensconced in the apparitional blaze of light at the top (A); and a cutaway view of Limbo at the lower left (H) where an angel announces the Incarnation. All these little scenes are lettered and identified by legends at the bottom of the picture just as in scientific illustrations. Incidentally, this same technique was used in contemporaneous frescoes painted by Pomerancio on the inside of the church of San Stefano Rotondo in Rome. This building was a training school for Jesuit novices. The paintings, intended to inspire the young missionaries to be, were of grisly martyrdoms, and the artist carefully showed saints with bodies dismembered, the severed limbs exploded apart and labeled with letters, just as in the anatomical diagrams of the time.

Nadal's illustrated book was taken to China by the missionaries as was Agostino Ramelli's. Furthermore, both illustrations were copied by native Chinese artists during the early seventeenth century. One of the first acts of the Jesuits after they established their mission in Peking in 1601 was to build a library for the latest European books on religion and science, as tools for proslytizing among the Chinese.[16] The Jesuits also encouraged

---

[16] This collection was known as the Pei-t'eng Library, named for the "North Church," one of the four Jesuit missions in Peking wherein the books were housed. The European contents of the original library (which began to be dispersed in the eighteenth century) have been catalogued by H. Verhaeren, C. M., *Catalogue of the Pei-t'ang Library*, Peking, 1944–1948 (3 vols.), with a condensed version in "La Bibliotheque Chinoise du Pet'ang," *Monumenta Serica*, 1939, *4.2*, pp. 605–626. See also J. Laures, S. J., "Die alte Missionsbibliothek im Pei-t'ang zu Peking," *Monumenta Nipponica*, 1939, 2.1, pp. 124–139; Henri Bernard-Maître, "Les Adaptationes Chinoises d'Ouvrages Europèens; Bibliographie chronologiques depuis la Venue des Portugais à Canton jusqu'a la Mission Française de Pékin," *Monumenta Serica*, 1945, *10*, (1-57), pp. 309–388; and Bernard-Maître, "Une Bibliothéque médicale de la Renaissance conservée a Pékin," *Bulletin de l'Université d'Aurore*, 1947, 29, pp. 99–118. My sincere thanks to Charles O'Neill, S. J., Director of the Institutum Historicum S. I. in Rome, for allowing me to do research in the Jesuit library and archives.

their converts to translate and publish some of these books in the Chinese vernacular. Figure 5.16 and 5.17 are wood-block prints copied by Chinese artists after Nadal's *Annunciation* and Ramelli's windlass pump, respectively. The first appeared in a Chinese language manual on the Rosary[17]; the second was included in a book entitled *Ch'i Ch'i T'u Shuo* published in 1627 by a Chinese convert named Wang Chêng. Wang Chêng was a scholar and admirer of the many European treatises on machines in the Jesuit library. With the aid of Johann Schreck, one of the most learned Jesuits, he selected some 50 pictures from among the various books, such as Ramelli's, and had them copied. His title translated means 'Diagrams and Explanations of Wonderful Machines (from the Far West).'[18]

One immediately notices in both of these copies how completely the Chinese artists have "orientalized" the scenes, substituting not only Chinese physiognomical types for the principal figures but Chinese-style isometric for Renaissance converging perspective. Chinese artists were also unfamiliar with *chiaroscuro*. Thus, the prints lack shading, which Europeans used commonly to enhance the illusion of the third dimension. Furthermore, the Chinese artists were unclear about the European conventions of exploded and transparent views. In the Chinese *Annunciation* after Nadal, all the miniature typological details have been omitted. In the print after Ramelli, we observe that the native illustrator has tried to be very literal in his copy, but with quite peculiar results.

Let us follow how the Chinese artist interpreted Ramelli's machine while avoiding any aesthetic judgment. We shall ask only whether or not the picture communicates information about how the well works; whether or not any viewer (Chinese or European) could make use of this illustration—as we assume he could utilize Ramelli's original—to build a working model from it. Our first observation confirms that the Chinese artist, who was unfamiliar with the transparent or cutaway view, was especially confused about the machinery that Ramelli showed beneath the ground. Indeed, as he had no parallel convention in his own style, he substituted for the cutaway edges of earth in the European original, a number of squiggly shapes which Chinese artists often used to denote apparitions or miraculous events (as in the Chinese *Annunciation* for

[17] This work, entitled in Chinese, *Song nien tchou konei tch'eng* ("Rules for the Recitation of the Rosary"), was published in Peking under the supervision of Father João da Rocha (1565–1623). An original copy is in the Archivio Romano della Compagnia di Gesù, Jap-Sin I 43. See also D'Elia, *Le origini dell'arte cristiana cinese*, p. 67ff.

[18] On the *Ch'i Ch'i T'u Shuo*, see Fritz Jäger, "Das Buch von den wunderbaren Maschinen; Ein Kapitel aus der Geschichte der abendländisch-chinesischen Kulturbeziehungen," *Asia Major*, 1944, (N.S. 1, n.1), pp. 78–96; also, Joseph Needham, *Science and Civilisation in China*, (Vol. 4.2), Cambridge, England, 1954, pp. 211–218. I am grateful to Mr. Chin-shing Huang of Harvard University for his invaluable help in translating the *Ch'i Ch'i T'u Shuo*, and also to Nathan Sivin, Professor of Oriental Studies at the University of Pennsylvania and editor of *Chinese Science*, for his assistance and comments.

FIGURE 5.16. *Woodcut Print of the Annunciation.* [*From João da Rocha, Song nien tchou konei tch'eng, c. 1620. Courtesy of the Institutum Historicum, S.I., Rome.*]

FIGURE 5.17. *Woodcut Print of Ramelli's Windlass Pump.* [*From Wang Chêng, Ch'i Ch'i T'u Shuo, 1627. Courtesy of the Harvard Yenching Library, Harvard University, Cambridge.*]

instance). In the meantime, the artist did not concern himself with the rope (see Fig. 5.14), which ran from the gear-driven reel, passed under the ground, and up again to the windlass. The artist did show a bit of this cord just below the well, but its crucial connection to the winding reel was ignored. Also, because he lacked a similar convention for the exploded view, the Chinese copied Ramelli's detail of the reel and gear at the lower left without understanding that it was the same component working together with other parts of the apparatus drawn at the lower right.

Is it possible that the Chinese artist possessed his own special conventions, understood by his own audience, for communicating information about such a machine? This seems doubtful, especially if we examine another Chinese copy of Ramelli's device published in 1726, in *T'u Shu Chi Ch'eng*, the great encyclopedia of the Ch'ing Dynasty (Figure 5.18). This print was not taken directly from Ramelli but was copied from

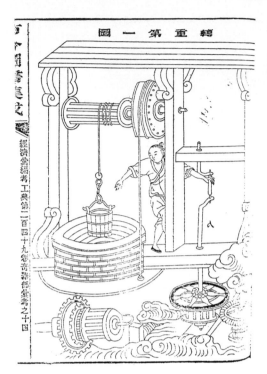

FIGURE 5.18. *Woodcut Print of Ramelli's Windlass Pump.* [*From T'u Shu Chi Chiêng, 1726, Vol. 1626–1628, Chapter 249. Courtesy of the Harvard Yenching Library, Cambridge.*]

the *Ch'i Ch'i T'u Shuo.* Here we see clearly that the second Chinese artist not only reproduced the same errors, but even misunderstood the earlier Chinese copyist's convention. This second artist was unsure of what the little squiggles represented, which the *Ch'i Ch'i T'u Shuo* illustrator substituted for the cutaway view. Instead of an apparition, the second artist thought these lines stood for water, so he added another convention, the common Chinese representation for billowing surf.

What are we to make of these strange incongruities in Chinese "scientific" illustration? It must be understood that the *Ch'i Ch'i T'u Shuo* (the rest of its 50-odd plates have all similar misinterpretations) is not an isolated exception. It can not be dismissed on the grounds that a more talented Chinese artist could have made truly intelligible copies. Not only do all Chinese pictures of technical subjects, in the hundreds of books published in China from the ninth to the nineteenth century, lack systematic *chiaroscuro* and linear perspective, but they are just as consistently impressionistic. They only suggest the forms and functions of the things represented and never show accurate dimensions or proportions

FIGURE 5.19. *Woodcut Print of Workmen Preparing a Mould for Casting a Bell.* [*From Sung Ying-hsing, T'ien Kung K'ai Wu, 1637. Courtesy of the Harvard Yenching Library, Cambridge.*]

to scale. This is true even in Chinese pictures of indigenous technical and scientific subject matter.

The Chinese illustrator was expected to be decorative, not didactic in his representations of the objects described in the verbal text. Figure 5.19 is of a page from perhaps the most famous Chinese technical treatise of the seventeenth century, *T'ien Kung K'ai Wu* ('Creation of Nature and Man') published in 1637.[19] It shows a scene of workmen preparing a mould for casting a bell, an art long practiced in China without any European influence. Figures 5.20 and 5.21 are of pages from China's most influential treatise on architecture, *Ying Tsao Fa Shih* ('Architectural Standards') first published in the twelfth century and reissued in numerous editions ever since (these illustrations are from an edition published in 1925). In the

---

[19] This work has been translated into English by E-tu Zen Sun and Shiou-Chuan Sun (Eds.), *Sung Ying-Hsing: T'ien-Kung Kai-Wu; Chinese Technology in the Seventeenth Century,* University Park, Pa., 1966.

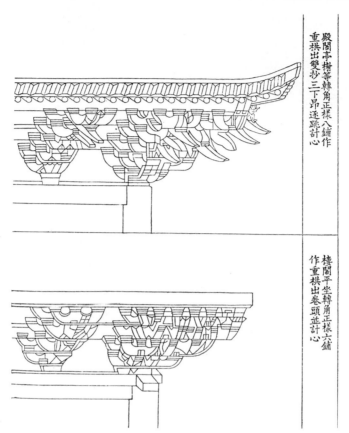

殿閣亭榭等轉角正樣八鋪作
重栱出雙抄三下昂逐跳計心

樓閣平坐轉角正樣六鋪
作重栱出卷頭並計心

FIGURE 5.20. *Woodcut Print of Two Architectural Roof Brackets.* [*From Li Chieh, Ying Tsao Fa Shih, c. 1103. Courtesy of the Harvard Yenching Library, Cambridge.*]

numerous details of buildings in this book, such as of composite brackets for supporting the roof cornice, and of the intricate wooden members composing them, the artist only wished to suggest the forms to the wood-carver, who was then expected to improvise and build the brackets as freely as his handicraft and imagination allowed. In no way can these pictures be compared to Western-style "shop drawings," in systematic isometric perspective, from which exact dimensions and proportions of parts can be translated to the object under construction.[20]

[20] Needham, in *Science and civilisation in China* (Vol. 4.3), pp. 107–114, has written that Chinese parallel perspective served in the same sense as do Western isometric machine-shop drawings. This is not so. While it may be, as Needham believes, that the original twelfth-century illustrations for *Ying Tsao Fa Shih* were accurate and approximately to scale, the fact that the subsequent copies became so inaccurate must show that Chinese artists had no consistent tradition or accepted conventions for drawing working diagrams as in the West.

One might wonder what Wang Chêng thought when he first examined the illustrations for his *Ch'i Ch'i T'u Shuo*. Like the mandarin he was, Wang Chêng seems not to have considered the artist as his intellectual and social equal and did not share with him a knowledge of how Western machines were supposed to work. Indeed, the Chinese mandarin class generally considered the mechanical arts to be socially demeaning. They enjoyed the results of a clever water pump, but the matter of its building was better left to laborers who would not be expected to work from pictures. In Europe, on the other hand, quite a different attitude was shared by many aristocrats (e.g., Galileo's own patron, the Grand Duke Ferdinand II of Tuscany, Francis Bacon in England, and Thomas Jefferson in America) rather, they felt that knowledge of technical matters was a social duty. In fact, the deluxe illustrated books we have discussed, such as Ramelli's, could only be afforded by the rich. I propose that this developing European attitude of sympathy for science and the mechanical arts was both incited and encouraged by the illustrations in such books. In China, as we have noted, the visual arts offered no encouragement to technology and science. Never, as far as I know, do we have a case where a Chinese invented a machine solely by means of pictures as did

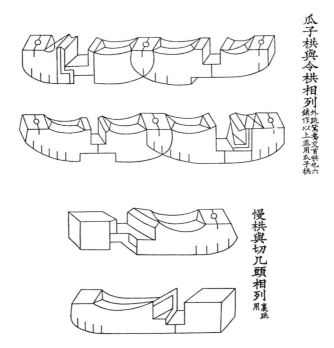

FIGURE 5.21. *Woodcut Print showing Carved Wooden Members of Roof Brackets.* [*From Li Chieh, Ying Tsao Fa Shih, c. 1103. Courtesy of the Harvard Yenching Library, Cambridge.*]

Taccola, Francesco di Giorgio, Leonardo, and Ramelli, or used pictures to solve problems of anatomy as did Vesalius. Separate geniuses of the arts and sciences, the Chinese had aplenty, but never were they combined in a single person. In fact, by Western standards, it is hard to comprehend how Chinese science and technology was able to progress at all with so little involvement of artists or pictures.

The relative states of the arts and sciences in China—and we should also include Japan—during the sixteenth and seventeenth centuries, offers a veritable laboratory for studying and isolating factors that promote or impede the growth of science and technology in any society. What did or did not happen in these oriental civilizations while the Jesuits were bombarding them with foreign ideas may reveal insights into the origins of our own Western scientific revolution. Art historians and psychologists with fluency in the Chinese and Japanese languages should do research in the school textbooks of China and Japan from the seventeenth through this century, to discover just when, and how much, Western-style illustrations replaced the native ones. Figures 5.22 and 5.23 are of pages from

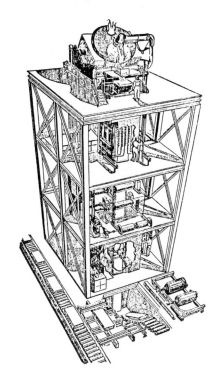

凝固。最后用工作輥以一定的速度夾住白热的鋼錠鬆緩把它拉出，經乙炔切割机切成一定長度的鋼錠。切割机的托架和鋼錠夾緊在一起，在切割时与鋼錠一起移动，切割好后与鋼錠脱开，很快的回到原来位置，开始切割下一块鋼錠。切下来的鋼錠轉成水平位置，用滾道送到各种型鋼的軋鋼机上，軋成各种所需的鋼材。用这种方法生产，全部生产过程只要4小时，回爐廢品只有9％。

用連續澆鑄鋼錠法，也可以澆鑄各种生鉄管子。澆出的鉄管质量很高，各部分的組織很均勻，机械性能很好，抗拉强度和抗穿强度比砂型鑄件高2.5—3倍。而且生产率也很高，每小时可鑄出3公尺長的鑄鉄管15—20根。

用連續澆鑄鋼錠法进行生产，不仅可以简化鋼材的生产程序，减少操作人員和輔助材料，并且可以大大改善劳动条件，所有的操作过程都可以广泛实行机械化和自动化。同时还能避免鋼錠的偏折，中心縮孔，和产生过大的結晶顆粒，从而提高鋼的质量。此外由于鋼錠兩端的缺陷少，可以不必大量切头，鋼錠的收获率高，用这种方法生产，設备简单，可以减少基本建設費用与經常維护費用。

連續澆鑄鋼錠法(右图)目前正被广泛采用，不久的將来也將在我国出現。这种现代先进的生产鋼材方法被采用以后，將为我国生产更多的鋼材。

FIGURE 5.22. *Electrotype Print Showing an Industrial Tower.* [*From Hsien-tai Chi-shu, 1957. Courtesy of the Harvard Yenching Library, Cambridge.*]

推动飞机以很快的速度前進。

在应用汽輪發动机的飛机中，用原子鍋爐代替汽輪发动机的鍋爐。使液体通过原子鍋爐（圖121）变成蒸汽，蒸气以极快速度投到汽輪机的輪叶上，汽輪机就帶着螺旋槳轉动起来，因而可以推动飛机前進。

应用原子能發动机的最大优点，就是不需要帶气，不需要帶很多燃料，这对于高空和长途飛行是非常有利的。原子能發动机不僅可以用在飛机上，也可以用在潜水艇，輪船和火車上。

将来的原子能飛机（圖122）和普通飛机不一样，飛机的头部就是駕駛員操縱室，發动机却在机尾。这是因为原子核分裂时有一种放射線，它能伤害人体，發动机放在机尾，再稍加防护設备，就能保証旅客們的安全。

原子能飛机的速度是超音速的。由于用原子能作动力，飛机可以几个月不着陆地，能繼續繞地球飛行好几十周。飛机机身非常巨大，能遠載許多旅客和大批物资。在机艙前部，有舒适的卧室、飯廳，还有放映电影的地方。机身中部可以裝运汽車、机器等各种物资器材，它比客艙大好几倍。再后面就是防护放射線的裝置。

水泵　原子鍋爐
冷凝器　汽輪機
圖121　原子能汽輪發动机

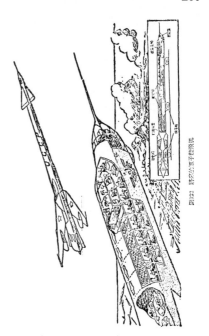

FIGURE 5.23. *Electrotype Print showing a Rocket Ship.* [*From Tzu jau Chang-shih Wen-ti Chieh-ta, 1956. Courtesy of the Harvard Yenching Library, Cambridge.*]

modern Chinese technical textbooks published in the 1950s under the present Communist regime. It is obvious from both figures that the illustrators have completely abandoned traditional Chinese forms in favor of Western-style chiaroscuro, perspective, and even the transparent view. I feel that such research will reveal a more than casual relationship between the influx of Western pictorial forms into these textbooks and the rate of expanding industrialization and adaptation to modern science in the East. If this could be proven, then we might infer that a similar relationship also existed in Renaissance Europe. At least we should have a *prima facie* case that Galileo could not have done what he did in Ming Dynasty China. He needed precisely the kind of visual education, the familiarity with perspective pictures in contemporaneous textbooks, only available in the school rooms of sixteenth-century Western Europe.

CONCLUSION

Scientists and historians of the future, I also predict, will study the visual arts not as mere passive reflectors of great ideas, but as active promulgators of those ideas. When the documents are finally in, and the arrival of the so-called Third World to scientific and technological parity with the Western nations is finally realized, it may well be understood that one of the fundamental problems revolutionary peoples of the twentieth century had to solve, transcending the polarized politics of capitalism and communism alike, was that of psychological adjustment to the peculiar visual conception of the natural world first set forth by the artists of the Renaissance.

ACKNOWLEDGMENTS

This chapter was delivered as a lecture at a conference entitled *Art and science in the Renaissance* sponsored by the Folger Shakespeare Library and the National Museum of Technology, Washington, D. C., October 28, 1978. I am grateful to the American Council of Learned Societies and the John Simon Guggenheim Memorial Foundation for their generous support of my research, and also to Harvard University for allowing me to use its vast library resources.

CHAPTER **6**
WILLIAM R. MACKAVEY

Exceptional Cases of Pictorial Perspective

Introduction 213
Close Viewing 215
Far Viewing 218
Trompe l'Oeil 220
References 223

INTRODUCTION

Pictures are magnificently robust and powerful in their ability to represent an object, scene, event, or person. Children, adults, and even many animals are quite capable of registering the essential similarities between an object and its counterpart in a picture. Even strong distortions such as those occurring in a caricature are apt to leave recognition unaffected, and indeed there is some evidence that the exaggerations of a caricature can actually facilitate recognition. It is as if the caricature has a superior fidelity. Such tolerance of distortion is testimony to the observer's ability to register, that is, to pick up the information-laden constants that continue throughout the transformations present in photograph, silhouette, cartoon, line drawing, caricature, etc.

The acceptability of most pictures is also unaffected by the particular viewing position of the spectator. In a crowded gallery, for example, a portrait does not look false to its observer by reason of viewing forced

213

The Perception of Pictures
Volume I

from some strange angle. The degree of distortion present in such a case can be seen by replacing the viewing eye with a camera and looking at the resulting picture of a picture. The side of the face nearer to the camera will then be seen stretched out, and the more distant side seen as foreshortened in the manner of certain anamorphic portraits such as William Scrot's classic ·Portrait of Edward VI (Leeman, 1976).

There is an interesting and revealing anecdote to be told about the difference between looking at a picture and a picture of a picture. A newspaper reporter, seeing only a photograph of the official portrait of the then Governor of the Commonwealth of Massachusetts, Frances X. Sargent, wrote a column ridiculing the bodily proportions displayed and deduced that a misshapen stand-in for the Governor must have been used for some parts of the commissioned work. The reporter simply failed to realize that in taking a photograph of a picture, the position of the camera is everything!

Given the power of a picture to provide a very serviceable resemblance to the original object, regardless of spectator position and across a very wide variety of picture types, those instances in which a distortion or falseness does intrude on perception are of special interest, and some of those instances will be considered in this chapter. First, how are we to understand the fact that most distortions, whether as the result of an artist's intent as in a caricature, or accidentally produced as in viewing a portrait from an eccentric viewing position, are not noticed as distortions? There appears to be a compensatory mechanism that operates with extreme effectiveness. The common view is that the presence of the picture surface itself is responsible for the compensation to distortion. Certainly there is generally more than enough information for the fact that one is looking at a picture. Much of it is broadly contextual (e.g., one is in a gallery or leafing through the pages of a magazine). Even in the absence of such broad contextural supports, in a contrived laboratory setting, for example, the picture surface will still reveal its two dimensionality by means of highlights, brush strokes, reflections, textures, and the like. Moreover, pictures provide neither binocular disparity nor motion parallax. Because of the former, the viewer is not provided with the disparate views that are required for stereopsis. Because of the latter, shifts in head or body position during viewing (or any movement of a hand-held photograph) do not produce differential movement of foreground and background objects. Pictured foreground objects do not "slide" past background objects as they would in the case of viewing a natural scene. In combination these factors provide an abundance of information for the presence of the picture surface and for triggering the compensatory mechanism. Occasionally however, not withstanding such information, the compensatory mechanism seems to fail and a picture will look quite false in its proportions or some other aspect. Three such situations of apparent failure of the compensatory mechanism will now be discussed. The situations involve close viewing, far viewing, and, finally, trompe l'oeil constructions.

CLOSE VIEWING

Particular problems are encountered whenever the station point for a perspective construction is very close to the subject. The simplest situation to imagine in this case is a photographer standing very near to the subject. A rough rule of thumb is that the station point should not come within the half measure of the subject, say within 3 ft. or so of a 6-ft. tall model. When the model is photographed from a near distance the viewer is apt to be frustrated when attempting to achieve a unitary and stable pictorial conception. The picture will provide not only the intended impression of looking at or toward the subject but will contain downward and upward views as well. One sees, in the same picture, not only the frontal torso, but shoe tops and the shadowy underside of the chin. The effect calls to mind certain of M.C. Escher's prints in which the components of the picture, seen in isolation and taken individually, are quite unremarkable, yet in combination reveal an impossible event such as a descending circular staircase that manages to return to its point of origin.

The problem of the too near station point is compounded when the object(s) of principal concern in the composition recede(s) in depth along the projected line of sight. Very near foreground objects will appear exaggerated or overscaled in size, and more distant objects, even those slightly more distant, will appear undersized. The reason for this resides in the form of the *visual angle function,* which is simply a descriptive measure of the size of an image within the eye as the distance of the imaged object from the eye is varied. In pictorial terms it refers to the size of the image on the picture surface as a function of the object's distance from the station point.

Whereas it is intuitively obvious that the visual angle of an imaged target must shrink as it recedes from view, the rate at which that shrinkage occurs is probably not so obvious. Figure 6.1 illustrates that a shift in the distance of a target located near to the viewer will have a much greater impact on visual angle than that same shift occurring at a greater distance. What this means in pictorial terms is that an object located near to a photographer, or to an artist drawing in strict perspective, will loom large and dwarf similar objects located at an even slightly greater distance. However "accurate" the picture, it will be lacking in "naturalness." The effect is suggested in Rembrandt's painting of *The Artist in His Studio* (Fig. 6.2).

Subtle instances of this effect can also be seen in some works of the

FIGURE 6.1. Rembrandt's *The Artist in his Studio*. **This painting illustrates the sort of size imbalance that can occur between a foreground object and a background object when a literal rendering of perspective is employed by the artist.** [*Courtesy of the Museum of Fine Arts, Boston.*]

Dutch realist Jan Vermeer, in his *Soldier and Laughing Girl,* for example. The size imbalance between the foreground soldier (too large) and the more distant (and too small) girl, and other similar instances, have encouraged the speculation that Vermeer must have made at least occasional use of an optical device such as the camera obscura in preparing his compositions. In these instances Vermeer would have been well advised to violate the canons of perspective and adopt a compromise in the service of more natural appearances.

The perceptual problems produced by a too near station point can be overcome by a forced positioning of the viewer so that the same visual geometry is presented for the picture and for its model; that requirement, however, is nearly impossible to implement in practice. If it can be managed the results are worth the effort. Even with one-eyed viewing, striking depth effects are possible.

A picture of a fountain composed of several figures against a background of buildings . . . is extremely confusing when viewed normally; but a lens brings the figures out clearly in depth, and a number of criss-crossing lines become jets of water, properly oriented in three dimensions [Schlosberg, 1941].

The purpose of the lens in this illustration is to enable the viewing of the photograph up close with accommodation more nearly appropriate to the apparent distance of the pictured object. For example, try looking at a number of high-quality photographs from a very near distance with the aid of a magnifying glass. The depth effect should be noticeably improved. (Low-quality photographs or halftones, when magnified, look too grainy and do not work well.)

As already indicated, a far simpler solution for the artist or photographer is to increase the distance to the subject to some substantial value. Leonardo da Vinci long ago suggested this simple device in the pages of his Notebooks filled with advice to painters. In the following excerpt he acknowledges the problem of controlling the spectator's position and proceeds to admonish the artist to stand away from the subject.

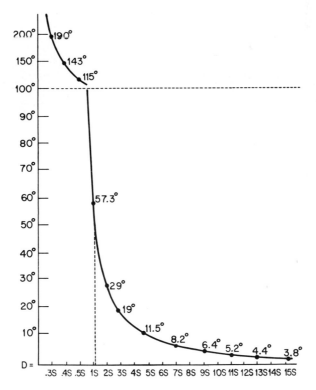

FIGURE 6.2. The visual angle function. The figure illustrates the fact that the size of an image will be affected much more by a given distance change (D) at a near distance than at a far distance. [*Courtesy of Margaret A. Hagen.*]

If you want to represent an object near to you which is to have the effect of nature, it is impossible that your perspective should not look wrong, with every false relation and disagreement of proportion that can be imagined in a wretched work, unless the spectator, when he looks at it, has his eye at the very distance and height and direction where the eye or the point of sight was placed in doing this perspective. . . otherwise do not trouble yourself about it, unless indeed you make your view at least 20 times as far off as the greatest width or height of the objects represented, and this will satisfy any spectator placed anywhere opposite to the picture [Richter, 1970, p. 271].

If, despite the hazards, an artist chooses a near station point, then some departure from a strict perspective construction will probably improve appearances. Size differences between near and more distant forms are

FIGURE 6.3. Mary Cassatt's *Mother and Child*. Do you feel that the face of the child seen reflected in the hand-held mirror is agreeably sized? [*Courtesy of the National Gallery of Art, Chester Dale Collection, Washington, D. C.*]

best reduced. The way this works can often be seen in paintings showing reflected or mirrored scenes. Before looking at any such painting, first perform this demonstration, borrowed from Gombrich (1960, p. 6). One may stand in front of a large sheet of paper or blackboard and imagine that surface to be a mirror in which he/she views his/her own reflection. If one sketches the outline of his/her imagined reflection (a crude effort will do), what one is apt to do is attempt a drawing that is more or less congruent with the contour of his/her own head. The intended scale between the drawn and actual head size is 1 : 1. If one repeats the exercise in front of a real mirror it immediately becomes clear that he/she should sketch the imagined reflection to half scale! This is an outstandingly compelling example of size constancy (i.e., the invariance of perceived size as a function of distance). Remember, the reflected counterpart stands equidistant on the other side of the mirror. Compare this with the treatment of a mirrored face chosen by Velasquez (*Venus and Cupid*), or Titian (*Venus with a Mirror*) or Mary Cassatt (*Mother and Child*). (See Figure 6.3.) Are the various solutions to the problem satisfying or troublesome?

FAR VIEWING

What of the pictorial representation of objects that are not in the near foreground, but rather presented as if at a great distance? There is perhaps less of a problem if only because distant objects will be drawn to reduced scale, will be less noticed, and are probably less thematically critical. Such images are, literally, in the background of interest and furnish the context for more focal material. There are, however, some interesting observations to be made.

When one peers into those portions of a canvas or photograph that present the images of objects at a great distance, the image sizes of similar objects will be fairly stable, no matter what their actual distances. That is, of course, required by the form of the visual angle function already discussed; at great distances any further increases in distance will have only trivial and perceptually insignificant effects upon visual angle. This conceptualization helps to articulate the paradox that is inherent in Mantegna's great painting of *The Dead Christ*.

In some aspects such as scale, great detail, clarity, as well as the absence of intruding foreground, the painting suggests that the viewer is stationed close to Christ's body. However, the correlative convergence that one expects to encounter while gazing from foot toward head and shoulders is lacking. Indeed, the absence of size scaling between the nearer and farther elements in the picture suggests quite the opposite, viz., that we are far removed and the resulting flattening of apparent depth is so strong as to resemble what is seen under conditions of optical magnification as through a telescope or binocular (see Lumsden, Chapter 3 of this volume).

By way of contrast, when Mantegna applied the same perspective treatment to the cherubic figures seen on the ceiling of the Ducal Palace in Mantua, the consequences seem far more natural. Because the spectator has little option but to view Mantegna's painting from a fair distance, what would otherwise be unacceptable becomes altogether natural and pleasing to the eye. Indeed in that setting the effect of the total painting is a highly successful trompe l'oeil with a strong impression of assorted heavenly and earthly forms returning the visitor's glances.

TROMPE L'OEIL

Successfully realized efforts at trompe l'oeil illusionism, such as Mantegna's ceiling painting, can have a marvelous impact; the painted surface drops away and the pigments are replaced by objects having depth and solidity. The effect is illustrated in Fig. 6.4 by the painting *Old Models* by the American artist William Harnett.

A fair claim to the zenith in trompe l'oeil illusionism can be made for a painting in the nave of the St. Ignazio Church in Rome. On that ceiling in the late 1600s, Fra Andrea Pozzo prepared a spectacular display. His painted illusion extends the apparent architecture of the church, 30-m overhead, so compellingly that it is simply impossible to segregate the painting from the architecture. The surface of the painting vanishes and one looks *into* the sky rather than *at* a painted ceiling. There are immense pillars extending heavenward, and the luminous canopy of the sky is filled with weightless suspended figures. Pirenne (1970) has described the scene as one "vast complicated piece of coloured sculpture."

The painting is meant to be viewed from the position of a marble disc on the floor of the nave. From that location, the illusion is complete. As one walks away from the marble disc, however, the painted supporting columns become deformed, they warp, and the ceiling sky seems to be on the verge of collapse; all this in sharp contradiction to the usual indifference of pictures to the position of the spectator.

If, as discussed in the "Introduction" of this chapter, it is the awareness of the picture's surface that prevents such distortions from being the typical occurrence when walking around a painting, then it is reasonable to attribute the rubbery quality of the Pozzo ceiling to the absence of perceived surfaceness. In view of the prevalence of the notion that it is the picture surface that triggers the perceptual compensation for viewing position, it is surprising that there is so little experimental work relevant to the issue, however, that is the case (Hagen, 1976). The greatest difficulty faced by this explanation, however, is that it fails to account for the per-

FIGURE 6.4. *Old Models* **by William Harnett, an example of the trompe l'oeil style of painting.**
[*Courtesy of the Museum of Fine Arts, Boston.*]

ceptual robustness of most trompe l'oeil paintings. Harnett's *Old Masters*, for example, looks quite undistorted in oblique view; the plasticity of the Pozzo ceiling is quite the exception, even for trompe l'oeil displays.

I believe that the principal factor contributing to the deformation of the painted architecture is to be found elsewhere—it is the peculiar way in which the real and the painted architecture interact with each other. When this is understood, it can be seen that Pozzo's painting behaves in essentially the same way that any picture behaves as one moves about, viz., it is altogether stable and in fact it is just this stability that is responsible for the interesting visual effects that are seen.

In order to understand this view, let us begin with a simpler, but formally equivalent example, an *en face* portrait. The drawn eyes that so effectively engage the viewer's eyes as he/she stands before a portrait continue to do so as he/she moves to either side. It is impossible to stand anywhere without having the subject of the portrait return the viewer's gaze—an eerie experience for many! The explanation of this effect is simple enough. The painting shows only a frontal view and no matter where we stand, only a frontal view will be revealed to us. There will *never* be a profile. Similarly, a portrait with the eyes averted will forever remain that way; it is impossible for a viewer to intercept that gaze by means of repositioning. This explanation accounts perfectly well for the deformations seen in the Pozzo ceiling as explained further.

One intermediate step may prove helpful and it involves a description of what happens when viewing another ceiling painting, this one painted by the Spanish painter Jose Maria Sert and located in the main lobby of the RCA Building in Rockefeller Center (New York, New York). The flat ceiling of the lobby is supported by a number of massive pillars and painted on the ceiling is a trio of Titans personifying Past, Present, and Future. The Titans are drawn in such a way that each appears to be astride a pair of these pillars. When standing directly beneath any one of the figures and looking directly up, it appears that body weight is carried equally by the two legs and in turn by each of the pillars underfoot. The principal axis of the Titan parallels a plumb line that runs directly to the spectator below, and, as one walks about the lobby floor, the figure of the Titan behaves exactly as do the eyes in the frontal portrait: orientation toward the spectator is maintained. Walking to one side causes the Titan to pivot and appear to transfer its weight to the far leg and pillar. Walking to the opposite side will of course cause the Titan to rock and transfer its weight once again. Throughout all of this, the columns, as real architectural structures, maintain their orientation with respect to gravity.

By now the analog to Pozzo's ceiling should be evident. Had the artist, Sert, chosen to draw the Titans as structural extensions of the supporting architectural columns, such rocking about as has been described would surely give the ceiling the appearance of collapse.

The critical factor producing the peculiar deformities seen in Pozzo's and Sert's ceiling paintings then is *not* the absence of surface information, but rather that each painting is intended to be integrated with the surrounding architecture. It is the contrasting geometric transformation exhibited by the two-dimensional painting on the one hand and the three-dimensional architecture on the other that destroys compatibility and introduces the appearance of distortion. It follows that were it possible to view each painting apart from its architectural setting, the movement of a spectator would produce transformations neither more nor less remarkable than are seen in other pictures. It now seems possible to include trompe l'oeil constructions as examples of the robustness to be seen in pictures—they no longer stand apart as exceptions.

REFERENCES

Gombrich, E. H. *Art and illusion*. Princeton, New Jersey: Princeton Univ. Press, 1960.

Hagen, M. A. Influence of picture surface and station point on the ability to compensate for oblique view in pictorial perception. *Developmental Psychology*. 1976, *12*, 57–63.

Leeman, F. *Hidden images*. New York: Abrams, 1976.

Pirenne, M. H. *Optics, painting, and photography*. Cambridge: Cambridge Univ. Press, 1970.

Richter, J. P. *The notebooks of Leonardo da Vinci* (Vol. 1). New York: Dover, 1970.

Schlosberg, H. Stereoscopic depth from single pictures. *American Journal of Psychology*. 1941, *54*, 601–605.

SARAH L. FRIEDMAN
MARGUERITE B. STEVENSON

CHAPTER **7**

Perception of Movement in Pictures

Introduction 225
Representational Information 226
    Single Viewpoint, Single Moment 227
    Multiple Viewpoints 228
    Metaphor 229
    Abstract Representations 230
The Effectiveness of Pictorial Movement Information—Experimental Evidence 236
    Single Viewpoint, Single Moment 236
    Multiple Viewpoints 243
    Metaphor 244
    Abstract Representations 246
A Continuum of Information Correspondence between Pictorial Indicators and the
    Environment 246
Summary 251
Appendix 1 252
Appendix 2 252
References 254

INTRODUCTION

This chapter reviews current information about pictorial representations of movement. It is possible to draw a two-dimensional picture that makes its viewers say the picture shows something or someone being moved or moving, as in the process of falling, being thrown, dancing, working, or jogging. Little has been written in the psychological literature

225

The Perception of Pictures
Volume I

ISBN 0-12-313601-6

about the understanding of such a two-dimensional representation of movement or about the correspondence between the information for environmental movement and the information for pictorial movement. The nature of the correspondence between environmental and pictorial movement is intriguing because it is so obvious that movement occurring over time cannot, in and of itself, be captured in two-dimensional representations. Even under the most unnatural observation conditions, the eye cannot be fooled by pictorial movement as might be the case with pictorial depth. Yet we feel that pictorial movement is compelling, that, over and above its informational value, it can also transmit a sense of movement.

We decided that the best way to learn about pictorial movement would be to survey actual pictures. We surveyed paintings, photographs, caricatures, cartoons, and diagrams produced by different cultures and during different historical periods. Based on this survey, we made a list of the types of information artists use for portraying movement in pictures. Once the pictorial indicators for movement had been enumerated, we became interested in the effectiveness of such indicators in inducing a correct understanding of pictorial movement.

We found a difference in the frequency with which the various pictorial movement indicators appeared in pictures. Existing experimental evidence indicated that developmentally and cross-culturally the indicators had not been equally comprehensible. These pieces of information, taken together suggested that pictorial movement indicators vary in the way they provide information about real movement.

Because indicators of pictorial movement share features with pictorial indicators that represent objects at rest, scenes and sound, it is possible that the nature of pictorial representation in general cannot be adequately described by a theory which does not specify different ways in which pictorial information can correspond to environmental information. On the practical side, the representational inequality of pictorial movement indicators has implications for the design of pictorial materials for intelligence tests and children's books. One would want to make sure that the pictorial indicators used in pictures will be designed so as to be understood by their readers.

REPRESENTATIONAL INFORMATION

Our first step toward learning about pictorial movement was to identify the representational information for movement in pictures from different cultures and different historical periods (see Appendix 1). In these pictures, we found that movement was represented by four types of indicators. Some pictures captured movement from a single vantage point at a single point in time; others used multiple viewpoints to represent movement. Movement was occasionally represented by borrowing information from one scene to represent movement in another. Finally, movement could be represented abstractly, independent of any pictorial object. More information about these indicators of movement is contained in the following discussions.

Single Viewpoint, Single Moment

The single viewpoint, single moment picture shows a momentarily frozen environment, as seen from one point of view. When a picture shows any randomly chosen moment of the process of movement, the depicted object will not necessarily suggest movement. For example, if a snapshot is taken of a man walking toward the camera when both his feet happen to be on the ground, the man may appear to be holding still, or the picture might appear ambiguous, with alternate interpretations being possible. For this reason, pictures using a single vantage point at a single point in time do not select just any view of any object at any point in the process of movement. The understanding of pictorial movement is more likely to occur if specific views and specific moments in the process of movement are represented. In the example of a man walking, pictorial movement would be more strongly suggested if the representation showed him at a sideways orientation. Therefore, single viewpoint pictures frequently indicate movement by showing a sideways orientation of the depicted object (Goodnow, 1978; Rovet & Ives, 1977).

Just as a particular view of an object can indicate movement, so can the choice of some particular moment at which the picture is recorded. Representations showing a figure at a moment in which its position differs substantially from an at-rest position are frequently used by artists. In such representations of human figures, the depicted body is frequently shown "leaning" or with a limb or part of the body shown in other than its relaxed position. The deviation from the resting position may involve a shift in the angle at which the object is commonly represented or a change in the spatial relationships among its components, as when a represented limb is bent at the knee or elbow. An example of a picture where movement is indicated only by deviation from the resting position can be seen in the picture of the curtain in Figure 7.1.

Some objects and scenes inherently suggest movement by their content. For example, there is no such thing as a still river or fire. Movement, therefore, is inferred in pictures of these subjects without additional indicators—the content forces the interpretation.

Similarly, the context in which objects are depicted may suggest movement: A skier with skis pointed down a hill must be moving. When an object such as a bird, plane, or swing is suspended in midair, it must also, of necessity, be moving. However, context usually serves to only enhance the impression of movement given by postural indicators. For

FIGURE 7.1. *Wind from the Sea* by Andrew Wyeth. [*From Andrew Wyeth by R. Meryman, 1968. Copyright 1968 by Mill Incorporated.*]

example, the pictorial movement shown in Figure 7.2 is conveyed by both postures and context. The people represented in this figure are shown wearing skates. The skates are accessories that enhance the perception of pictorial movement, but the skates by themselves do not force an interpretation of pictorial movement—for it is possible to stand still on the ice when wearing skates. In most pictures of movement, context, by itself, does not permit an understanding of pictorial movement.

Other scenes strongly suggesting movement show the path an object has taken. Footprints on the sand, ski tracks on fresh snow, skate marks on ice, wheel marks in mud, dust kicked up by a horse, the wake behind a swimmer or a ship, or arrows next to an object all indicate the path of movement. In Mexican art, footprints are used to show the path of travel (Smith, 1968).

Multiple Viewpoints

Another way of representing movement pictorially is to show an object or a part of an object at successive moments. In this way, a selection of the changes occurring with time is recorded as multiple images. For ex-

FIGURE 7.2. Detail from *Scene on the Ice* by Henrick Avercamp. [*Courtesy of the Ailsa Mellon Bruce Fund, National Gallery of Art, Washington, D.C.*]

ample, Figure 7.3 records the story of Salome by placing her figure in different parts of the picture so as to show her movement over time. A dancer with multiple arms and legs to show movement is indicated in Figure 7.4.

Metaphor

Aspects of the environment that are unlikely to occur together in the real world may be represented side by side in a picture so as to suggest movement. In other words, movement is suggested through a pictorial metaphor.[1] For example, the artist may add arms and legs to an object that is limbless in reality, or a vehicle may be shown in a "human" posture with its front wheels raised off the ground. Marks showing the pattern of movement may be borrowed from water or snow to show the path of motion in the air. Steam or exhaust may be placed behind an object that in fact leaves none. For example, in cartoons the pictorial movement of humans is frequently accentuated by lines or a blur even though real human movement produces no such effects.

Photographs of moving objects are often taken by leaving the camera's

---

[1] The use of the word "metaphor" as an appropriate descriptor of this class of pictures was suggested to us by John M. Kennedy.

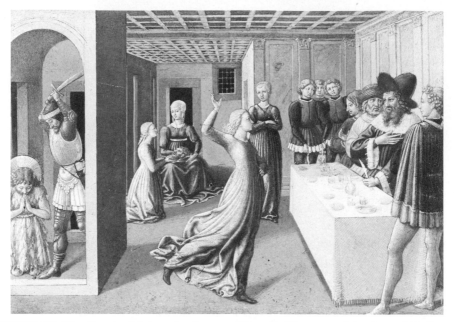

FIGURE 7.3. *The Dance of Salome* by Benozzo Gozzoli. [*Courtesy of the Samuel H. Kress Collection, National Gallery of Art, Washington, D.C.*]

shutter open for a relatively long period of time. The effect is a picture of the object with a blur next to it. For this reason, one can argue that many of the metaphors for movement are imitations of photographic effects rather than pictorial metaphors. We have found, however, that artists used pictorial metaphors to show movement before the invention of the camera. Figure 7.5 is an eleventh- or twelfth-century Japanese picture of a child flying down from heaven on a cloud. The lines show the path of movement of the wheel through the air, even though such marks would not actually be seen in the environment—had a child with a wheel come through the air.

Abstract Representations

Pictorial movement may be indicated without any pictorial object. As can be seen in Figure 7.6, angular and curved lines convey a strong impression of movement without the depiction of any object. An abstract way of representing movement is also used in diagrams. For example, movement of soldiers can be shown by arrows on a map without the depiction of a single soldier (Figure 7.7).

The representational indicators for depicting movement in pictures have been presented one-by-one. This is, however, not the way they usually appear in pictures. In pictures, movement is frequently represented by a combination of indicators, providing the viewer of the picture with redundant information. For example, in Figure 7.2 the movement of the skaters is suggested both by their postures and by the context (ice, people wearing skates).

In looking through picture books of different cultures and historical periods, we noted that the pictorial movement indicators we have identified have been used with differing frequency throughout history. Our impression is that movement has been most commonly represented by postures deviating from the resting position and by contextual information. Moving people and animals have been shown leaning forward with bent limbs since the earliest cave paintings. Raised swords and bows have added contextual information to hunting scenes. Figure 7.8 shows an Aboriginal cave painting with these pictorial movement indicators.

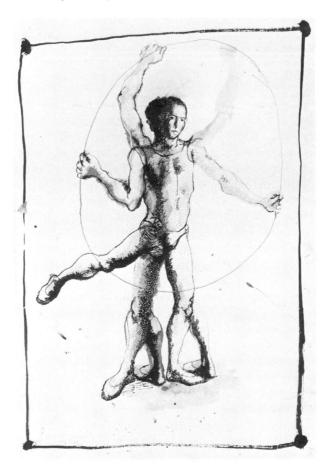

FIGURE 7.4. A Dancer by Pavel Tchelitchew. [*Courtesy of the Ella Gallup Sumner and Mary Catlin Sumner Collection, Wadsworth Atheneum, Hartford, Connecticut.*]

FIGURE 7.5. *Child Attendant Flying Down from Heaven on a Cloud.* [*From Pagent of Japanese art, by Tokyo National Museum Staff, 1952, Copyright 1952 by Kodansha Ltd. Publishers. Reprinted by permission.*]

Figure 7.9 shows an example of Aegaen art from the fifteenth century B.C. in which costumed figures with raised arms indicate dancing. Pictorial indicators other than those of postures deviating from the resting position and of context have been used infrequently in the pictures we viewed.

We checked our impressions about the incidence of the different pictorial movement indicators with a small survey of pictures. We examined the two-dimensional art of 13 cultural or artistic periods (see Appendix 2). In each period, pictures were looked at until 25 pictures with information about movement were found. Each picture was then examined to determine whether movement was indicated by postures deviating from the resting position, by contextual information, by metaphor, or whether the picture had a content that forced an understanding of pictorial movement. We reached consensus in our evaluation of each picture. The sources viewed included ancient cave paintings; Egyptian tomb paintings; Greek vase paintings; Medieval; Renaissance; Baroque; Realism; Oriental; American; French Fauvism; and German Blaue Reiter paintings; illustrations in contemporary childrens' books; and contemporary newspaper comics. Our selection of art pictures can in no way be considered a random sampling of the representational art of each period because we relied on the selection of each book's author. These authors' selections, however, probably were not influenced by movement information and therefore should include a reasonable collection of movement pictures from the periods examined.

Table 7.1 summarizes the results of this survey. The number of pictures we viewed in order to find 25 representations of movement suggests the

FIGURE 7.6. *Racing Automobiles* by Balla. [*Courtesy of the Stedelijk Museum, Amsterdam.*]

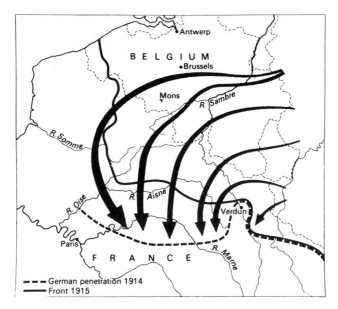

FIGURE 7.7. Map from a school textbook showing the German attack on France 1914–1918.
[*From A. W. Gattrell & Co. and in Britain in the modern world: The twentieth century by A. M. Newth, Penguin Education, 1967, p. 38. Reprinted by permission.*]

FIGURE 7.8. A group of four running women. *(From Australia-Aboriginal Paintings—Arnhem Land.[Unesco world art series]: New York Graphic Society Ltd. and United Nations Educational, Scientific, and Cultural Organization. Reprinted by permission.)*

FIGURE 7.9. Ring with ritual scene. [*From Aegean art: The origins of Greek art by P. Demargne, 1964. Copyright 1964 by Thames and Hudson, Ltd. Reprinted by permission.*]

frequency with which movement was represented in each period. Movement pictures were most common in Greek vase painting and most rare in French Fauvism. Every picture included postural information for movement—the person, object, or animal represented was not shown in a resting position. In most pictures of people, contextual information was added to the postural information to indicate movement. The contextual information included, for example, holding a weapon, carrying a burden, sitting on a horse, playing a musical instrument, or performing such work as sewing or digging.

Some artists chose to depict things that are necessarily moving: moving water in a waterfall, river, or waves; fire; a bird or person suspended in the air; or a sailboat with full sails. The information necessitating an interpretation of movement was most common in the work of the American artist, Marin. It was absent or nearly absent from the ancient Egyptian and Greek art we included.

Only three of the art pictures surveyed showed movement by recording

TABLE 7.1
Results of a Cross-Cultural Survey of Pictures Showing Movement

Cultural period	Number of pictures viewed to find 25 pictures of movement	Pictorial movement indicators			
		Posture	Content	Necessitat-ing	Metaphor
Ancient cave paintings	70	25	9	—	—
Egyptian tomb paintings	66	24	17	1	—
Greek vase paintings	34	25	19	1	—
Mediaeval (Giotto; Martini)	80	25	15	7	4
Renaissance (da Vinci; Michelangelo)	58	25	18	4	3
Baroque (Rubens; Fragonard)	104	25	13	9	3
Realism (Goya; Delacroix)	89	25	17	4	—
Oriental (Kokusai)	50	25	20	9	—
American (Marin)	63	25	12	17	—
French Fauvism (Matisse; Marquet; Derain)	181	24	21	10	—
German Blaue Reiter (Macke; Kandinsky)	117	25	11	5	—
Contemporary children's books	34	25	18	6	7
Contemporary newspaper comics	41	25	5	5	7

NOTE: The sources for the pictures are in Appendix 2.

the path that an object had taken, and all were by the Fauvist artist, Marquet. Five of the pictures in children's books and four of the cartoon frames employed this information to convey an impression of movement. The artists in the Medieval, Renaissance, and Baroque periods drew wings on people (or angels), which may be metaphoric movement information. Other metaphoric information appeared as lines and limbs next to or attached to a nonliving object. These indicators were found in children's books and in comic strips. We did not find pictures with multiple viewpoints of a whole figure or parts of it.

In conclusion, we have identified different types of pictorial information for movement: (a) single viewpoint, single moment, which includes postural deviations from the resting position, sideways orientation, path of the object, and context information; (b) multiple viewpoints; (c) metaphor; and (d) abstraction. In looking at pictures from different historical and cultural periods we found that movement has most frequently been represented by postural deviations from the resting position and by context. The other types of information have become widely used only recently as ways of representing movement.

Because the various types of information have not appeared with equal frequency in the pictorial art of different cultures and periods, we became interested in whether these methods of movement indication are psychologically equally effective. In order to answer this question we turned to the experimental evidence.

THE EFFECTIVENESS OF PICTORIAL MOVEMENT INFORMATION—EXPERIMENTAL EVIDENCE

In our search for experimental evidence concerning the effectiveness of pictorial movement indicators, we found developmental and cross-cultural studies in which individuals responded to pictures showing movement. In the developmental studies, performance of different age groups was compared. In the cross-cultural studies, the performance of individuals with different degrees of exposure to a pictorial culture was compared. By combining information from both of these approaches, it is possible to infer the relative contribution of experience and maturation to the understanding of pictorial information for movement. Table 7.2 lists studies dealing, directly or indirectly, with pictorial movement perception and indicates the methodological features of these studies.

Single Viewpoint, Single Moment

Several types of representational information convey the impression of movement by capturing a scene from one viewpoint at one moment

TABLE 7.2
Studies in Which Responses to Pictorial Movement Indicators Were Recorded

Authors	Year published	Number of movement pictures	Representational indicators studied	Experimental task	Developmental paradigm	Cross-cultural paradigm
Amen, E.	1941	5	Postural	Verbal description of pictures' content	X	—
Klopfer, B. et al.	1941	?	Postural	Verbal description of pictures' content	X	—
Ford, M.	1946	?	Postural	Verbal description of pictures' content	X	—
Hemmendinger, L.	1951		Postural	Verbal description of pictures' content	X	—
Werner, H., & Wapner, S.	1954	1	Orientation	Indicating midline of field	—	—
Wapner, S., & Werner, H.	1957	4 pairs	Postural	Adjusting speed of two moving belts	X	—
Winter, W.	1963	2	Path of movement	Verbal description of pictures and answers to specific questions	—	X
Duncan, H. F. et al.	1973	5	Path of movement, multiple	Answers to specific questions	X	X
Kennedy, J. M., & Ross, A. S.	1975	2	Content	Answers to questions	X	X
Friedman, S. L., & Stevenson, M. B.	1975	45	Postural, path-of-movement, multiple	Classification of pictures	X	—
McCarrell, N.	1976	16	Postural	Recognition task	X	—
Brooks, P.	1977	18	Path-of-movement	Cued recall task	X	—

237

in time. As reviewed previously, these include postural information, information from the orientation of a figure, the content of the picture, the context of the picture, and the depiction of a path of movement. There is developmental and cross-cultural evidence about the effectiveness of several of these techniques.

POSTURAL

Deviations from the resting position are effective pictorial indicators of movement for young children. Amen's data (1941) show that 3-year olds (but not 2-year olds) report seeing movement in pictures with postural information (see Figure 7.10). Methodological improvements might allow confirmation of anecdotal evidence that children even below age 2 can understand pictorial movement. In the studies by Wapner and Werner (1957), Friedman and Stevenson (1975), and by McCarrell (1976), 4-, 5-, and 6-year olds responded accurately to pictorial postures that deviated from the resting position (see Figures 7.11, 7.12, and 7.13).

A curious finding is that the effectiveness of the postural deviation

FIGURE 7.10. Stimulus material from Amen (1941). [*From "Individual differences in apperceptive reaction: A study of the response of preschool children to pictures" by E. W. Amen, Genetic Psychology Monographs, 1941, 23, 319–385. Reprinted by permission.*]

FIGURE 7.11. Stimulus material from Wapner and Werner (1957). [*From Perceptual development by S. Wapner and H. Werner, 1957. Copyright 1957 by the Clark University Press. Reprinted by permission.*]

indicator appears to decline with increasing age. In the study by Wapner and Werner (1957), individuals were asked to adjust the speed of two moving belts that varied in both their rate of movement and in the pictorial posture (at rest versus deviating from the resting position) of the figures drawn on them. The speed adjustment performance of 16- to 19-year-olds was not affected by the postural movement indicators of the pictorial figures. The speed adjustment performance of younger individuals, however, was affected by the pictorial movement information. The most affected was the performance of the 6- to 7-year-olds, who made the moving belt with the information for pictorial movement move about 45 mm/sec slower than the moving belt without pictorial movement information. The latter belt was moving at 133 mm/sec. In the same vein, Friedman and Stevenson (1975) found that research participants 12 years

FIGURE 7.12. Stimulus materials from Friedman and Stevenson (1975). [From "Developmental changes in the understanding of implied motion in two-dimensional pictures" by S. L. Friedman and M. B. Stevenson, Child Development, 1975, 46, 773–778. Copyright 1975 by The University of Chicago Press, Chicago. Reprinted by permission.]

FIGURE 7.13. Hippopotamus and Dog. [*From "Children's detection and use of dynamic information in still pictures" by Nancy McCarrell, Paper presented at the symposium on "The extraction of information from pictures," The Society for Research in Child Development, Denver, Colorado, 1976*]

and older classified pictures with postural indicators of movement as representing movement between 50 and 60% of the time. Between 70 and 80% of the time, 4- and 6-year olds classified the same pictures as showing movement. Additional support is added by McCarrell (1976) who found that postural, pictorial movement indicators facilitated recognition memory in kindergarteners more than in third graders (exact ages are not reported).

In summary, the effectiveness of the postural information for portraying movement was found to vary differentially with subject age. Children younger than 3 did not use this pictorial information in describing what they saw in pictures. Between the ages of 3 and 10, children demonstrated distinct awareness of the presence of postural information for pictorial movement. Older individuals seemed to make less use of the same pictorial information. The behavior of the older individuals might well be the result of learning new ways for understanding pictures. For example, older children may have learned the demand for redundancy in information provided by pictures, or that sources of information within a picture should not contradict one another. In other words, experimental pictures might have been adequate for the younger subjects but might have been poor depictions for the more sophisticated, older subjects.

Studies of the development of responses to Rorschach ambiguous inkblots (Ford, 1946; Hemmendinger, 1951; Klopfer, Kelley, & Pietrowski, 1941) show similar results. Those inkblots suggesting pictorial movement postures to adults (i.e., those eliciting responses such as "dancing," "lifting," "bowling") are given movement responses by many 6- and 7-year olds. Nine-year olds are the most responsive to pictorial postures in the Rorschach blots. However, by 10 years, movement responses to the same inkblots decline.

In the context of discussing the postural information for pictorial movement, it is important to note that not all postural information should be considered equally effective. Arnheim (1971, pp. 407–408) points to the superior effectiveness of extreme and exaggerated postures. Friedman and Stevenson's (1975) data partially support Arnheim's opinion: Figures in a "running" posture with one leg stretched out front and the other stretched out back were classified as moving more often than were those in the "walking" posture with both feet on the ground and one leg bent at the knee. In the environment, animal and human active movement involves the bending of limbs at the knees or the elbows. Friedman and Stevenson (1975) found that pictures in which the figure's limbs were represented as bent were more frequently classified as showing movement than control figures that depicted the same postures with straight limbs.

ORIENTATION

The effect of a figure's or an object's pictorial orientation on the understanding of pictorial movement can be inferred from a study by Werner and Wapner (1954 and Figure 7.14). These authors have shown that adults perceive a figure facing the right edge of the page as being closer to it than a similar figure facing the left edge of the page.

CONTENT

Only one study has used pictures that necessitate a perception of pictorial movement because of the inherent motion of the object depicted. Kennedy and Ross (1975) used pictures of a fire and a river (see Figure 7.15) in their study of the schooled and unschooled members of a non-pictorial culture. They found that their subjects could identify the two pictures correctly despite the absence of any other pictorial movement information in the pictures. We have not found experimental evidence about the effectiveness of context and literal path-of-movement information in eliciting a correct interpretation of pictorial movement.

FIGURE 7.14. Bird or airplane from H. Werner and S. Wapner (1954). [From "Studies in physiognomic perception: I effect of configural dynamics and meaning induced sets on the position of the apparent median plane" by H. Werner and S. Wapner, Journal of Psychology, 1954, 38, 51–65. Copyright 1954 by The Journal Press. Reprinted by permission.]

FIGURE 7.15. **Fire and river from Kennedy and Ross (1975).** [*Reprinted from "Outline picture perception by the Songe of Papua" by J. M. Kennedy and A. S. Ross, Perception, 1975, 4, 391–406. Copyright 1975 by Pion Ltd., Reprinted by permission.*]

Multiple Viewpoints

The understanding of pictorial information about movement conveyed by representations of multiple body parts improves with both age and acculturation. Friedman and Stevenson (1975) showed their subjects three pictures with multiple body parts: one with two extra legs, one with two extra heads, and one with four extra arms (see Figure 7.12). Out of all the opportunities to classify, almost 80% of the time 4-year olds classified these pictures as showing movement, and in more than 90% of the time older subjects did the same. Cross-cultural evidence suggests that experience with pictures plays a role in the development of the ability to correctly interpret pictures with multiple body parts. Duncan, Gourlay, and Hudson (1973) interviewed South African children in Grades 1–5 who had differing amounts of exposure to Western culture and its pictures. The subjects were of European, rural Zulu, urban Zulu, rural Tsonga, and urban Tsonga backgrounds. These children were shown a picture of a child with three heads (one facing the viewer and two facing sideways) and with lines indicating the path of movement encircling the head (see Figure 7.16–H-4). Only 3% of the rural Zulus, 14% of the rural Tsongas, but 35% of the urban Zulus and 24% of the urban Tsongas thought that the multiple head represented a head in movement. However, 86% of the White South Africans interpreted the head as moving. Data from these

Picture H-4   Picture H-2

FIGURE 7.16. **Boy and dog from Duncan, Gourlay, and Hudson (1973).** [*Reprinted from H. F. Duncan, N. Gourlay, and Wm. Hudson, A study of pictorial perception among Bantu and white primary school children in South Africa, p. 26. (Human Sciences Research Council Series No. 31), © Witwatersrand University Press, Johannesburg, 1973.*]

two experiments suggest that the understanding of the multiple information for pictorial movement is acquired with exposure to a pictorial
culture and that, within the Western culture, this understanding is present
as early as 4 years old.

Metaphor

Developmental and cross-cultural evidence suggests that movement
indicated metaphorically is better understood by older and more acculturated subjects. Friedman and Stevenson (1975) found that less than 30%
of the responses that 4 year olds and 6 year olds gave to nine pictures
with movement metaphors (see Figure 7.12) were movement responses.
In fact, a similar percentage of movement responses were given to figures
with *no* pictorial movement information. By contrast, 12 year olds and
20 year olds gave movement responses in about 70% of the opportunities
to classify these pictures. This was the same percentage as that for the
pictures with postural indicators of movement. When Brooks (1977) compared 8-, 12-, and 15-year-olds on their ability to remember pictures that
contained or lacked metaphoric path-of-movement information (see Figure 7.17), she found that the path-of-movement information facilitated
the recall of pictures by the two older age groups but especially by the
oldest group. Similarly, in the South African study by Duncan and his

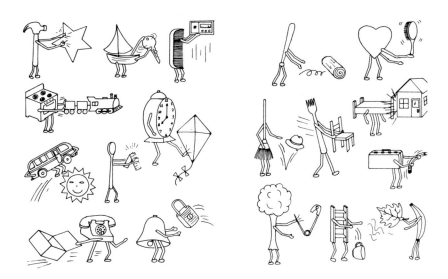

FIGURE 7.17 Pictures with action lines from Brooks (1977). [*From ''The role of action lines
in children's memory for pictures'' by P. H. Brooks, Journal of Experimental Child Psychology,
1977, 23, 98–107. Copyright 1977 by Academic Press, Inc., New York.*]

colleagues (1973), metaphoric path-of-movement information (see Figure 7.16–H-2) was correctly interpreted more often by subjects in the higher school grades.

Although the above studies suggest that age (i.e., maturation or increased exposure to pictures) affects the understanding of pictorial metaphors, the cross-cultural comparisons stress the importance of exposure to a pictorial culture for the understanding of the same information. In the study by Duncan *et al.* (1973), subjects were shown a picture of a dog running and wagging its tail (Figure 7.16–H-2). The movement of the tail was indicated by circular marks around it. In response to the question of what were the marks around the tail, only 1% of the rural Zulus, 3% of the rural Tsongas, 18% of the urban Zulus, 14% of the urban Tsongas, but 75% of the Europeans gave a correct answer. Another South African study (Winter, 1963) also showed that metaphoric information for movement (see "impact" lines in Figure 7.18) is misunderstood by those with little European background. The available evidence leads to the view that the understanding of the metaphoric information develops later than the understanding of postural or multiple information. It also indicates that exposure to Western pictorial representations (possibly "action" comics and cartoons) contributes toward an earlier and better understanding of the metaphoric pictorial information for movement.

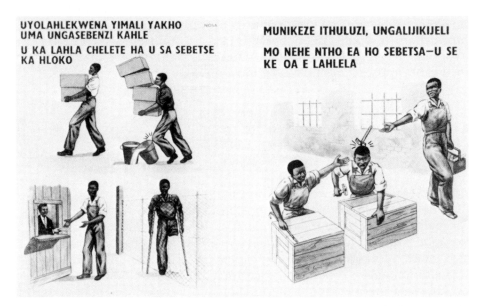

FIGURE 7.18. Safety posters from Winter (1963). [*From "The perception of safety posters by Bantu industrial workers" by W. Winter, Psychologia Africana, 1963, 10, 127–135. Copyright 1963 by Psychologia Africana. Reprinted by permission.*]

Abstract Representations

The studies discussed previously are the only studies we found in our search for experimental data to tell us about the effectiveness of the different types of pictorial information for movement. We did not find any experimental research about abstract pictures that convey the impression of movement.

The findings of the developmental studies show that the effectiveness of postural, multiple viewpoint, and metaphoric information changes with the age of the picture viewer. It seems that in order to understand these types of information people must either reach a particular level of cognitive maturity or learn the association between the types of information and what they represent. The cross-cultural studies have not systematically explored the effectiveness of the postural pictorial information, but they have explored the effectiveness of multiple viewpoint and metaphoric information. These studies show that the effectiveness of multiple viewpoint and metaphoric information depends at least in part on the viewers level of exposure to a pictorial culture.

Our survey of the experimental evidence underscores the fact that there is still limited research concerning the understanding of pictorial movement indicators. We would like to see a systematic effort to study, both developmentally and cross-culturally, the effectiveness of *all* the indicators we have enumerated. Equally important would be a research effort of studying the effectiveness of different combinations of pictorial movement indicators as most pictures of movement contain redundant information. It would be of special interest to find out which indicator combinations are only informative of the artist's intention and which create a lively impression of pictorial movements.

A CONTINUUM OF INFORMATION CORRESPONDENCE BETWEEN PICTORIAL INDICATORS AND THE ENVIRONMENT

The evidence just reviewed shows that indicating movement by postural deviations from the resting position is common historically and is easily understood by all the individuals studied. Indicating movement by metaphors is less prevalent in art and is a relatively poor source of pictorial movement information for young and/or unacculturated individuals.

The differential effectiveness of pictorial movement indicators took us by surprise. Theories about the relationship between pictorial and environmental information (Arnheim, 1971; Gibson, 1977; Gombrich, 1960; Goodman, 1968) suggested that all types of pictorial information should be equally effective in eliciting a correct interpretation.

It is informative to review the theoretical work about the relationship between pictorial indicators and the environment they represent. A correct reading of representational pictures involves an ability to detect an equivalence between pictorial forms and their environmental referents. Yet, there are many differences between the two. Consider the fact that a picture is a flat surface, whereas our world is three dimensional. The pictorial shapes are very rarely of the same size, color, and texture as those of the objects represented. Frequently the content of a picture is out of context relative to its surroundings. Although the perceived spatial relationships between real objects change as their viewer moves around, the perceived spatial relationships between depicted objects remain constant. The perception of real movement most commonly occurs when an object is in the process of changing its position relative to other objects, but pictorial movement does not involve such change over time. The perception of real sound involves the auditory modality, yet it is possible to indicate sound through pictures.

Despite these differences between pictures and the environment, the power of pictures to evoke the environment is compelling. What are the bases for our capability to detect an equivalence between pictures and the environment? The answer to this question depends on the theory one subscribes to. Gibson (1971, 1977) argues that pictures provide their observer with the same kind of information as the environment. The accuracy of the information is independent of the degree to which the pictures replicate the visual sensations provided by the environment. This is possible because different optic arrays can contain the same information without having the same stimulus energies at all points. The information Gibson refers to is that of the distinctive features and invariants that are equivalent in the real and pictorial optic arrays.

Unlike Gibson, Arnheim (1971) argues that a picture is a visual interpretation of reality and that the correspondence between a picture and what it represents is based on both equivalence of structure and some agreed on convention. He makes the point that the structure of the pictorial shapes should deviate as little as possible from the structural concept the viewer has of the forms to be represented. In his treatment of "tension" (1971, Chapter 9), Arnheim (1971) explains that the perception of pictorial movement is not a product of learning to associate particular pictorial shapes with real movement, rather, the perception of equivalence is due to the dynamic brain processes activated by pictorial shapes that are balanced in a "dynamic composition (p. 416)."

Gombrich (1960) goes a step further in emphasizing the conventional aspects of pictures. According to him pictorial representations are compositions of pictorial schemes. These schemes are culture specific; they do not possess objective likeness to the environment, rather, they represent it and do not provide their viewers with the wealth of information given by the environment. A picture suggests the environment by pre-senting a relational model that is in agreement with the relationships existing in the environment. Familiarity with the pictorial vocabulary is necessary but not sufficient for seeing a correspondence between a pic-ture and its real subject: Pictures as a rule lack pieces of information about their referents and sometimes offer contradictory information. Therefore, the viewer of a picture must generate and test hypotheses regarding the meaning of the picture before he or she can discover the correspondence between the pictorial and the real. Consequently, the seeing of a correspondence between pictorial and real movement de-pends on the interpretations that viewers give these pictures (Gombrich, 1960).

Goodman (1968) is the most extreme proponent of the view that pic-torial representation does not require that pictures replicate any of the information available in the environment. In other words, his views are diametrically opposed to the views expressed by Gibson (1971). Goodman claims that pictorial representation can be achieved by an arbitrary system for depicting almost anything. The correctness of pictures is dependent on how informative the artist chooses to be within a given system. Ac-cording to Goodman (1968), the perceived realism of pictures depends on the viewers' familiarity with the pictorial system of representation: "If representation is a matter of choice and correctness a matter of in-formation, realism is a matter of habit (p. 38)."

In summary, Gibson, Arnheim, Gombrich, and Goodman do not agree on the nature of the correspondence between pictures and the environ-ment represented. These authors do, however, share an important as-sumption: Each writes about pictures in a manner implying that pictures (i.e., all pictures) obey a principle or set of principles of correspondence to the environment.

If all pictorial information is representational according to the same set of principles, then all pictorial information should be equally effective in eliciting correct interpretations of pictorial materials. The results of the experimental studies we surveyed show that pictorial information is not equally effective for young children or for partially acculturated individ-uals. This fact suggests to us that pictorial movement indicators do not correspond to the environment according to one set of representational principles.

We believe that the understanding of a pictorial indicator by subjects who are of different cognitive or pictorial naivety can be used as an in-direct measure of the correspondence between pictorial and environ-mental information. Pictorial information that is understood correctly by very young subjects probably does not call for mature cognitive function, nor for the learning of associations between pictorial shapes and aspects of the environment. For example, there is evidence that pictures of objects are understood by 5- and 6-month-old American infants (DeLoach, Strauss, & Maynard, 1977; Dirks & Gibson, 1977; Rose, 1977) and by individuals who live in nonpictorial cultures (for review, see Hagen & Jones, 1978). As these pictures of objects are so readily understood, the correspondence between the pictorial and environmental information for specifying objects is probably self-evident, even though there are many differences between the picture and what it portrays.

When there is a developmental improvement in the understanding of a correspondence between the pictorial and environmental information, it is not clear whether the improvement is due to cognitive maturation or to the learning of associations between the pictorial and environmental information. For example, Friedman and Stevenson (1975) found that pictures in which movement was indicated by metaphoric information were correctly interpreted more frequently by older subjects. This could be explained by either increased cognitive maturity with increased age or by an increased opportunity to learn associations. In such cases, comparisons of the performance of members of pictorial cultures with that of people having little or no pictorial culture highlights the role of learning as separated from maturation regarding the ability to understand pictures. Although Duncan et al. (1973) and Friedman and Stevenson (1975) did not use the same pictorial materials, the Duncan et al. cross-cultural findings suggest that the correct understanding of metaphoric pictorial movement information calls for the learning of associations between pictorial and environmental information. In cases where acculturation is not shown to be responsible for age changes in the understanding of pictures, one could infer that the equivalence between pictorial and environmental information becomes self-evident with sufficient maturation.

Although the data about the effectiveness of pictorial movement indicators are far from complete, they suggest that the indicators can be placed on a continuum in terms of the information correspondence between them and the environment. At one extreme of the continuum are the pictorial indicators spontaneously recognized by a naive viewer as representative of the environment. Postural deviations from the resting position provide examples of such indicators. At the other extreme of the continuum are indicators that are arbitrary and must be learned as one learns words labeling objects and events. Arrows showing the direction of movement are an example of this end of the continuum. In between are pictorial indicators that require an ability to notice pictorial analogies (e.g., pictorial metaphors). Once such metaphors are noticed, they are grasped as meaningfully related to their environmental referents.

We do not believe that our proposition regarding a continuum of information equivalence between pictorial indicators and the environment is specific to pictorial movement indicators. Three of the four representational indicators are not unique to representations of movement. They are to be found in pictures of objects, spatial relationships and sound:

1. When an object is represented or when spatial relationships among objects are represented, they are usually shown from a single perspective that does not record all the environmental information about the referents. For example, if the front of an object is recorded, its sides and its back are missing from the picture. When sound production is represented it is often shown by a posture (mouth open, fingers touching a keyboard) seen at one moment in time from one point of view.

2. Pictures of objects and pictures of scenes sometimes show multiple viewpoints. For example, to show a face, some cubists combine front and profile views in the same painting (e.g., Cooper, 1971). In oriental art, part of a scene may be drawn from one viewpoint, part from another (Willetts, 1965). Some modern artists also show multiple viewpoints of the same scene in a single picture (Escher, 1967).

3. Pictorial metaphors are also used in pictures other than pictures of movement (Goodman, 1968; Kennedy, 1976). These metaphors interpret the depicted environment as when conveying mood by usage of specific colors or by use of specific gestures in an inappropriate context (e.g., dark colors to show sadness; broad smiles by attendants of a funeral). Pictorial metaphors often convey abstract ideas such as peace or friction (e.g., a dove carrying an olive leaf flying between leaders of countries at war; "lightening" lines at a site of friction).

Our proposition regarding a continuum of information correspondence between pictorial indicators and the environment provides a framework for research and theory development about the nature of this correspondence. We are currently testing the proposition in a developmental study of the understanding of pictorial sound indicators. Our proposition also has practical implications. In the United States children are introduced to picture books during their first year. Yet, the material presented in such books is not always geared to the picture-reading abilities of young children. For example, contemporary children's picture books make use of pictorial movement information that young children have not been able to correctly interpret in experimental presentations (Friedman & Stevenson, 1975). In order to design pictures that will be understood by their prospective readers, it is necessary to have information about the type of pictorial information which can be understood by children of different ages.

Another application is to intelligence tests. In the United States, intelligence of children is evaluated by tests that rely on responses to pictorial materials. This means that the evaluations are determined, to some extent, by the ability to understand pictures. This ability may or may not be related to the mental maturity of the child. Because performance on intelligence tests determines many school experiences of children, it is important to make sure that these tests use pictures that children of the same level of maturation but of different cultural experiences understand in the same way.

SUMMARY

This chapter is about pictorial information for movement. We refer to information in two-dimensional pictures that evoke a perception of active or passive movement. In looking at pictures from different historical and cultural periods we have identified pictorial indicators for movement:

1. There are indicators depicting a selected single moment of the process of movement as seen from a specific point of view.
2. There are indicators showing an object (living or still) or part of it at selected successive moments.
3. There are indicators suggesting movement by showing side-by-side aspects of the environment that are unlikely to occur together in the environment.
4. There are abstract lines or shapes that have the power to suggest movement.

We noticed that only the first type of indicators have been used frequently in art of different cultures and periods.

A limited body of psychological research suggests that the different pictorial indicators for movement are not equally effective—they are first understood at different ages. The understanding of some indicators has been studied cross-culturally and was found to depend on the amount of exposure to a pictorial culture (more exposure was associated with better understanding). The varied effectiveness of the pictorial indicators for movement suggested to us that these indicators are also varied in terms of their correspondence to the environmental movement they represent. We consequently hypothesized that these indicators could be placed on a continuum of information correspondence to the environment. At one extreme of the continuum are the pictorial indicators spontaneously recognized as representative of the environment. At the other extreme of the same continuum are indicators that are arbitrary and must be learned by a process of association. Because pictorial indicators for movement share characteristics with pictorial indicators of objects, scenes, and sounds, we suggest that the latter may also be varied in terms of their information correspondence to the environment.

ACKNOWLEDGMENTS

The authors wish to thank R. Arnheim, H. Gardner, J. J. Gibson, E. H. Gombrich, N. Goodman, R. N. Haber, M. A. Hagen, J. M. Kennedy, R. W. Pickford, and R. D. Walk for their critical reading of this manuscript. Thanks also go to M. Lybarger and J. Kay for assistance with the second survey of pictures.

APPENDIX 1

Art books used in our initial survey of pictorial techniques for representing movement:

Bland, D. *A history of book illustrations.* Berkeley, California: Univ. of California Press, 1969. Pp. 34, 37, 52.
Brett, G. *Kinetic art: The language of movement.* New York: Reinhold, 1968. P. 14.
Cassou, J. *Picasso.* New York: Hyperion Press, 1940. P. 126.
Demargne, P. *Aegean art: The origins of Greek art.* (The arts of mankind). France: Thames & Hudson, 1964. Pp. 177, 179, 192, 195, 198.
Donadoni, S. *Egyptian Museum Cairo.* In A. Mondadori (Ed.), *Great museums of the world.* New York: Simon and Schuster, 1969. Pp. 23, 123, 139.
Duncan, D. D. *Picasso's Picassos.* New York: Harper, 1962. Pp. 146, 149, 156.
Fisher, R., & Reff, T. *Picasso.* New York: Tudor, 1967. Plate 50.
Grimme, E. G. *Unsere Liebe Frau.* Germany: Verlag M. DuMont Schauberg, 1968. Plates 21, 25, 60.
Fry, R., Binyon, L., Siren, O., Rackham, B., Kendrick, A. F., Winkworth, W. W. *Chinese art: An introductory handbook to painting, sculpture, ceramics, textiles, bronzes, minor arts.* London: B. T. Batsford, 1935. Plate 9.
Haftmann, W. *Painting in the twentieth century.* Washington, D. C.: Praeger, 1965. Pp. 116, 122, 156.
Huyghe, R. *Art treasures of the Louvre.* New York: Harry N. Abrams, 1960. Plates 44, 45, 46, 48.
Kingman, L., Foster, J., & Lantoft, R. G. *Illustrations of children's books: 1957–1966.* Boston: Horn Book, 1968. Pp. 8, 40, 49, 51.
Longstreet, S. *The dance in art.* Alhambra, California: Borden, 1968.
Maringer, J., & Bandi, H. G. *Art in the ice age—Spanish Levant art, arctic art.* New York: Praeger, 1953. Pp. 77, 121, 124.
Lockwood, A. *Diagrams.* New York: Watson-Guptill, 1969. Pp. 76, 77, 116, 122.
Meyer, F. *Marc Chagall: Life and work.* New York: Harry N. Abrams. Pp. 233, 267, 371.
Rowland, K. *The shapes we need (looking and seeing).* New York: Van Nostrand Reinhold, 1965. P. 102.
Rowland, K. *Learning to see Book III. Movement.* New York: Van Nostrand Reinhold, 1969. Pp. 1, 2, 3, 5, 6, 12.
Singh, M. *Himalayan art, Unesco art books.* Greenwich, Connecticut: New York Graphic Society Ltd., 1968. Pp. 26, 85, 90, 91, 154, 170, 276.
Staff Members of the Tokyo National Museum (Ed.). *Pageant of Japanese art* (Painting 1, Vol. 1). Tokyo: Toto Bunka. Pp. 3, 26, 27, 39.
Stubbe, W. *Graphic arts in the 20th Century.* New York: Praeger, 1962. P. 217.
The New Brunswick Museum, Saint John, N. B. *Arctic values,* 1965 (Nov. 19–Dec. 19). Pp. 56, 61.
United Nations Educational, Scientific, and Cultural Organization. *Australia Aboriginal paintings.* New York: New York Graphic Society, 1954.

APPENDIX 2

Art books used in our second survey of pictures showing movement:

American

Helm, M. *Jean Marin*. Boston: Pellegrini & Cudahy, 1948.

Ancient Cave Painting

Gardi, R., & Tschudi, J. *Felsbilder der Sahara*. im Tassili n'Ajjer:Bern, Stuttgart, Hallwag, 1969.
Ucko, P. J., & Rosenfeld, A. *Palaelithic cave art*. New York: McGraw-Hill, 1967.

Baroque

Anaoff, A. *L'Oeuvre dessiné de Fragonard*. Paris: Catalogue Raisonne, 1968.
Smith, E. L. *Rubens*. London: Spring Books, 1964.

Children

Flack, M. *Angus and the cat*. Garden City, New York: Doubleday, 1931.
Mother Goose nursery rhymes. New York: Platt & Munk, 1953.
Rey, M. *Curious George flies a kite*. New York: Houghton Mifflin, 1958.
Scarry, R. *Please and thank you book*. New York: Random House, 1973.
Scuss, Dr. *Green eggs and ham*. New York: Beginner Books, 1960.

Egyptian Tomb Painting

Christiane Desroches-Noblecourt. *L'art Egyptian*. Paris: Presses Universites de France, 1962.
Smith, W. S. *Ancient Egypt*. Boston: Museum of Fine Arts, 1960.

French

Derain, A. *Exposition Derain*. Paris: Galerie Schmit, 1976.
Guichard-Meilli, J. *Henri Matisse*. Paris: Fernand Hazen, 1967.
Marquet. *Exposition Marquet*. Paris: Galerie Schmit, 1967.

German

Bovi, A. *Wassily Kandinsky*. Firenze: Sansoni, 1970.
Kunstverein, F. *Ausust Macke*. Hamburg: Kunstverein, 1969.

Greek Vase Paintings

Cook, R. M. *Greek art, its development, character, and influence*. London: Trinity Press, 1972.

Mediaeval

Grosebruch, M. *Glotto di Bondone*. Koln, Germany: M. Dumont Schauberg, 1962.

Newspaper Comics

The Washington Post, November 28, 29, 1977.

Oriental

Grilli, E. *Katsushika Hokusai*. Tokyo: Charles E. Tuttle, 1955.
Perzynski, F. *Hokusai*. Bielefeld and Leipzig: Valhagen & Klasing, 1908.

Realism

Arts Council of Great Britain. *Delacroix*. London: Arts Council, 1964.
Ganter, J. *Goya*. Berlin: Mann, 1974.

Renaissance

Allodili, E. *Michelangelo*. Florence, Italy: Novissima Enciclopedia Monografica Illustrata, 1928.
Bode, W. von. *Leonardo da Vinci*, Mit 73 abbildugen. Berlin: G. Grote, 1921.
Clement, C. *Michelangelo*. New York: Scribner & Welford, 1882.

REFERENCES

Amen, E. W. Individual differences in apperceptive reaction: A study of the response of preschool children to pictures. *Genetic Psychology Monographs*, 1941, *23*, 319–385.
Arnheim, R. *Art and visual perception*. Berkeley: Univ. of California Press, 1971.
Brooks, P. H. The role of action lines in children's memory for pictures. *Journal of Experimental Child Psychology*, 1977, *23*, 98–107.
Cooper, D. *The cubist epoch*. New York: Phaidon, 1971.
DeLoach, J. S., Strauss, M. S., & Maynard, J. *Infants' recognition of pictorial representations of real objects*. Unpublished paper presented at the Biennial Meeting of the Society for Research in Child Development, New Orleans, 1977.
Dirks, J., & Gibson, E. Infants' perception of similarity between live people and their photographs. *Child Development*, 1977, *48*, 124–130.
Duncan, H. F., Gourlay, N., & Hudson, W. *A study of pictorial perception among Bantu and White primary school children in South Africa*. Johannesberg: Witwatersrand Univ. Press, 1973.
Escher, M. C. *The graphic work of Escher*. Meredith Press, 1967.
Ford, M. *The application of the Rorschach test to young children*. Minneapolis, Minnesota: Univ. of Minnesota Press, 1946.
Friedman, S. L., & Stevenson, M. B. Developmental changes in the understanding of implied motion in two-dimensional pictures. *Child Development*, 1975, 46, 773–778.
Gibson, J. J. The information available in pictures. *Leonardo*, 1971, *4*, 27–35.
Gibson, J. J. The ecological approach to the visual perception of pictures. *Leonardo*, 1977, *12*.
Gombrich, E. H. *Art and illusion* (2nd ed.). Princeton, New Jersey: Princeton Univ. Press, 1960.
Goodman, N. *Languages of art: An approach to a theory of symbols*. Indianapolis, Indiana: Bobbs-Merrill, 1968.

Goodnow, J. J. Visible thinking: Cognitive aspects of change in drawings. *Child Development*, 1978, *49*, 637–641.

Hagen, M. A., & Jones, R. K. Cultural effects on pictorial perception: How many words is one picture really worth? In R. D. Walk, & H. L. Pick, Jr. (Eds.), *Perception and experience*. New York: Plenum, 1978.

Hemmendinger, L. *A genetic study of structural aspects of perception as reflected in the Rorschach test responses.* Unpublished doctoral dissertation, Clark University, 1951.

Kennedy, J. M., & Ross, A. S. Outline picture perception by the Songe of Papua. *Perception*, 1975, *4*, 391–406.

Kennedy, J. M. Pictorial metaphor: A theory of movement indicators in static pictures. Paper presented at the *Information through Pictures Symposium*, Swarthmore College, 1976.

Klopfer, B., Kelley, D. M., Pietrowski, Z. Rorschach reactions in early childhood. *Rorschach research exchange*, 1941, *5*, 1–23.

McCarrell, N. Children's detection and use of dynamic information in still pictures. Paper presented at the symposium on *The extraction of information from pictures*, The Society for Research in Child Development, Denver, Colorado, 1976.

Rose, S. A. Infants' transfer of response between two-dimensional and three-dimensional stimuli. *Child Development*, 1977, *48*, 1086–1091.

Rovet, J., & Ives, W. W. *Graphic orientations of familiar and novel objects: A developmental and cross-cultural study.* Unpublished manuscript, Hospital for Sick Children, Toronto, Ontario, Canada, 1977.

Smith, B. *Mexico, a history in art.* New York: Harper, 1968. Pp. 68, 124, 132, 133, 138, 139.

Wapner, S., & Werner, H. *Perceptual development.* Worcester, Massachusetts: Clark Univ. Press, 1957.

Werner, H., & Wapner, S. Studies in physiognomic perception: I. Effect of configurational dynamics and meaning induced sets on the position of the apparent median plane. *The Journal of Psychology*, 1954, *38*, 51–65.

Winter, W. The perception of safety posters by Bantu industrial workers. *Psychologica Africana*, 1963, *10*, 127–135.

Willetts, W. *Foundations of Chinese art: From neolithic pottery to modern architecture.* New York: McGraw-Hill, 1965.

CHAPTER **8**

D. N. PERKINS
MARGARET A. HAGEN

Convention, Context, and Caricature

Introduction 257
A for Instance 261
Measuring Consistency in Caricaturing 268
A Test of Transfer 271
Negation and Recognition 275
    Recognition Blocked by Contraindication 277
    Recognition from Partial Evidence 277
Three More Theories of Caricature 278
Caricature and Convention 282
References 285

INTRODUCTION

Caricatures are no joke, at least not for those who would understand the perception of pictures. Although manifestly distorted, caricatures nevertheless prompt recognition. One recognizes which president, senator, or celebrity appears in a cartoon, although the rendering of the face ranges far from realistic portrayal. What theory of perception explains this? In fact, we will have to ponder no less than five theories before reaching a tentative decision. We begin by bracketing the possibilities with two extreme theories: the *tag* and *superportrait* accounts of caricature recognition.

257

The Perception of Pictures
Volume I

In an essay entitled "The Mask and the Face," E. H. Gombrich perhaps best expresses a tag theory (Gombrich, 1972). Gombrich mentions one especially striking example, that of Hitler's financial wizard, Hjalmar Schacht, who apparently wore a high-starched collar. Over a period of time, a greatly exaggerated collar could replace Schacht's face entirely in caricature (Gombrich, 1972, pp. 12–13). Gombrich (1972) calls such a representation the *mask* rather than the *face*: "The mask here stands for the crude distinctions, the deviations from the norm which mark a person off from others. Any such deviation which attracts our attention may serve us as a tab of recognition and promises to save us the effort of further scrutiny (p. 13)."

In an earlier essay, Gombrich (1963) mentions other examples about which a similar point could be made. One caricature of Theodore Roosevelt represented the vigorous president as a bull moose with the Roosevelt glasses and grin. The cartoon was inspired by Roosevelt declaring himself to be as healthy as a bull moose. Another caricature depicted Roosevelt as the Democratic donkey, his cigarette holder jauntily clamped in his smiling mouth. In these, as in the Schacht example, a couple of idiosyncracies carry the point and little of the shape of the face appears.

What do such caricatures imply about how they are recognized? These pictures *tag* their subjects by one or two salient traits, much as do nicknames like "slim" or "red." However, such tags give recognition little to go on and therefore recognition must rely considerably on context and convention. First, context contributes by providing other clues outside the face (e.g., the donkey or bull moose in the Roosevelt cartoons), signs of place (e.g., Whitehouse or United Nations building in the background), and captions. Second, context assists by narrowing the field of individuals: Ordinarily, only the newsworthy are caricatured. In an extreme case, the context may help so much that one can dispense with the face. Blatant examples occur when the caricaturist simply labels a collar or cuff with the person's name, as often happens with less well-known public figures.

Recognition also may depend on the viewer's knowledge of conventions for depicting the individual. The Roosevelt cartoons possibly illustrate this, but Schacht's collar surely does. At first, the collar alone would have been confusing. But over time, it became an established part of the way Schacht was caricatured. Finally, the collar could replace the face altogether because it had acquired a conventional significance.

A tag theory of caricature recognition in general would claim that all or most caricatures followed the Schacht or the Roosevelt models. Gombrich does not assert this himself, although his examples show that at least some caricatures function like tags. As an account of caricature, a tag theory has two particular claims to make. First, *caricatures reflect very few distinguishing attributes of the true face.* Second, *experience with a face from personal contact, photographs, television appearances, and so on does not prepare one to recognize the face in caricature.* Recognition requires the support of a directive context and/or an established convention.

A study by T. A. Ryan and Carol Schwartz (1956) suggests a contrasting account of caricature recognition, although Ryan and Schwartz neither examined portrait caricatures nor even employed the term caricature. Ryan and Schwartz wondered what mode of representation would best communicate complex spatial arrangements. They investigated four kinds of representations: photographs, shaded drawings, line drawings, and cartoons. According to Ryan and Schwartz (1956), the cartoons "distorted the figure to emphasize the essential spatial relationships involved (p. 61)." They used a tachistoscope to expose depictions of a hand in various postures, a set of knife switches in several on and off arrangements, and cut-away views of valves in a steam engine at four points in the engine cycle. Each subject was asked to reproduce the configuration seen—shaping his hand as the pictured hand, adjusting the knife switches as shown, or picking out the right stage of the engine cycle. The experimenters kept increasing the exposure time until a subject succeeded. Ryan and Schwartz found that the cartoon representation produced the most rapid response for the valves and the switches. Though cartoons proved only third best for the hand, the averaged results also favored the cartoons.

Ryan's and Schwartz's cartoons could as easily be called caricatures. Ryan and Schwartz talk of emphasizing essential spatial relationships, and this recalls the way portrait caricaturists themselves often characterize their art. Caricaturists say they highlight the most salient features of the face, using exaggeration to make them even more salient (Berger, 1952; Rother, 1966). E. J. Gibson (1969, pp. 102–105) has suggested much the same account, and so have we (Goldman & Hagen, 1978; Perkins, 1975a,b).

Of course, it must be acknowledged that a caricature omits much about the face. Lost are the precise proportions and small details. The caricatured nose does not represent the length of the true nose. But at the same time, caricature preserves the trends of attributes with respect to population norms (Perkins, 1975 a). That is, in caricature, a long nose gets longer, a short nose shorter, a strong chin stronger, a weak chin weaker. These examples are some of the "crude distinctions, the deviations from the norm" of which Gombrich writes. However, caricature may involve not just one or two such tags, but indications of the trends of many attributes. The caricature would *show* these trends more plainly than even the real face.

All this amounts to what we will call a *superportrait* theory of caricature recognition. The superportrait theory makes claims just opposite to those of the tag theory: *Caricatures reflect many distinguishing attributes of the true face* (trends although not exact attributes). Second, *familiarity with the real face allows recognition of caricatures with little help from context and convention, swifter and more accurate recognition than from pho-*

tographs, conventionally realistic paintings, or even the real face itself.

In addition to the theoretical contrast they suggest, Gombrich, on the one hand, and Ryan and Schwartz, on the other, deal with differing functions of caricature. The newspaper and periodical caricatures discussed by Gombrich illustrate the *reference* function. The caricatured face contributes to recognizing the cartoon subject. The audience comes prepared to discern the reference by prior knowledge of the person's face, and perhaps of context and convention. Ryan and Schwartz, in contrast, discuss an informing function of caricature. The viewer comes to the caricature not already knowing its subject, but intending to learn the look of the subject. Both functions appear valuable, and the educational potentials of the informing function have been explored only minimally.

It is noteworthy that the tag and superportrait theories appraise differently the effectiveness of these functions. The superportrait theory allows reference to be accomplished easily, by a rendering of the face alone. The tag theory asks much more of the audience—a knowledge of context and convention to support recognition. The superportrait theory holds a caricature to be the very best way to inform. However, the tag theory has the caricature informing only about one or two, often superficial idiosyncracies. One is left with the question of how and how well do caricatures inform and refer. The answer requires testing the two theories.

To explore this issue is to ask fundamental questions about a phenomenon of pattern recognition. It might be thought that the answers would hold true for human pattern recognition in general. Face recognition easily might be taken as a typical case. Viewers would differentiate faces by the same processes and with combinations of the same generic set of attributes as they would use to differentiate Cadillacs from Fords, or turkeys from chickens.

But in fact, three lines of experimental evidence show face recognition to be a rather special matter. People recognize individuals of their own race better than individuals of other races (Galper, 1973; Malpass & Kravitz, 1969; Shepherd, Deregowski, & Ellis, 1974). Although photographic positives and negatives present the same amount of information in a technical sense, subjects perform better on face recognition paradigms with positives (Galper, 1970; Galper & Hochberg, 1971; Phillips, 1972). Similarly, performance is better on upright versus inverted faces (Goldstein, 1975; Hochberg & Galper, 1967). All three findings show face recognition to be more than an instance of a general ability. Indeed, we are inclined to think that there is no such general ability to which face recognition somehow is an exception. Rather, recognition routinely would be specialized to its various needs: differentiating faces, makes of automobiles, words, or whatever.

What does all this mean for the present inquiry? On the one hand, it says that our consideration of face and caricature recognition concerns only a special case. But on the other hand, it allows that the special case might be typical in its broad characteristics of the many other special cases comprising a perceiver's powers of recognition. Accordingly, later in this chapter we will venture some general remarks on recognition and on the reading of representations other than caricatures.

A FOR INSTANCE

The tag and superportrait theories disagreed twice. The first contention concerned the extent to which caricatures used distinguishing attributes of the true face. That issue invited a case-study approach, one pursued through this and the next section. The case study began with the possibility that the Schacht and Roosevelt caricatures were atypical. How would caricaturists routinely treat the visage of a public figure? To study their use of distinguishing attributes, locating attributes common to caricature and face would not suffice. The attributes would have to be distinguishing both of caricatures as caricatures of that person, and of the real face as the face of that person. Furthermore, the attributes would need to differentiate caricature and face not only logically, but perceptually, contributing to the wholistic "look" of the face. Only then might such attributes be the physical basis for the quick reflexive recognition of real face and caricature alike.

One of us started such an investigation in 1970, examining caricatures of Richard Nixon (Perkins, 1975b). Thirty-eight caricatures were collected from magazines and newspapers. Six photographs of Richard Nixon were found to compare with the caricatures. Finally, caricatures and photographs of other individuals provided a comparison sample.

After some effort, four attributes were isolated that might distinguish caricatures of Richard Nixon from the caricatures of others. To this point, we have spoken carefully of "attributes" or "properties" rather than "features," because the latter has a somewhat narrower connotation. However, the attributes found could quite appropriately be called features. All four appear clearly in Figure 8.1 by Levine.

1. *Elongate nose.* The typical nose in a Nixon caricature proved long and fairly narrow, sloping downward from the face. Often, but not as consistently, the nose would curl upward and/or swell toward the tip. Frequently the artist would add a vertical seam at the end.
2. *Hairline with bays.* The caricature by Levine also shows the typical treatment of Nixon's hair and hairline. A lock ascending from the forehead divides it into two bays.
3. *Box chin.* The chin juts below the main line of the face.
4. *Jowls.* Self-explanatory.

To what extent did these features distinguish caricatures of Richard

Running Harder . . . .

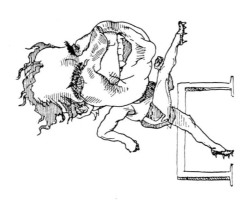

Running . . . .

Running too Hard.

FIGURE 8.1. Caricatures of Richard Nixon by David Levine. [*Reprinted with permission from The New York Review of Books, Copyright © 1963–1979, New York Reviews Inc.*]

Nixon from caricatures of other prominent inidividuals? First, nearly all Nixon caricatures included all four features. Second, caricatures of other individuals most typically did not include any of these features. Consider the nose for instance. The standard "big nose" one associates with caricature was found to be quite different—larger overall, fat rather than narrow. The long narrow Nixon nose did not appear frequently in caricatures of others. The same could be said of the other features. Consequently, in combination, the four features differentiated Nixon caricatures very well.

Did these features correspond to attributes of Nixon's real face? The six photographs of Richard Nixon were compared with the photographs of other individuals. The photographs disclosed a nose of long and thin appearance and one especially sharp photo revealed the vertical seam in the tip of the nose. There was evidence also for the upward curl: The bridge of the nose near the eyes looked more vertical than near the tip. However, no clear evidence of the swollen nose tip appeared. The hairline and jowls showed in nearly all the photographs. The chin proved somewhat more subtle, but two or three of the six photographs revealed a distinct discontinuity in the outline of the lower face.

However logically distinguishing, did the four features contribute to the intuitive appearance of a caricature as a Nixon caricature? Again proceeding informally, Perkins (1975b) investigated whether this was so by initially investigating how necessary these features were for a recognizable Nixon caricature. Perkins systematically altered a caricature by Levine so as to eliminate features. Figure 8.2a is a tracing of a caricature by Levine. Figures 8.2c, d, e, and f copy the original except that jowls, hairline, chin, and nose, respectively, were drawn in a different manner. All four features were modified together in Figure 8.2b.

The drastic treatment in Figure 8.2b clearly destroyed the drawing's visual identity as a Nixon caricature. The modification of individual features certainly, and in a couple of cases considerably, degraded the identity. Redrawing other Nixon caricatures revealed that the changed feature which had the most effect depended on the caricature and the modification. However, changing a feature to be contrary to the characteristics discussed always had some effect on the visual identity.

The implications need careful formulation. One might say that the *absence* of certain features impaired the visual identity, but this would be misleading. In Figure 8.2, features were not merely masked, but actually replaced by other renderings. The different renderings provided visual evidence against the perception of the picture as being a Nixon caricature. Indeed, the sample of Nixon caricatures included one displaying Nixon only from the nose up. Easily recognizable, this picture urged that *negation* of features, more than concealment of features, was the issue. An indication that the face did *not* possess a key feature would mar, al-

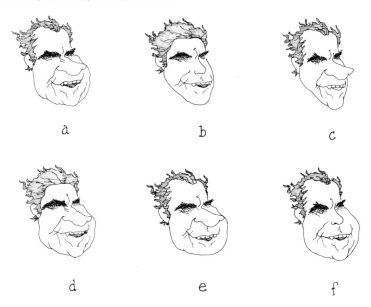

FIGURE 8.2. A caricature by Levine traced (a) and modified to eliminate all four key features (b), jowls (c), hairline (d), box chin (e), and long nose (f).

though not always seriously, the "look" of a Nixon caricature. Perkins (1975b) coined a term for this, calling the features "rather necessary" instead of strictly necessary for an adequate caricature.

Would the four features also prove "rather sufficient"? That is, would including the four features nearly guarantee a recognizable caricature of Richard Nixon? Here the answer was no. One could easily draw a poor caricature incorporating the four features—Figure 8.3 for instance. However, this did not mean that the four features did not help in caricaturing Richard Nixon. For example, in the course of the work Perkins became able to do a tolerable caricature of Nixon, using the features as a rough recipe (Figure 8.4). Additionally, Perkins used the four features in a brief lecture on caricature, discussing some of the themes of this chapter. He invited audience members to attempt caricatures of Nixon from photographs before and after the lecture. The "before" attempts rarely had the look of Nixon caricatures. Although the "after" attempts could not be called good caricatures, audience members following the formula of the four features achieved markedly better results. Figure 8.5 includes "before" and "after" examples. So, the four features encompass much of what goes into a recognizable Nixon caricature, even though they do not provide a sure recipe.

In summary, we have described four features that distinguish caricatures of Richard Nixon from caricatures of other individuals. We have

FIGURE 8.3. A deliberate miss–incorporating all four key features but not resembling a caricature of Richard Nixon. [*From Perkins, D. N., Studies in the Anthropology of Visual Communication, 1975b. Reprinted by permission.*]

also found these to be part of Richard Nixon's actual face, and features, we might add, that would differentiate his face from most others. We have argued that the features are relevant to the "look" of a Nixon caricature. The four are "rather necessary" and, if not sufficient, at least contribute considerably to an adequate caricature. The success of these also argues that several more key attributes exist and could be specified.

We have not offered any evidence that the four features contribute to the recognition of Richard Nixon from his real face, although that seems wholly plausible. Police use a device called an Identikit which allows various types of noses, hairlines, and so on to be overlaid to create a composite depiction of a criminal from witnesses' descriptions. That such composites do lead to identifications suggests that the four features described for Nixon are features of importance in recognizing real faces.

FIGURE 8.4. Caricatures of Richard Nixon by Perkins. [*From Perkins, D. N., Studies in the Anthropology of Visual Communication, 1975b. Reprinted by permission.*]

FIGURE 8.5. Caricatures made from photographs of Richard Nixon by a member of a lecture audience before (top) and after (bottom) explanation of the key features. [*From Perkins, D. N., Studies in the Anthropology of Visual Communication, 1975b. Reprinted by permission.*]

Accordingly, the case study of Nixon caricatures by Perkins favored the superportrait theory. As they draw, caricaturists apparently render several trends of the face with considerable care and consistency. Nevertheless, the informal nature of this case study necessitated the following, more careful study.

MEASURING CONSISTENCY IN CARICATURING

Goldman and Hagen (1978) reasoned that if Perkins' (1975b) analysis of caricature was correct, then nearly all artists should use what he called the "rather necessary" key features consistently over time, unless the real face itself changed. On the other hand, Goldman and Hagen speculated, stylistic differences among artists and the changing political climate might lead to much less regularity than Perkins' informal survey suggested. The Watergate incident had resulted in an increasingly negative political climate for Richard Nixon. Therefore, Goldman and Hagen undertook a more methodical longitudinal analysis of caricatures of Richard Nixon, one involving measurements of the photographed and caricatured face. Two sorts of consistency were tested: consistency in the features chosen for most exaggeration, and consistency in degree of exaggeration.

TABLE 8.1
Feature Ratios of Caricatures of Richard Nixon Ranked by

Artist	Vertical head, length nose	Vertical head, length jowl	Length nose, length fore	Length nose, length ear	Length jaw, width jaw
Cummings	9	10	5	8	11
Behrendt	11	10	9	7	3
Marlitte	9	11	10	6	2
Whitte	11	10	9	8	4
Staskyl	10	7	9	8	11
Oliphant	9	10	7	8	11
Herblock	9	8	7	9	11
Wright	5	11	10	9	6
Lurie	8	3	7	5	11
Simpson	10	11	8	9	5
Hill	11	3	8	10	9
Engle	10	11	9	8	4
Davis	4	10	2	5	3
Hayden	10	4	9	8	11
Fisher	10	7	9	8	11
Scrawls	11	10	9	8	5
Sanders	11	9	10	8	3
Mean rank	9.4	8.6	8.1	7.7	7.3

The investigators obtained measurements of Richard Nixon's face in preparation for assessing the exaggeration in caricatures. Five photographs of Richard Nixon from 1973 were measured by two independent judges, and 11 mean feature ratios (MFR) were calculated. Two corresponded to features emphasized by Perkins (1975b): vertical head length/jowl length and vertical head length/nose length. The investigators selected nine other feature ratios somewhat arbitrarily as ratios that plausibly might differentiate faces and mediate recognition. All the ratios are named along the top of Table 8.1.

The investigators searched news and political periodicals from 1973 to obtain 100 caricatures from 17 artists. From these, 1 caricature was selected randomly to represent each artist, and the 11 MFRs were calculated for each caricature. Then, for each MFR in every caricature, a deviance score was computed—the percentage of deviance from the mean photographic ratio (MPR). A deviance score of 0% occurred when a MFR of a caricature equalled the MPR. For each artist's drawing, the 11 MFRs then were ranked from 1–11 starting at the least to the most deviance from the MPR. Table 8.1 lists the rank orders of the MFRs for each of the 17 artists, and the mean rank for each ratio at the bottom.

Three types of anlayses were performed on these ranks. First, a Kendall Coefficient of Concordance was computed ($W = 0.597$, $X^2(10) = 101.43$, $p < .001$). This indicated great consistency in the exaggerated features.

Degree of Distortion Relative to Ratios of Photographs

Length nose, eye eye	Vertical head, length fore	Length nose, length jaw	Vertical head, width fore	Vertical head, length ear	Vertical head, eye eye
7	6	1	3	4	2
8	6	5	2	4	1
7	8	1	4	3	5
7	6	1	3	5	2
5	6	1	3	4	2
6	4.5	1	2	4.5	3
6	3	1	4	5	2
4	8	3	2	7	1
10	1	9	4	2	6
7	3	2	4	6	1
6	2	7	5	4	1
7	6	1	5	3	2
9	7	11	6	1	8
7	3	5	2	1	6
6	5	4	1	3	2
7	6	4	2	3	1
7	5	6	4	2	1
6.8	4.9	3.6	3.4	3.4	2.7

Second, a Friedman analysis of variance for ranked data was performed ($F = 83.13$, $p < .001$). This showed that the mean ranks for feature ratios differed significantly from chance ranking. Third, a parametric analysis of variance was performed with post-hoc comparisons in order to identify which feature ratios differed significantly from each other in rank. The main effect for rank was significant ($F(10,170) = 19.2$, $p < .02$). Post-hoc comparisons indicated that of the 55 possible pairs of feature ratios, 31 differed in rank with $p < .05$ at least.

Goldman and Hagen argued that these analyses supported several conclusions about the consistency hypotheses. The analyses revealed great consistency across artists in the features selected for exaggeration in caricature. A feature ratio greatly distorted by one artist was nearly always greatly distorted by the others. Furthermore, the degree to which a particular feature ratio was distorted relative to other ratios was very consistent across artists. Finally, the most distorted feature ratios were those involving jowl and nose length. This is not surprising and agrees with Perkins' observations and what seems apparent on examining a few caricatures of Richard Nixon. These results provide a numerical justification for such impressions and disclose no unexpected prominence of less superficially salient features.

In order to examine consistency within an artist and across time, the work of five very prolific artists was analyzed for the years 1972 and 1973, a period in which Richard Nixon's public image underwent a rapid decline. The five artists selected were Oliphant, Herblock, Wright, Lurie, and Hayden. Mean deviance scores for each artist for each year were calculated as described previously. Rank order correlation coefficients were calculated for each of the artists across the years. For four of the five artists, Lurie excepted, there were significant correlations between the ranked feature ratios for 1972 and 1973.

However, the absolute size of the distortions changed considerably, increasing from a mean of 56% for 1972 to a mean of 61% in 1973, a significant difference. This increase appeared in 9 of the 11 MFRs. An analysis of photographs of Richard Nixon during that period revealed that the only feature ratios actually to change in his face were those involving the length of the jowl. Thus, although some of the increase in distortion from 1972 to 1973 evident in the caricatures might have been due to real change in the face, most was not. Goldman and Hagen argued that the greater distortion was due primarily to the increasingly unfavorable political climate.

It should also be noted that although the analysis of consistency across artists revealed great consistency in which features were most exaggerated, there were great stylistic differences in the degree of exaggeration from artist to artist. The mean degree of exaggeration was 53% in 1972 for the group as a whole, but the means for individual artists ranged from a low of 12% for Davis to a high of 86% for Fisher.

In summary, Goldman's and Hagen's results, together with Perkins' previous work, were consistent with a superportrait theory of caricature and inconsistent with a tag theory. Goldman and Hagen confirmed Perkins' claim that different artists exaggerated the same features in caricatures of Richard Nixon. Apparently, caricaturists base their creations on the same several salient features of the subject's face. Exaggerations already worked upon a face by nature determine *what* will be emphasized in a caricature. However, the artist chooses *how much* and *how* to exaggerate according to his stylistic bias and his perception of the political climate.

A TEST OF TRANSFER

Whatever attributes caricature and face might share, the superportrait and tag theories differed on another point: Would experience with the face prepare for recognition of caricatures, and would experience with caricatures allow recognition of the face? Where the first issue addressed invited a case-study approach, this one permitted a straightforward experimental investigation. Subjects could view representations of unfamiliar persons in one medium—caricature or photograph. They then could attempt to pick out representations of the same persons from a larger set of representations in the other medium. Success would mean that viewing faces in the one medium permitted recognition in the other.

The present authors conducted just such an experiment, using 54 three-quarter face photographs of individuals unfamiliar to the subject population, 54 profile photographs of the same individuals, and 54 caricatures in three-quarter face, drawn by an artist of seeming competence. Figure 8.6 illustrates two sets of photographs and their corresponding caricatures. Photographs and caricatures of 15 persons were selected randomly as a training set. Each subject viewed a set of 15 three-quarter or profile photographs, or caricatures, spending about 3 sec on each picture. Then the experimenter showed the subject each picture from the set of 54 three-quarter or profile photographs, or caricatures, in a fixed random order. The subjects indicate the pictures they thought represented persons from the original set of 15. All possible transfers were examined, 20 subjects to each condition. Table 8.2 summarizes the conditions and the results, listing for each condition the mean number of the initial 15 persons recognized among the test set, and the mean number of mistaken identifications, along with standard deviations.

Statistical tests examined whether the subjects discriminated the per-

FIGURE 8.6. Sample photographs and caricatures used in the transfer experiment.

sons previously viewed at a better than chance level, and whether performance on the nine conditions differed. For the former, t tests showed that the number of correct discriminations and false alarms differed significantly from chance in each of the nine conditions. Regarding contrast among the conditions, analyses of variance revealed highly significant differences among both the number correct and the false alarms over the nine conditions ($p < .0001$). Duncan, multiple range, post-hoc comparisons showed significant differences between many of the individual conditions.

In particular, the results refuted the tag theory. The tag theory predicted

FIGURE 8.6. continued

that a caricature of a face would not prepare a viewer to recognize that face elsewhere, nor would exposure to the face prepare the viewer to recognize a caricature of it. However, according to the t tests described, performance on all conditions exceeded chance, $p < .01$ for the caricature to profile photograph condition and $p < .005$ for all other conditions. Even so, it should be noted that, on the average, subjects correctly identified less than half, and as few as a third, of the persons they had seen in the conditions using caricatures with photographs. Obviously, subjects were not discriminating very well.

The results also refuted the superportrait theory. The superportrait the-

TABLE 8.2
Mean Correct Identifications and False Alarms for the Transfer Experiment, Ordered from Most to Least Correct Conditions

Condition	Number correct (maximum 15)		False alarms (maximum 39)	
	M	SD	M	SD
3/4 photo–3/4 photo	13.0	2.2	1.7	2.7
Profile photo–profile photo	11.9	1.7	3.1	2.5
Caricature–caricature	11.6	2.1	5.0	4.2
3/4 photo–profile photo	9.8	3.0	5.3	3.9
Profile photo–3/4 photo	8.5	3.1	5.6	4.6
3/4 photo–caricature	7.2	2.1	9.8	4.0
Caricature–3/4 photo	6.3	2.1	9.7	4.7
Caricature–profile photo	5.8	2.4	11.8	5.7
Profile photo–caricature	5.0	2.6	6.9	4.3

ory of caricature predicted that a caricature would inform a viewer even better than a photograph. A viewer that saw caricatures rather than photographs would recognize other photographs of the same people better, and a viewer that saw photographs would recognize caricatures better than other photographs of the same people. However, Table 8.2 indicates just the opposite. The four conditions combining caricatures with photographs uniformly produced fewer correct identifications and more false alarms than the two photograph–different-photograph conditions. The pairwise differences reached statistical significance at the .01 level. However, the three-quarter-photograph–caricature condition did not differ significantly from the profile-photograph–three-quarter-photograph condition in correct identifications, or the photograph–different-photograph conditions in false alarms.

In fact, the simple lesson of Table 8.2 is that the more alike the modes of representation, the more viewing prepares for later recognition. The best performance occurred in the conditions where the viewer tried to identify the same pictures he viewed originally. Apparently, the viewer took advantage of characteristics not invariant in different views, but specific to the one view. The worst performances occurred when the viewer tried to identify persons he had seen both in a different pose (i.e., three-quarter or profile) and in a different medium (i.e., caricature or photograph). Conditions that involved only one of these contrasts produced intermediate performances. With a few exceptions, this pattern is confirmed by statistically significant differences among the conditions.

As the case study described earlier already had challenged the tag theory, it is unfortunate that the present findings should refute the only other theory under consideration. Perhaps special circumstances could explain away the findings—the caricatures may have been poorer than they appeared, or the three-quarter and profile photographs may have been too similar though representing different viewpoints. Possibly caricatures could prove their superiority over photographs taken on different occasions, with different backgrounds, involving varied poses. Perhaps. However, this sounds too much like making excuses. If caricatures are superportraits, that "super" ought to mean something so that a seemingly competent caricature should overcome the disadvantages mentioned and produce better recognition despite them.

In summary, the conclusions from the case study favored a superportrait over a tag theory. However, the conclusions from the present experiment argue against both theories. Apparently, neither theory is applicable and another is required.

NEGATION AND RECOGNITION

In fact, three new alternative theories will be considered. In order to describe these, we will need to discuss some properties of pattern recognition systems in general. Two characteristics of recognition which proved prominent in the case study of Nixon suggest a simple model of pattern recognition. In particular, we concluded that Nixon caricatures were identified by means of key attributes; recognition might not occur if the caricature negated even a couple of key attributes, but recognition might occur when the stimulus presented only a couple, masking the rest. To generalize, recognition that something belongs to a particular category would depend on a set of key attributes. Negation of a few key attributes would suppress recognition of the something as belonging to that category. However, recognition might occur with only a few key attributes presented and others obscured. Models of recognition with these characteristics we termed *negation models*.

At this point, three questions deserve attention: What besides the Nixon study recommends a negation model of recognition; how does a negation model differ from other views of recognition; and, is there any reason to think that a negation model applies to face recognition as it seems to apply to caricature recognition? As to the first question, consider a simplified characterization of a pattern recognition system. Suppose that the task of the system is to identify which (if any) of a set of known and mutually exclusive categories contains a given stimulus, and suppose that each category is described by a list of attributes. Any example of the category has all the attributes and anything having all the attributes belongs to the category. In other words, the attributes provide necessary and sufficient conditions.

Consider how the recognition process optimally would use these attributes. A single negation of a key attribute should exclude the associated category. This is an extreme version of the principle stated above—that negation of only a few key attributes blocks recognition. However, a stimulus need not either present or negate an attribute, but instead might offer *no* information one way or the other. If a stimulus presented a few key attributes of one category, and negated none, the few attributes might well suffice to exclude all alternative categories. Therefore, recognition could occur based on partial evidence. In summary, an idealized pattern recognition system would behave in accordance with a negation model. Indeed, there would be no tolerance at all for negated attributes.

Of course, a practical pattern recognition system operating on these principles would have to allow more leeway. Noise might cause spurious negations and some attributes might weigh against, but not entirely exclude, a particular categorization, so a practical, pattern recognition system would have more tolerance for negations. Also, an actual psychological process might not identify a category even when all others were logically excluded, because it might not employ "look up" procedures that functioned reliably on sparse evidence. That is, situations could arise rather like needing to look up a word in a dictionary but only knowing how the word ended, not how it began.

Now consider how the negation model contrasts with another familiar conception of recognition. Often it is suggested that recognition depends on the degree of match between stimulus and attributes: The recognition process selects the category with the most matches to the stimulus. According to this theory, an attribute negated counts equally but oppositely from the same attribute presented. This is so even if different attributes are differently weighted. Therefore, a category with many attributes presented but also several negated could be chosen over one with fewer attributes presented but none negated. However, other models of pattern recognition, such as Feigenbaum's EPAM theory (Feigenbaum, 1961; Simon & Feigenbaum, 1964) function differently. They are varieties of negation models where a negated attribute weighs much more heavily against a category than the same attribute presented weighs for it. In fact, strictly speaking, a presented attribute only weighs for its category by excluding other categories that require contrary attributes. In the ideal, the whole process is one of excluding mismatches, rather than weighing matches.

We already have noted that caricature recognition displays symptoms of the negation model. Now we need to compare the processes of recognizing caricatures and faces. Is there any reason, besides plausibility, to think that the negation model applies to face recognition? (If there is such a reason, it does not mean faces and caricatures are recognized by virtue of the same attributes. That would remain to be argued.) In fact, some empirical investigations do support a negation model of face recognition, although they do not address the question as directly as one would like.

Recognition Blocked by Contraindication

We discussed how the negation of key features weakened a caricature's appearance as a Nixon caricature. One qualification is required. This phenomenon is not precisely blocked recognition, but rather degraded resemblance. However, we presume that the two go hand in hand.

Evidence of blocking in face, rather than caricature, perception comes from a study by Bradshaw and Wallace (1971). The investigators used an Identikit to assemble pictures of faces from the variety of noses, eyes, and other features provided. The faces were exposed in pairs, and subjects were asked to decide as quickly as possible whether the two faces were identical. The more features differing between the two faces, the more quickly subjects responded. This supported a serial feature-checking account of the matching task over a parallel "gestalt" theory because, in the latter, the wholistic apprehension of the faces would predict no faster response to greater discrepancy. Bradshaw and Wallace concluded that the comparison process sequentially tested for matching features, that it stopped upon finding a discrepancy, and that features, once tested, were not retested.

Again, as with our observations on Nixon, these findings do not refer directly to recognition. Matching is not recognition, as Bradshaw and Wallace explicitly acknowledged. Furthermore, Bradshaw and Wallace found no difference between photographic positives and negatives on their task, although other investigators have found performance to be better using positives in the recognition paradigms (Galper, 1970; Galper & Hochberg, 1971; Phillips, 1972). Thus some differences obtain between the two tasks. Nevertheless, the findings at least detect differential weight given to negation in a face perception task.

Recognition from Partial Evidence

Earlier, we mentioned encountering a readily recognizable caricature of Nixon, visible only from the nose up. Goldstein and Mackenberg (1966) offered some experimental evidence of face recognition from partial views. Goldstein and Mackenberg examined face recognition in kindergarten, first-, and fifth-grade children. Their stimuli were photographs of classmates, photographs that had been identified by the subjects 2 weeks earlier. During the experiment, Goldstein and Mackenberg presented the photographs with various parts of the face masked. We will summarize the performance of the fifth graders, presuming them to be closest to adult competence. The fifth graders identified 95% of the photographs exposed from the middle of the nose up and 70% of those exposed from the eyebrows up. However, the figure dropped to 45% for exposure below the center of the nose, and for exposure of a horizontal bar-shaped region including the eyes and the bridge of the nose. In general Goldstein and Mackenberg's study demonstrated that familiar faces often are recognizable from only partial feature exposure.

To conclude, we should stress that only a crude description of a negation model has been offered. In this description attributes either do or do not count, but in real circumstances perhaps different attributes weigh somewhat more or less. When we speak of a few key attributes, the number is vague, and, even then, how are attributes to be counted? Nixon's nose, for instance—long, thin, perhaps curled upward and with a seam at the end—is that one attribute, two, or four? Despite these caveats, the notion of a negation model will help in reconsidering caricature recognition.

THREE MORE THEORIES OF CARICATURE

This chapter began with the puzzle caricatures posed. Manifestly distorted, why should a caricature prompt recognition? The simple explanation rests in the fact that caricatures are not entirely distorted. They do preserve some characteristics of the true face. Although exact measures are not usually depicted correctly, the trends of the face relative to population norms are. Therefore, someone might conclude that recognition succeeds simply because caricatures speak more loudly of less. They compensate for providing less evidence to the viewer by making the most distinguishing trends blatant.

The negation model proves its value here by showing how such an account underrates the paradox of caricature recognition. A caricature does not just omit exact attributes, it misrepresents them. Nixon's nose is long, but not *that* long. However correct the caricature in trend, it negates exact attributes of the subject's true face. Accordingly, recognition might be blocked by the inaccuracies of caricature. Instead, recognition occurs. What theories of caricature accommodate that fact?

Three alternatives seem possible. One asserts that exact measures simply are not key attributes for recognition of the true face. Consequently, the inaccuracies of caricature do not negate key attributes nor block recognition. Rather, the perceiver's recognition system reacts to the caricature essentially as it would to a photograph. This thesis will be called the *identity theory*. The word "identity" of course, does not imply that a viewer would confuse caricatures with real faces or photographs. The identity theory holds that the features making individuals recognizable are the same in caricature as in real faces or photographs.

We will call a second account the *tolerance theory*. In this theory, exact measures do function as key attributes in normal face recognition. Although the negation model permits some negation even of key attributes, the tolerance theory asserts that caricature recognition depends on greater tolerance for the negation of key attributes.

The *selection theory* is the remaining possibility. If negated exact attributes are not simply tolerated, then they must be discounted precisely because they are exact attributes. In identifying caricatures, the recognition process is retuned to respond selectively to trend attributes. Recognizing caricatures requires testing the stimulus against the trend information implicit in the mnemonic record of exact attributes. Or perhaps, recognition of normal faces uses both exact and trend attributes, and recognizing caricatures requires ignoring negation of exact attributes.

Which theory is best? We reject the tolerance theory as implausible by the following argument. The tolerance theory must presume that normal recognition depends both on trend and exact attributes, because greater tolerance for negation would not help if recognition employed only exact attributes in the first place. However this has an odd consequence: One could trade off the negation of trend attributes against the negation of exact attributes. A caricature could negate trends of the true face, but compensate for such negation by presenting some exact attributes. A precise depiction of one part of the face could compensate for outright disregard for the true face in another part. Imagine what this would mean in a particular case. Suppose one tried to caricature Nixon with a short nose and no jowels, but a meticulously drawn hairline and box chin. It would be unlikely that the results would look anything like a Nixon caricature. Accurate depiction in one place will not necessarily compensate for negation of key trends in another.

The other two theories remain. Two kinds of evidence would favor the identity theory. First, the theory predicts that exact attributes are irrelevant to the recognition of real faces. Second, it predicts that relatively few trend attributes are operative, because the case study of Nixon concluded that the four features considered constituted a good part of what made a Nixon caricature recognizable. Research on face recognition provides evidence for both these points.

Regarding the first point, Harmon (1973) tested the recognition of images of faces, blurred so that fine detail and exact contour were obscured. Faces that were blurred so much that eyes and mouth were simply darker regions of fog were recognized 85% of the time. (see Figure 8.7.).

Regarding the second point, Harmon also investigated the number of dimensions needed to differentiate faces. Harmon (1973) discovered that 21 dimensions sufficed to thoroughly sort a population of 256 portraits of white, unbearded males without glasses and from 20- to 50-years old.

FIGURE 8.7. Photographed and blurred photographed used in Harmon's experiment. The picture on the right was recognized 85% of the time. [Reprinted by permission of Dr. Leon Harmon. From Haron, Leon, "The recognition of faces," Scientific American, 1973 (Nov.), 229 (5), 70–84. Courtesy of Scientific American and Bell Laboratories.]

Some of the dimensions were: hair from full to bald; forehead receding, vertical, or bulging; nose short, medium, or long. Subjects chose the 10 measures they thought to be most prominent or differentiating for a particular photograph. In fact, these measures very reliably selected that face from the population, even though frequent errors in estimation occurred. Of course, Harmon's findings do not stem from a direct study of recognition. They do, however, show that relatively few dimensions of a trend character suffice to differentiate faces. Furthermore, they show subjects to be sensitive to a particular face's extremes in trend. Finally, another finding does relate something like extremes in trend to actual recognition performance. An experiment by Going and Read (1974) revealed that photographed faces independently rated high in uniqueness were better recognized than those rated low.

However, other arguments count against the identity thesis and favor the selection theory. For one, our own findings revealed recognition of caricatures to be *worse* than recognition of photographs. This might mean that exact attributes facilitated the recognition of the photographs. Harmon's findings do not necessarily deny this. Harmon found a high recognition rate on fuzzy photographs, but certainly not a perfect one. The loss of accuracy in that case could be essentially the same loss that we found between photographs and caricatures.

For another argument against the identity theory, the selection theory allows the recognition of real faces to depend in part on details. Therefore, one might expect details to be irrelevant as compared with the broad characterizing power of the trend attributes, yet, findings from a different area entirely argue that incidental details can function in recognition. Paul Kolers (1973, 1974) has investigated memory for the typography of sentences—their appearance in normal text, or text inverted and reflected in various ways. It is natural to suppose that only the meaning of text would be remembered, or at most the words. Kolers was able to show otherwise. Subjects could differentiate significantly often between sentences they had read before and those they had not, and they proved able to distinguish between those they had read before in the same typography versus a different typography. The sentences of various categories were shuffled together and the subjects were not aware on the initial reading that they would need to attempt such a task. Apparently incidental aspects of linguistic stimuli remain in memory and function in recognition. Such an occurrence in language makes it all the more likely that exact attributes of a face also would figure in recognition.

At the moment, formal experimental evidence offers no definitive solution to the identity versus selection theory controversy. The arguments both ways are suggestive, but not conclusive. However, we would propose that everyday experience casts an important vote. The identity theory appears insufficient, whereas the selection theory appears more sound. The evidence from this comes from the recognition of likenesses. For example, suppose one strolls along the sidewalk regarding passers-by. Various recognition experiences can occur.

1. Sometimes an individual may strike one as someone else—a friend, a celebrity, or a political figure. One actually mistakes him for another person, even if only for a moment.
2. Sometimes an individual strikes one as *looking like* someone else; one notes the likeness, but, from the first, one also perceives it to be only a likeness.
3. One proceeds down the street deliberately looking for likenesses. Individuals that would not otherwise have struck one as looking like others suddenly do.

Cases 2 and 3 speak directly to present concerns. One could consider the passer-by as a sort of "caricature" of the other identity recognized—the friend, celebrity, or political figure. With this translation, do the acts of recognition fit the identity or the selection theory? Well, the identity theory holds that "caricature" and subject share the same key attributes, the attributes that contribute to recognition. Therefore, the passer-by would be mistaken for someone else. However, this does not happen in cases 2 and 3. Instead, the passer-by is recognized as looking like, but not just like, someone else. Contrary evidence in the pedestrian's face must have warned against an outright mistake. Therefore, recognition occurred despite the negation of key attributes. Apparently, the selection theory applies.

These examples show that face recognition involving selection can occur, not only through deliberate effort, but also spontaneously. That such spontaneous recognition happens makes it all the more plausible an explanation for caricature recognition. Subjectively, the perceiver in cases 2 and 3 seems to be ignoring details and responding to the trends of the face. This suggests that recognizing the likeness of one face to another is a phenomenon quite akin to recognizing caricatures. The selection theory would account parsimoniously for both.

CARICATURE AND CONVENTION

The selection theory posits a perceptual process that we call *selective recognition*. It would be surprising if selective recognition did not operate in many other contexts besides caricature. This closing section undertakes two tasks considering the nature and variety of selective recognition and considering how the concept might clarify the role of convention in representation.

One might think selective recognition is a matter of direction of gaze. Certainly by looking in one area, a viewer excludes evidence elsewhere, evidence which otherwise might block recognition. By looking only at part of a face, a viewer may recognize a likeness to someone that otherwise he would not discern. Accordingly, direction of gaze is an element of selective recognition—but only one element. Caricatures are recognized but a viewer hardly can point his eyes just at the trends and not at the rest.

One might think of selective recognition as a matter of gaze plus attention. A viewer need not attend to everything before his eyes, and recognition might arise only from the attributes attended to. No doubt there is some truth in this, but this also is an insufficient characterization of selective recognition. In regarding a long-nosed caricture one doesn't attend just to the trend attribute and not to the exact attribute—only to the being long and not to the length. On the contrary, one takes note of and delights in the length of the nose. However, one does not let the length weigh as counter-evidence. Therefore, something attended to nevertheless can be discounted in recognition.

These examples suggest that selective recognition depends on a number of processes which accomplish selection. The output of these processes feeds into a rapid "look-up" system. The "look-up" system reports any identification based on the attributes it receives. Further selective scrutiny may depend on the result of the "look-up" report. The "look-up" process also is influenced strongly by the expected or desired type of identification. For instance, if one looks for likenesses of friends in the faces of strangers, one tends to find such likeness, but if one looks for likenesses of celebrities, one tends to find those.

The examples discussed so far have concerned selective recognition in caricature and face perception. However, the perception of many other likenesses would appear to depend on selective recognition. Consider, for instance, likenesses encountered about the home. A coke bottle may strike one as a person, the front of one's house as a face, a shiny pen as a rocket, and so on. These perceptions require discounting negative evidence. Otherwise, one would mistake bottle for person, facade for face, or pen for rocket, rather than just apprehending a likeness.

Considering the preceding examples, one might think that selective recognition involved only a response to trends. But selectivity can function in other ways too. One can look, for example, to see what other objects the color or texture of something brings to mind. Perhaps one recognizes the color of ones coat in the color of a leaf. In such instances, details rather than trends are scrutinized and recognition is based on similarities between parts or aspects of things. Such varied examples suggest a relationship between selective recognition and metaphor. Indeed, many "dead" metaphors of our language record likenesses of one object to another, for example, saw horse, ear of corn, or eye of a potato (although in an important way, talk about metaphors as a matter of likeness is misleading; for the needed reservations, see Black, 1962, Chapter 3; Goodman, 1968, pp. 77–78; and Perkins, 1978, in the present context). Also, many metaphors in poetry may arise from, and certainly stimulate in the reader recognition of likenesses in appearance. Perkins (1978) has discussed these matters in a paper entitled "Metaphorical Perception."

Metaphor aside, the concept of selective recognition clarifies the role of conventionality in picturing. Two senses of convention need to be distinguished. First, pictures may be conventional in employing particular arbitrary symbols established by prior practice. As discussed earlier, a few caricatures in fact do this, but we argued that caricatures in general are not of that sort. Second, sometimes it is said that systems of picturing, rather than particular images, are conventions, because viewers supposedly must adapt their viewing to the peculiarities of a system, for instance Rennaissance perspective or cubism. In affirming a selection theory of caricature recognition, we are also affirming the conventional nature of caricature in this second sense, because the viewer must learn the appropriate selectivity.

Often, the position that pictures are conventional is taken to imply that learning to "read" such pictures is an extended process like learning to read text. However, this does not follow from the kind of conventionality associated with selective recognition. On the contrary, a viewer might orient to caricature as a mode of representation rather quickly, at least in a rough way. Suppose, for example, that a person unfamiliar with caricatures encounters one, knowing that the drawing depicts a real person. The viewer finds that nose, cheeks, and chin have proportions exceeding the normal range of human variation. Clearly, he cannot take these parts as exact representations of the subject. Accordingly, the viewer might conclude that he should discount metric accuracy as an informative characteristic of the depiction. In this way, the caricature itself would have revealed the selectivity required to decode it.

Of course, we do not suggest that the normal process of recognizing a caricature resembles this account, since most persons have already learned the appropriate selectivity. Nor do we even suggest that reasoning as explicit as the reasoning in the previous paragraph occurs when people encounter caricatures for the first time. However, it is generally recognized that people approach symbols expecting them to be meaningful, and, when the symbols initially resist interpretation, people search for ways in which they could be meaningful. The point is that caricature, although conventional in the specified sense, also would seem to lend itself to the perceiver's effort to find an appropriate selectivity.

This account of the role of convention in caricature plausibly applies to more realistic modes of representation also. At first thought, that is not obvious, because while caricatures present their subjects in a distorted way, realistic pictures do not. It's tempting to conclude that what we called the "identity theory" of recognition applies to realistic pictures, because they seemingly present the same information the perceiver uses in recognizing objects in real scenes. However, many have pointed out thta realistic pictures do not replicate all features of the things they represent. One does not interpret a black-and-white photograph as depicting a gray world full of gray people, nor a flat picture as depicting a two-dimensional world. The human pattern recognition system might abide by the identity theory and be indifferent to these differences. However, it seems more likely that features like color and three-dimensional form perceived stereoscopically function in recognizing real objects, and that therefore realistically pictured objects need to be viewed with a selectivity appropriate to them, just as do caricatures. In that sense, realistic pictures as well as caricatures would be conventional. However, as with caricatures, the selectivity required for properly "reading" realistic pictures would seem to lend itself to quick discovery (see Jones and Hagen, Volume II of The perception of pictures, Chapter 6).

In this way, the case of caricature and the concept of selective recognition provide a perspective on conventionality quite different from the usual one, the one that interprets conventionality by analogy with language and the conventional labels of a language. To a considerable extent, the conventions involved in realistic picturing and the additional ones involved in caricaturing are relatively economical general rules, rather than large sets of arbitrary associations. Furthermore, the rules do not introduce new relationships between the representation and the referent, relationships irrelevant to perceiving real scenes, but rather select among familiar relationships. These circumstances help to make a rough adaptation to a system of picturing like caricature relatively easy, perhaps so easy that one is tempted to ask why such a system should be called conventional at all. However, there is a ready answer. Ease of learning is one thing and conventionality something else. Easy to acquire or not, the appropriate selectivity remains logically and functionally crucial. Not to realize this would be to understand the recognition of caricatures and pictures in general according to the identity theory and to miss the fundamental nature of the phenomenon.

REFERENCES

Berger, O. *My victims: How to caricature.* New York: Harper, 1952.

Black, M. *Models and metaphors: Studies in language and philosophy.* Ithaca, New York: Cornell Univ. Press, 1962.

Bradshaw, J. L., & Wallace, G. Models for the processing and identification of faces. *Perception and Psychophysics,* 1971, *9*(5), 443–448.

Feigenbaum, E. A. The simulation of verbal learning behavior. *Proceedings of the Western Joint Computer Conference,* 1961, 121–132.

Galper, R. E. Recognition of faces in photographic negative. *Psychonomic Science,* 1970, *19*(4), 207–208.

Galper, R. E. "Functional race membership" and recognition of faces. *Perceptual and Motor Skills,* 1973, *37*(2), 455–462.

Galper, R. E., & Hochberg, J. Recognition memory for photographs of faces. *American Journal of Psychology,* 1971, *84*(3), 351–354.

Gibson, E. J. *Principles of perceptual learning and development.* New York: Meredith, 1969.

Going, M., & Read, J. D. Effects of uniqueness, sex of subject, and sex of photograph on facial recognition. *Perceptual and Motor Skills,* 1974, *39*(1), 109–110.

Goldman, M., & Hagen, M. A. The forms of caricature: Physiognomy and political bias, *Studies in the Anthropolgy of Visual Communication,* 1978, *5,* 30–36.

Goldstein, A. G. Recognition of inverted photographs of faces by children and adults. *Journal of Genetic Psychology,* 1975, *127*(1), 109–123.

Goldstein, A. G., & Mackenberg, E. J. Recognition of human faces from isolated facial features: A developmental study. *Psychonomic Science,* 1966, *6,* 149–150.

Gombrich, E. H. The cartoonist's armory. In *Meditations on a hobby horse and other essays on the theory of art.* London: Phaidon, 1963.

Gombrich, E. H. The mask and the face: The perception of physiognomic likeness in life and art. In E. H. Gombrich, J. Hochberg, & M. Black (Eds.), *Art, perception and reality.* Baltimore: Johns Hopkins Univ. Press, 1972.

Goodman, N. *Languages of art.* New York: Bobbs-Merrill, 1968.

Harmon, L. D. The recognition of faces. *Scientific American,* 1973, *229*(5), 70–84.

Hochberg, J., & Galper, R. E. Recognition of faces: I. An exploratory study. *Psychonomic Science,* 1967 *9*(12), 619–620.

Kolers, P. A. Remembering operations. *Memory & Cognition,* 1973, *1*(3), 347–355.

Kolers, P. A. Two kinds of recognition. *Canadian Journal of Psychology,* 1974, *28*(1), 51–61.

Malpass, R. S., & Kravitz, J. Recognition for faces of own and other race. *Journal of Personality and Social Psychology,* 1969, *13*(4), 330–334.

Perkins, D. A definition of caricature. *Studies in the Anthropology of Visual Communication,* Spring 1975, *2*(1). (a)

Perkins, D. Caricature and recognition. *Studies in the Anthropology of Visual Communication,* Spring 1975, *2*(1). (b)

Perkins, D. Metaphorical perception. In E. Eisner (Ed.), *Reading, the arts and the creation of meaning.* Reston, Virginia: National Art Education Association, 1978.

Phillips, R. J. Why are faces hard to recognize in photographic negative? *Perception & Psychophysics,* 1972 *12*(5), 425–426.

Rother, E. Drawing caricatures. *Design,* 1966 *67*(4), 12–15.

Ryan, T. A., & Schwartz, C. B. Speed of perception as a function of mode of representation. *American Journal of Psychology,* 1956, *69,* 60–69.

Shepherd, J. W., Deregowski, J. B., & Ellis, H. D. A cross-cultural study of recognition memory for faces. *International Journal of Psychology,* 1974, *9*(3), 205–212.

Simon, H. A., & Feigenbaum, E. A. An information-processing theory of some effects of similarity, familiarization, and meaningfulness in verbal learning. *Journal of Verbal Learning and Verbal Behavior,* 1964, *3,* 385–396.

Subject Index

A

Abstraction and movement in pictures, 230, 233
effectiveness of, 246
Adjacency and retinal image, 10
Agricola, George Bauer, 197–199
Alberti, 11, 37, 40, 49, 59
Ambiguity of pictorial representation, 48–49
Anamorphic art, 138
Angular perspective, 56–57
Art and cartography, 182

B

Bacon, Roger, 185
Balla, 233
Binocular scale of space, 9
Brown, Harcourt, 180, 182
Brunelleschi, 49, 67, 188, 191

C

Canonical form, 24–25
Caricature recognition, 257–285
context and, 258
convention and, 282–285
face recognition and, 260–261, 271–278
identity theory of, 278–282
negation models and, 275–278
selection theory of, 279–282
superportrait theory of, 259–260, 268, 271, 273–274
tag theory of, 257–259, 260, 271, 273–274
tolerance theory of, 279
Caricatures, 38
convention and, 282–285
facial attributes and, 261–268
mask in, 258
measuring consistency in, 268–271
perception of, 24
"rather necessary" features and, 265–266
reference function of, 260
of Richard Nixon, 261–271, 278
Cartesian coordinate system, 41–45
Cartography and art, 182
Cartoons and spatial relationships, 259
Cassatt, Mary, 218
Chêng, Wang, 203–205, 259
Chiaroscuro, definition of, 180
Ch'i Ch'i T'u Shuo, 203–205
Children's books and movement in pictures, 250–251
Chinese art
Ch'i Ch'i T'u Shuo and, 203–205
conventions in, 203–206
Jesuits and, 202–203
parallel perspective in, 208
Pei-t'eng Library and, 202–203
Renaissance art compared with, 182
scientific illustration in, 202–211
T'ien Kung K'ai Wu ("Creation of Nature and Man") and, 207
Western art influence on, 210–211
Ying Tsao Fa Shih ("Architectural Standards") and, 207–208
Chinese attitudes toward scientific development and mechanical arts, 209–210
Chou Ch'en, 187–188
Christian religion
optics and, 188
Renaissance art and, 202
Close viewing and compensation, 215–218
Compensation
close viewing and, 215–218
distortion and, 213–215
failure of, 215–222
far viewing and, 218–220
for geometric distortion, 156–175
ground plane grid and, 75
magnification and, 159–175
minification and, 159–175

in parallel perspective, 57–58
perceptual assumptions and, 158–175
picture surface and, 221–222
slant and, 166–168
stereopsis and, 157
trompe l'oeil and, 220–222
for viewing point, 137–175
virtual space and, 159–175
Context and caricature recognition, 258
Continuity in spatial relations, 65–66
Convention and caricature, 282–285
Convergence information and spatial relations, 63

D

Depth compression and viewing point dislocation, 146
Distal and proximal stimulus, 4–5
Distance
gradient for texture size and, 80
height in picture plane and, 87
horizon line and, 83–84
magnification and, 93
size perception and, 102
Distance perception
magnification effect on, 154
viewing distance effect on, 151–152
virtual space effect on, 151–152
Distance point and parallel lines, 56
Distortion
in architecture and painting, 222
familiarity and, 156–157
horizon line and, 85–86
of interobject distance, 92, 94, 99–103, 124, 126
magnification and, 92–93
minification and, 126–134
motion as cause of, 93, 117–126, 127–132
of object distance, 92
of shape, 92–93, 103–107, 124–127
of slant, 92–93, 103–107, 124–127
veridical perception and, 107
of virtual space, 149–150, 156–157
Dual reality of pictures, 12
developmental aspects of, 15–21
illusion and, 28
station point and, 16–21
Dürer, Albrecht, 11, 189–191

E

Eastern art versus Renaissance art, 182, 185–189
Edge direction and horizon line, 84–85
Elevation in orthographic projection, 43–45
En face portrait, 221–222
Escher, M.C., 215
Euclid on optics, 6, 37
European attitudes toward scientific development, 209–210
Exploded view and Renaissance art, 192–194

F

Face recognition, 260–261
caricature recognition and, 271–278, *see also* Caricature recognition
negation models and, 275–278
Far viewing and compensation, 218–220
Flatness of pictures, 12–14, *see also* Dual reality of pictures
Frescoes, 182–187

G

Galileo, 181, 209, 211
Geographical slant
horizon line and, 85
optical slant and, 81–82
"Geometrical" as term, 148
Giorgio Martini, Francesco di, 189, 192, 195–197, 210
Giotto, 182–185
Gradients and spatial relations, 76–82
Grid, *see* Ground plan grid
Grosseteste, Robert, 185
Ground plane
horizon line of, 50–52
optical contact and, 72–73
trace line of, 50–52
Ground plane grid, 50, 50–59
compression and, 75
object distance and, 74–76
object size and, 73–76
station point and, 68–70

H

Harnett, William, 220–221
Harvey, William, 181

Height in picture plane, 86–87
Height projection, 59, 60
Holbein, Hans, 189
Horizon line, 82–86
  distance and, 83–84
  distortion and, 85–86
  edge direction and, 84–85
  geographical slant and, 81–82, 85
  of ground plane, 50–52
  height in picture plane and, 86–87
  scale and, 62
  size and, 82–83
  station point and, 51–52, 68
Horizon-ratio relation, 59–60, 82

I

Identity theory of caricature recognition,
  278–282
Illusion and perception, 25–28
  dual reality of pictures and, 28
Illustrative techniques in Renaissance art,
  197–211
Intelligence tests and movement in pictures,
  250–251
Invariants, pictorial, 62–66
  optic array and, 65
Inventive imagination and pictures, 195
Isomorphism of perceived and virtual space,
  148–149

J

Jacopo, Mariano di, 191–197
Jesuits and Pei-t éng Library, 202–203
Johann II of Bavaria, 182

L

Levine, David, 261–265
Light
  absorption of, 6
  depth in reflected, 10–14
  information in, 33–35
  in natural environment, 35–36
  reflectance of, 5–6
  retinal image and projection of, 6–7
Linear perspective, 188
  spatial layout through, 140–143
Lorenzetti, Ambrogio, 185–186

M

Magnification, 91, 92–126
  compensation and, 159–175
  distance of observation and, 93
  distance perception and effect of, 154
  distortion caused by motion and, 93,
    117–126
  distortion of interobject distance and,
    99–103, 124
  distortions of shape and, 124–125
  distortion of slant and, 124–125
  macrostructure and, 123
  microscopy and, 123–126
  microstructure and, 123
  object distance and, 99–103
  optical slant perception and, 111–112
  "paradoxical skid" and, 123
  projected visual angle and, 98
  slant and, 151, 166–167
  space perception and effects of, 97–126,
    151–154
  texture density and effect of, 107–111
  three-dimensionality and, 99
  velocity and, 117–122, 125–126
  viewing distance and, 169
  viewing point dislocation and, 143–144
  virtual orientation and, 164
Mantegna, 218–220
Marquet, 236
Messina, Antonello da, 188–189
Metaphor, selective recognition and, 283
Metaphor and movement in pictures,
    229–230, 232, 236
  effectiveness of, 244–246
Mexican art, 228
Minification, 91, 126–134
  compensation and, 159–175
  distortion of interobject distance and, 126
  movement as cause of distortions, 127–132
  slant and, 166, 168
  viewing distance and, 170
  virtual orientation and, 165
Monocular viewing, 114
Motion
  distortion caused by, 93, 117–126, 127–132
  "paradoxical skid" due to, 123
Motion parallax, 63–64
Motion scale of space, 8–9
Movement in pictures, perception of, 225–251
  abstraction and, 230, 233, 246
  children's books and, 250

content and, 227, 242
context and, 227–229
cross-cultural survey of, 235
environmental and pictorial information
and, 246–251
information effectiveness of, 236–246
intelligence tests and, 250–251
metaphor and, 229–230, 232, 236, 244–246
Mexican art and, 228
multiple viewpoints and, 228–231, 243–244
orientation information and effectiveness
of, 242
posture and, 228, 231–236
representational information for, 226–236
single viewpoint, single moment and,
227–228, 236–242
studies of responses to, 237
Multiple viewpoints and movement in pictures, 228–231
effectiveness of, 243–244

N

Nadal, Hieronymus, 200–202
Negation models, 275–278
Nixon, Richard, 261–271, 278
"Normal" viewing, 132
Nutius, Martinus, 200

O

Object distance
ground plane grid and, 74–76
magnification and, 99–103
Object size
ground plane grid and, 73–76
mean magnitude estimates as function of,
162, 163
Oblique perspective, 60
Observation distance and visual angle, 97,
100, 131
Occlusion
pictorial representation and, 46–48
spatial relations and, 71–72
One-point perspective, 57
Optic array, 36–37
invariants and, 65
picture plane and, 39–40
redundancy of information and, 66
as term, 35

Optical contact and ground plane, 72–73
Optical slant, 76–77
definition of, 103
determining, 103–111
geographical slant and, 81–82
gradient for texture size and, 79
lens focal length and, 112–114
magnification effect on perception of
111–112
perpendicular object motion and, 122–123
station point variation and, 114–116
Optics
changes produced by eye, 10
Christian religion and, 188
of scenes, geometrical, 4–10
Orthographic projection, 41–48
elevation in, 43–45
limitations of, 48–62
perspective representation from, 47
picture construction from, 45–48
plan in, 43–44
use of, 45–48
vanishing point and, 46
Outline drawings, perception of, 23–24

P

Panofsky, Erwin, 179–180
"Paradoxical skid," 123
Parallel lines and distance point, 56
Parallel perspective, 56–58
Pei-t éng Library, 202–203
Perception, errors in, 21–23
Perceptual assumptions and compensation,
159–175
Perspective
angular, 56–57
artificial versus natural, 40
Chinese parallel, 208
close viewing and, 215–218
definition of, 6–7
exceptional cases of, 213–222
linear, see Linear perspective
natural versus artificial, 40
oblique, 60
one-point, 57
parallel, 56–57
perception error and, 21
rules of, 11–12
three-point, 60
two-point, 57

Perspective constructions, 48–62
  historical techniques of, 49
  from orthographic projections, 47
  rules of 41–45
  scale and, 61–62
Perspective transformation, 7
  movement and binocularity as cause of, 7–8
  Renaissance painters and, 11
Picture, definition of, 35
Picture-in-a-picture perception, 173–174
Picture as window in Renaissance art, 183–188
Picture perception and scene perception compared, 3–4, 15
Picture plane, 38–40
  center of, 39
  definition of, 39
  height in, 86–87
  optic array and, 39–40
  visual pyramid and, 36
Picture surface observation rules, 114–116
Pictures and inventive imagination, 195
Pictorial compensation, 138
Pictorial constancy, 138
Pictorial and environmental information, 246–251
Pictorial representation
  ambiguity of, 48–49
  occlusion and, 46–48
Pictorial space perception, 148–156
Plan in orthographic projection, 43–44
Plantin, Christophe, 200
Point-projection theory of pictorial information, 38
Pomerancio, 202
Posture and movement in pictures, 228, 231–236
  effectiveness of, 238–242
Pozzo, Fra Andrea, 220–222
Printing press effect on Renaissance art, 189–211
  "image culture" caused by, 190
Projected visual angle
  magnification distortion and, 97–98
  observation distance and, 97, 100
Projective model of vision, 35–38
  limitations of, 37–38
Proximal and distal stimulus, 4–5

R

Ramelli, Agostino, 197–200, 202–205, 210
Rembrandt, 215–217

Renaissance art, 179–212
  characteristics of, 181–185
  Chinese art compared with, 182
  Christian religion and, 202
  Eastern art versus, 182, 185–189
  exploded view and, 192–194
  illustrative techniques in, 197–211
  picture-as-window in, 183–188
  printing press advent and, 189–211
  rotated view and, 194
  scientific development and influence of, 179–181
  time and space unity in, 202
  transparent view and, 195–197
Renaissance painters and perspective transformation, 11
Retinal image
  adjacency and, 10
  eye rotation and changes in 8
  head movement and changes in, 8–9
Rocha, Father João da, 203–204
Rodler, Hieronymus, 182–183
Roosevelt, Theodore, 258
Rotated view and Renaissance art, 194

S

Sargent, Frances X., 214
Scale, 71
  horizon line and, 62
  perspective construction and, 61–62
  trace line and, 62
Schacht, Hjalmar, 257–258
Schön, Erhard, 182
Schreck, Johann, 203
Scientific development
  European attitudes toward, 209–210
  Renaissance art influence on, 179–181
  social attitudes toward, 209–210
Scientific illustration
  in Chinese art, 202–211
  of Leonardo da Vinci, 190–191
Scrot, William, 214
Selection theory of caricature recognition, 279–282
Selective recognition, 282–285
  metaphor and, 283
Sert, Jose Maria, 222
Shape, distortions of, 92–93, 103–107, 124–127
Shear
  space perception and effect of, 155–156
  viewing point dislocation and, 144–148
  in virtual space, 146

Single viewpoint, single moment in pictures, 227–228, 236–242
Size, *see also* Magnification; Minification
    horizon line and, 82–83
    station point and, 80
    viewing distance effect on, 154
    viewing-point dislocation effect on, 150–151
Size constancy, 218
Size imbalance and close viewing, 215–218
Size scaling and far viewing, 218–220
Slant
    compensation and. 166–168
    distortions of, 92–93. 103–107, 126–127
    magnification and, 151
    picture plane location information and, 172–173
Space perception from pictures, 3–29, 148–156
    isomorphism and, 148–149
    magnification effect on, 97–126
Space scales, 7–9
    correlation among, 9–10
Spatial layout
    fundamental concepts of, 33–41
    geometry of, 33–88
    through linear perspective, 140–143
Spatial relationships
    cartoons and, 259
    continuity and, 65–66
    convergence information and, 63
    geometrical information for, 62–88
    gradients and, 76–82
    importance of, 88
    motion parallax and, 63–64
    occlusion and, 71–72
    optical contact and, 72–73
    redundancy of information and, 66
    scale and, 71
    station point and, 66–71
    stereoscopic information and, 63
    texture information and, 73–76
Spatial representation, synthesis of, 140–141
Station point
    changes in position of, 40–41
    definition of, 40
    dual reality of pictures and, 16–21
    eye movements and, 20
    finding, 66–71
    ground plane grid and, 68–70
    head movement and, 20
    horizon line and, 51–52, 68
    optical slant and variations in, 114–116
    size and, 80

Stereopsis and compensation phenomena, 157
Stereoscopic information and spatial relations, 63
Superportrait theory of caricature recognition, 259–260
Surface scale of space, 7
Surround of pictures, 12
Synthesis of spatial representation, 140–141

T

Taccola, 191–197, 210
"Telephoto effect," 139
Telescope viewing, 114
Texture density and magnification, 107–111
Texture gradient and magnification, 102
Texture size as gradient, 77–80
Texture and spatial relations, 73–76
Three-point perspective, 60
T'ien Kung K'ai Wu ("Creation of Nature and Man"), 207
"Time to collision" equation, 120–122
Titian, 218
Tolerance theory of caricature recognition, 279
Trace line
    of ground plane, 50–52
    scale and, 62
    vanishing point and, 54–56
Transparent view and Renaissance art, 195–197
Trompe l'oeil and compensation, 220–222
T'u Shu Chi Ch'eng, 205–206
Two-point perspective, 57

V

Vanishing point
    definition of, 53
    edge direction and, 84–85
    finding, 54
    horizon line and 53–54
    in linear perspective, 141
    orthographic projection and, 46
    perpendicular lines and, 56–57
    trace line and, 54–56
Velasquez, 218
Veridical perception, 107
Vermeer, Jan, 216
Viewing distance
    distance perception and effect of, 151–152

magnification and, 169
minification and, 170
signal-to-noise ratio and, 159
size and effect of, 154
Viewing point compensation, 137–175
Viewing point, correct, 139, 158
Viewing point dislocation
  depth compression and, 146
  distortion of virtual space caused by, 149–150
  effects of, 143–148
  magnification and, 143–144
  shear and, 144–148
  size and effect of, 150–151
  virtual space and effect of, 156
Vinci, Leonardo da, 11, 189, 210, 217
  scientific illustrations of, 190–191
Virtual orientation, 161–168
  magnification and, 164
  minification and, 165
Virtual space, 139
  compensation and, 159–175
  distance perception and effect of, 151–152
  distortion of, 150
  familiarity and distortion of, 156–157

isomorphism of, 148–149
shear in, 146
viewing point dislocation effect on, 156
Visual angle function, 215, 217
Visual angle and observation distance, 131
Visual field reduction effects, 116–118
Visual pyramid and picture plane, 36

W

Wechtlin, Hans, 197
Wyeth, Andrew, 228

X

X–Y–Z coordinate system, 41–45

Y

Ying Tsao Fa Shih ("Architectural Standards"), 207–208